C000229037

GUIDE TO THE W

north west
& the pennines

Also available:

Nicholson Guide to the Waterways
1. Grand Union, Oxford & the South East
2. Severn, Avon & Birmingham
3. Birmingham & the Heart of England
4. Four Counties & the Welsh Canals
6. Nottingham, York & the North East
7. River Thames & the Southern Waterways
8. Scotland – the Highland and Lowland Waterways

Nicholson Inland Waterways Map of Great Britain

Published by Nicholson
An imprint of HarperCollins*Publishers*
77–85 Fulham Palace Road
Hammersmith, London W6 8JB

www.collins.co.uk
www.bartholomewmaps.com

First published by Nicholson and Ordnance Survey 1997
Reprinted 1998
New edition published by Nicholson 2000, 2003

Copyright © HarperCollins*Publishers* Ltd 2003

This product uses map data licensed from Ordnance Survey® with the permission of
the Controller of Her Majesty's Stationery Office.
© Crown copyright 1999. All rights reserved.

Ordnance Survey is a registered trade mark of Ordnance Survey, the national mapping
agency of Great Britain.

The representation in this publication of a road, track or path is no evidence of the existence
of a right of way.

Post Office (PO) is a trade mark of Post Office Limited in the UK and other countries.

Researched and written by David Perrott and Jonathan Mosse.
Designed by Bob Vickers.

The publishers gratefully acknowledge the assistance given by British Waterways and
their staff in the preparation of this guide.

Grateful thanks is also due to the Environment Agency and members of the
Inland Waterways Association, CAMRA representatives and branch members.

Photographs reproduced by kind permission of Derek Pratt Photography.

Every care has been taken in the preparation of this guide. However, the Publisher accepts no
responsibility whatsoever for any loss, damage, injury or inconvenience sustained or caused
as a result of using this guide.

The Publisher makes no representations or warranties of any kind as to the operation of the websites
and disclaims all responsibility for the content of the websites and for any expense or loss incurred by
use of the websites.

All rights reserved. No part of this publication may be reproduced, stored in a retrieval
system or transmitted in any form, or by any means, electronic, mechanical, photocopying,
recording or otherwise without the prior written consent of the publishers and copyright owners.

Printed in Hong Kong.

ISBN 0 00 713668 4
PJ11167 03/3/63.5

The publishers welcome comments from readers. Please address your letters to:
Nicholson Guides to the Waterways, HarperCollins Reference,
HarperCollins Publishers, Westerhill Road, Bishopbriggs, Glasgow, G64 2QT or
email nicholson@harpercollins.co.uk

Wending their quiet way through town and country, the inland navigations of Britain offer boaters, walkers and cyclists a unique insight into a fascinating, but once almost lost, world. When built this was the province of the boatmen and their families, who lived a mainly itinerant lifestyle: often colourful, to our eyes picturesque but, for them, remarkably harsh. Transporting the nation's goods during the late 1700s and early 1800s, negotiating locks, traversing aqueducts and passing through long narrow tunnels, canals were the arteries of trade during the initial part of the industrial revolution.

Then the railways came: the waterways were eclipsed in a remarkably short time by a faster and more flexible transport system, and a steady decline began. In a desperate fight for survival canal tolls were cut, crews toiled for longer hours and worked the boats with their whole family living aboard. Canal companies merged, totally uneconomic waterways were abandoned, some were modernised but it was all to no avail. Large scale commercial carrying on inland waterways had reached the finale of its short life.

At the end of World War II a few enthusiasts roamed this hidden world and harboured a vision of what it could become: a living transport museum which stretched the length and breadth of the country; a place where people could spend their leisure time and, on just a few of the wider waterways, a still modestly viable transport system.

The restoration struggle began and, from modest beginnings, Britain's inland waterways are now seen as an irreplaceable part of the fabric of the nation. Existing canals are expertly maintained while long abandoned waterways, once seen as an eyesore and a danger, are recognised for the valuable contribution they make to our quality of life, and restoration schemes are integrating them back into the network.

This series of guides offers the most comprehensive coverage of Britain's inland waterways, all clearly detailed on splendid Ordnance Survey® maps. Whether you are boating, walking, cycling or just visiting, these books will give you all the information you need.

▌ CONTENTS

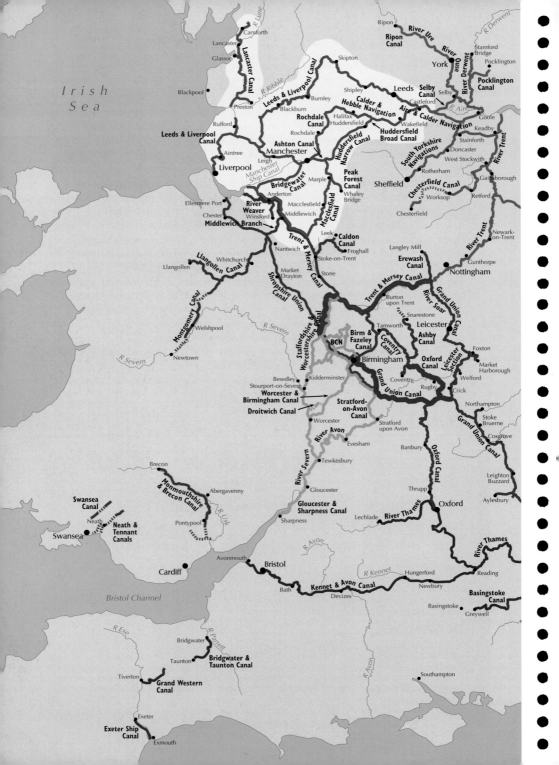

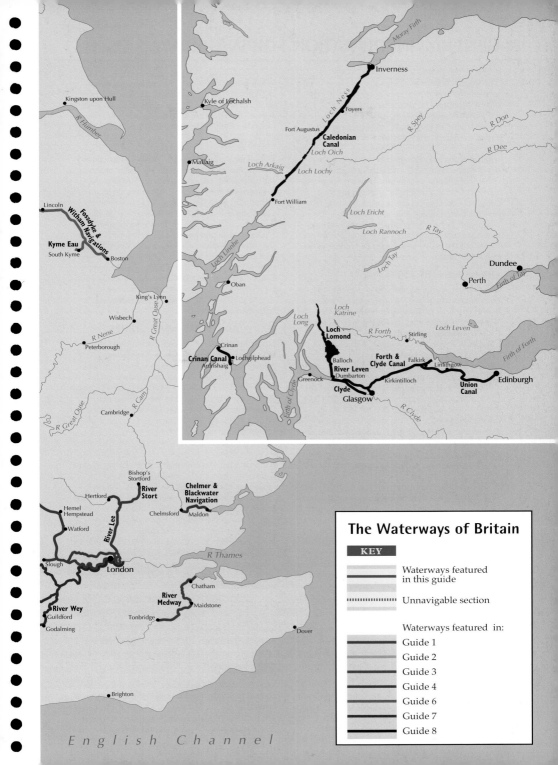

Kingston upon Hull

R Humber

Lincoln

Fosdyke & Witham Navigations

Kyme Eau

South Kyme

Boston

King's Lynn

Wisbech

R Nene

R Great Ouse

Peterborough

R Great Ouse

Cambridge

R Cam

Bishop's Stortford

River Stort

Chelmer & Blackwater Navigation

Hertford

Chelmsford

Maldon

Hemel Hempstead

Watford

River Lee

Slough

London

R Thames

Chatham

River Wey

River Medway

Maidstone

Guildford

Tonbridge

Godalming

Dover

Brighton

English Channel

Moray Firth

Inverness

Kyle of Lochalsh

Foyers

Fort Augustus

Caledonian Canal

R Spey

R Don

Loch Ness

Loch Oich

R Dee

Mallaig

Loch Arkaig

Loch Lochy

Fort William

Loch Ericht

Loch Linnhe

Loch Rannoch

R Tay

Dundee

Loch Tay

Perth

Firth of Tay

Oban

Loch Long

Loch Katrine

Loch Lomond

R Forth

Stirling

Loch Leven

Crinan

Crinan Canal

Lochgilphead

Ardrishaig

Balloch

Forth & Clyde Canal

Falkirk

Linlithgow

River Leven

Dumbarton

Kirkintilloch

Union Canal

Edinburgh

Greenock

Firth of Forth

Firth of Clyde

Clyde

Glasgow

R Clyde

The Waterways of Britain

KEY

Waterways featured in this guide

Unnavigable section

Waterways featured in:

Guide 1

Guide 2

Guide 3

Guide 4

Guide 6

Guide 7

Guide 8

GENERAL INFORMATION FOR WATERWAYS USERS

The slogan 'Waterways For All' was coined to take account of the wide diversity of people using the inland waterways for recreation.

Today boaters, walkers, fishermen, cyclists and gongoozlers (on-lookers) throng our canals and rivers, to share in the enjoyment of a quite amazing waterway heritage. British Waterways (BW), along with other navigation authorities, is empowered to develop, maintain and control this resource in order to maximise its potential. It is to this end that a series of guides, codes, and regulations have come into existence over the years, evolving to match a burgeoning – and occasionally conflicting – demand. Set out below are key points as they relate to everyone wishing to enjoy the waterways. Please see the inside front cover for details on how to contact British Waterways.

LICENSING – BOATS

The majority of the navigations covered in this book are controlled by BW and are managed on a day-to-day basis by local Waterway Offices. Waterway Managers are detailed in the introduction to each waterway. All craft using BW waterways must be licenced and charges are based on the length of the craft. This licence covers all navigable waterways under BW's control and in a few cases includes reciprocal agreements with other waterway authorities (as indicated in the text). BW and the Environment Agency now offer an optional Gold Licence which covers unlimited navigation on the waterways of both authorities. Permits for permanent mooring on the canals are also issued by BW. For further information contact BW Customer Services. You can download licence fees and charges and an application form from the BW website.

BW and the Environment Agency operate the Boat Safety Scheme, setting technical requirements for good and safe boat-building practice. A Boat Safety Certificate or, for new boats, a Declaration of Conformity, is necessary to obtain a craft licence. For powered boats proof of insurance for Third Party Liability for a minimum of £1,000,000 is also required. Further details from BW Customer Services. Other navigational authorities relevant to this book are mentioned where appropriate.

LICENSING – CYCLISTS

Not all towpaths are open to cyclists. This is because many stretches are considered to be too rough or narrow, or because cyclists are considered to cause a risk to other users. Maps on the BW website show which stretches of towpath are open to cyclists, and local offices can supply more detailed information relevant to their area. A cycle permit is required (except on the Caledonian and Crinan Canals), and this is available free of charge (except for the Kennet & Avon Canal, where a charge is made) from BW Customer Services.

When using the towpath for cycling, you will encounter other towpath users, such as fishermen, walkers and boaters. The Waterways Code gives advice on taking care and staying safe, considering others and helping to look after the waterways.

TOWPATHS

Few, if any, artificial cuts or canals in this country are without an intact towpath accessible to the walker at least. However, on river navigations towpaths have on occasion fallen into disuse or, sometimes, been lost to erosion. Considerable efforts are being made to provide access to all towpaths, with some available to the disabled. Notes on individual waterways in this book detail the supposed status of the path, but the indication of a towpath does not necessarily imply a public right of way or mean that a right to cycle along it exists. Maps on the BW website show all towpaths on the BW network, and whether they are open to cyclists. Motorcycling and horse riding are forbidden on all towpaths.

INDIVIDUAL WATERWAY GUIDES

No national guide can cover the minutiae of individual waterways and some Waterway Managers produce guides to specific navigations under their charge. Copies of individual guides (where they are available) can be obtained from the Waterway Office detailed in the introduction. Please note that times – such as operating times of bridges and locks – do change year by year and from winter to summer.

STOPPAGES

BW works hard to programme its major engineering works into the winter period when demand for cruising is low. It publishes a *National Stoppage Programme* and *Winter Opening Hours* leaflet which is sent out to all licence holders, boatyards and hire companies. Inevitably, emergencies occur necessitating the unexpected closure of a waterway, perhaps during the peak season. You can check for stoppages on individual waterways between specific dates on the BW website. Details are also announced on lockside noticeboards and on Canalphone (*see* inside front cover).

STARTING OUT

Extensive information and advice on booking a boating holiday is available on the BW website. Please book a waterway holiday from a licenced operator – only in this way can you be sure that you have proper insurance cover, service and support during your holiday. It is illegal for private boat owners to hire out their craft. If in doubt, please contact BW Customer Services. If you are hiring a canal boat for the first time, the boatyard will brief you thoroughly. Take notes, follow their instructions and *don't be afraid to ask* if there is anything you do not understand. BW have produced a short video giving basic information on using a boat safely. Copies of the video, and the *Boater's Handbook*, are available free of charge from BW Customer Services. Sections of the *Boater's Safety Toolkit* can also be downloaded from the internet, *see* www.aina.org.uk.

GENERAL CRUISING NOTES

Most canals are saucer-shaped in section so are deepest at the middle. Few have more than 3–4ft of water and many have much less. Keep to the centre of the channel except on bends, where the deepest water is on the outside of the bend. When you meet another boat, keep to the right, slow down and aim to miss the approaching craft by a couple of yards: do not steer right over to the bank or you are likely to run aground. If you meet a loaded commercial boat keep right out of the way and be prepared to follow his instructions. Do not assume that you should pass on the right. If you meet a boat being towed from the bank, pass it on the outside. When overtaking, keep the other boat on your right side.

A large number of BW facilities – pump outs, showers, electrical hook-ups and so on – are operated by pre-paid cards, obtainable from BW regional offices; local waterways offices (*see* introductions to individual navigations); lock keepers and some boatyards within the region. Cards are available in £5, £6, £10 and £15 denominations. Please note that if you are a weekend visitor, you should purchase cards in advance.

Speed
There is a general speed limit of 4 mph on most BW canals. This is not just an arbitrary limit: there is no need to go any faster and in many cases it is impossible to cruise even at this speed: if the wash is breaking against the bank or causing large waves, slow down.

Slow down also when passing moored craft, engineering works and anglers; when there is a lot of floating rubbish on the water (and try to drift over obvious obstructions in neutral); when approaching blind corners, narrow bridges and junctions.

Mooring
Generally speaking you may moor where you wish on BW property, as long as there is sufficient depth of water, and you are *not causing an obstruction*. Your boat should carry metal mooring stakes, and these should be driven firmly into the ground with a mallet if there are no mooring rings. Do not stretch mooring lines across the towpath. Always consider the security of your boat when there is no one aboard. On tideways and commercial waterways it is advisable to moor only at recognised sites, and allow for any rise or fall of the tide.

Bridges
On narrow canals slow down and aim to miss one side (usually the towpath side) by about 9 inches. *Keep everyone inboard when passing under bridges*, and take special care with moveable structures – the crew member operating the bridge should be strong enough and heavy enough to hold it steady as the boat passes through.

Tunnels
Make sure the tunnel is clear before you enter, and use your headlight. Follow any instructions given on notice boards by the entrance.

Fuel
Hire craft usually carry fuel sufficient for the rental period.

Water
It is advisable to top up daily.

Lavatories
Hire craft usually have pump out toilets. Have these emptied *before* things become critical. Keep the receipt and your boatyard will usually reimburse you for this expense.

Boatyards
Hire fleets are usually turned around on a Saturday, making this a bad time to call in for services. Remember that moorings at popular destinations fill quickly during the summer months, so do not assume there will be room for your boat. Always ask.

LOCKS AND THEIR USE

A lock is a simple and ingenious device for transporting your craft from one water level to another. When both sets of gates are closed it may

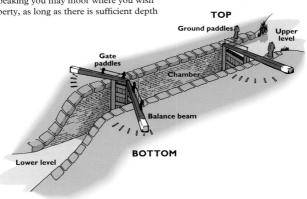

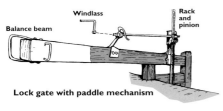

Lock gate with paddle mechanism

be filled or emptied using gate or ground paddles at the top or bottom of the lock. These are operated with a windlass.

General tips
• Make safety your prime concern. *Keep a close eye on young children.*
• Always take your time, and do not leap about.
• Never open the paddles at one end without ensuring those at the other end are closed.
• Never drop the paddles – always wind them down.
• Keep to the landward side of the balance beam when opening and closing gates.
• *Never* leave your windlass slotted onto the paddle spindle – it will be dangerous should anything slip.
• Keep your boat away from the top and bottom gates to prevent it getting caught on the gate or the lock cill.
• Be wary of fierce *top gate* paddles, especially in wide locks. Operate them slowly, and close them if there is *any* adverse effect.
• Always follow the navigation authority's instructions, where these are given on notices or by their staff.

PLANNING A CRUISE

Many a canal holiday has been spoiled by trying to go too far too fast. Go slowly, don't be too ambitious, and enjoy the experience. Note that mileages indicated on the maps are for guidance only.

A *rough* calculation of time taken to cover the ground is the lock-miles system:

Add the number of *miles* to the number of *locks* on your proposed journey, and divide the resulting figure by three. This will give you a guide to the number of *hours* it will take. But don't forget your service stops (water, shopping, pump out), and allow plenty of time to visit that special pub!

TIDAL WATERWAYS

The typical steel narrow boat found on the inland waterways system has all the seagoing characteristics of a bathtub, which renders it totally unsuitable for all-weather cruising on tidal estuaries. However, the more adventurous will inevitably wish to add additional 'ring cruises' to the more predictable circuits within the calm havens of inland Britain. Passage is possible in most estuaries if careful consideration is given to the key factors of weather conditions, tides, crew experience, the condition of the boat and its equipment and, perhaps of over-riding importance, the need to take expert advice.

In many cases it will be prudent to employ the skilled services of a local pilot. Within the text, where inland navigations connect with a tidal waterway, details are given of sources of both advice and pilotage. It is also advisable to inform your insurance company of your intention to navigate on tidal waterways as they may very well have special requirements or wish to levy an additional premium. This guide is to the inland waterways of Britain and therefore recognizes that tideways – and especially estuaries – require a different approach and many additional skills. We therefore do not hesitate to draw the boater's attention to the appropriate source material.

GENERAL

Most inland navigations are managed by BW or the Environment Agency, but there are several other navigation authorities responsible for smaller stretches of canals and rivers. For details of these, contact the Association of Inland Navigation Authorities at www.aina.org.uk or BW Customer Services. The boater, conditioned perhaps by the uniformity of our national road network, should be sensitive to the need to observe different codes and operating practices. Similarly it is important to be aware that some waterways are only available for navigation today solely because of the care and dedication of a particular restoration body, often using volunteer labour and usually taking several decades to complete the project. This is the reason that, in cruising the national waterways network, additional licence charges are sometimes incurred. The introduction to each waterway gives its back-ground history, details of recent restoration (where relevant) and also lists the operating authority.

BW is a public corporation, responsible to the Department of Environment, Food and Rural Affairs and, as subscribers to the Citizen's Charter, they are linked with an ombudsman. BW has a comprehensive complaints procedure and a free explanatory leaflet is available from Customer Services. Problems and complaints should be addressed to the local Waterway Manager in the first instance – the telephone number is listed in the introduction to individual waterways.

The Inland Waterways Association campaigns for the 'conservation, use, maintenance, restoration and development of the inland waterways', through branches all over the country. For more information contact them at PO Box 114, Rickmansworth, WD3 1ZY, telephone 01923 711114, fax 01923 897000, email iwa@waterways.org.uk or visit their website at www.waterways.org.uk.

BRITISH WATERWAYS EMERGENCY HELPLINE

Emergency help is available from BW outside normal office hours on weekdays and throughout weekends via British Waterways' Emergency Helpline (*see* inside front cover). You should give details of the problem and your location.

▌AIRE & CALDER NAVIGATION

MAXIMUM DIMENSIONS

River Lock to Leeds Lock
Length: 143'
Beam: 17'
Headroom: 12'

Leeds Lock to Castleford
Length: 200'
Beam: 20'
Headroom: 12'

Castleford to Wakefield
Length: 140'
Beam: 17'
Headroom: 12'

MANAGER

01977 554351
enquiries.castleford@britishwaterways.co.uk

MILEAGE

LEEDS to
Castleford: 10 miles, 5 locks
Wakefield: 17¹/2 miles, 10 locks including
Fall Ing

SAFETY NOTES

BW produce excellent *Cruising Notes* for
pleasure boaters using this waterway, obtain
by telephoning the manager's office. This is
both a commercial waterway and one
developed from a river navigation: both pose
their own disciplines highlighted in the notes.
Each lock on the waterway has a set of traffic
lights both upstream and downstream of the
lock chamber. The purpose of these lights is
to convey instructions and advice to
approaching craft.

Red light
Stop and moor up on the lock approach. The
lock is currently in use.

Amber light *(between the red and green lights)*
The lock keeper is not on duty. You will need
to self-operate.

Green light
Proceed into lock.

Red & green lights together
The lock is available for use. The lock keeper
will prepare and operate the lock for you.

Flashing red light
Flood conditions – unsafe for navigation.

Most lock approach moorings are immediately
upstream and downstream of the lock
chamber. However, **please note:**

1 Knostrop Lock downstream approach
   mooring is located alongside the lock
   bulnose.

2 Locks at Leeds, Lemonroyd, Castleford,
   Woodnook and Broadreach allow access
   to river sections of the navigation. For
   interpretation of river level gauge boards
   see Safety Notes in the introduction to the
   Calder & Hebble Navigation on page 40.

3 There is a safe haven mooring immediately
   upstream of Lemonroyd Lock.

All locks between Leeds and Wakefield
(except Fall Ing Lock) are equipped with
VHF Marine Band Radio. They monitor and
operate on channel 74.
In an emergency non-VHF users contact
the manager's office or out of office hours
telephone 0800 47 999 47. Mobile phone
users telephone 01384 215785.

Aire & Calder Navigation

Introduction

The River Aire was first made navigable to Leeds in 1700, and rapidly became a great
commercial success, taking coal out of the Yorkshire coalfield and bringing back raw
wool, corn and agricultural produce. Improvements were then made to the difficult
lower reaches, with first Selby and later Goole becoming Yorkshire's principal inland
port. The opening of the New Junction Canal in 1905 further secured its suitability
for commercial traffic, which until recently amounted to some 2 million tonnes a
year, mainly coal, sand and petroleum. With the completion of coal extraction at the
St Aidens opencast site, together with the unacceptably high sulphur content of the
material from Kellingley colliery, coal carrying has suddenly drawn to a halt.
However, petroleum tonnages are on the increase while the quantities of sand and
gravel carried by barge to Lafarge's Whitwood terminal look to be extremely healthy.

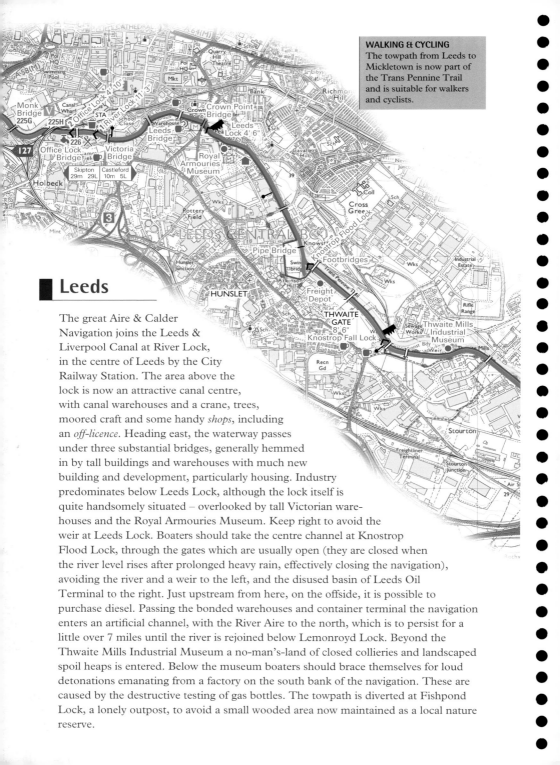

WALKING & CYCLING
The towpath from Leeds to Mickletown is now part of the Trans Pennine Trail and is suitable for walkers and cyclists.

Leeds

The great Aire & Calder
Navigation joins the Leeds &
Liverpool Canal at River Lock,
in the centre of Leeds by the City
Railway Station. The area above the
lock is now an attractive canal centre,
with canal warehouses and a crane, trees,
moored craft and some handy *shops*, including
an *off-licence*. Heading east, the waterway passes
under three substantial bridges, generally hemmed
in by tall buildings and warehouses with much new
building and development, particularly housing. Industry
predominates below Leeds Lock, although the lock itself is
quite handsomely situated – overlooked by tall Victorian warehouses and the Royal Armouries Museum. Keep right to avoid the
weir at Leeds Lock. Boaters should take the centre channel at Knostrop
Flood Lock, through the gates which are usually open (they are closed when
the river level rises after prolonged heavy rain, effectively closing the navigation),
avoiding the river and a weir to the left, and the disused basin of Leeds Oil
Terminal to the right. Just upstream from here, on the offside, it is possible to
purchase diesel. Passing the bonded warehouses and container terminal the navigation
enters an artificial channel, with the River Aire to the north, which is to persist for a
little over 7 miles until the river is rejoined below Lemonroyd Lock. Beyond the
Thwaite Mills Industrial Museum a no-man's-land of closed collieries and landscaped
spoil heaps is entered. Below the museum boaters should brace themselves for loud
detonations emanating from a factory on the south bank of the navigation. These are
caused by the destructive testing of gas bottles. The towpath is diverted at Fishpond
Lock, a lonely outpost, to avoid a small wooded area now maintained as a local nature
reserve.

NAVIGATIONAL NOTES

1 All the locks on the Aire & Calder operate mechanically. Lock keepers move from lock to lock, primarily to operate them for commercial traffic. They will assist boaters through locks whenever possible but all locks can now be self-operated. Obey the traffic light signals.

2 Remember that this is a river navigation. Many of the locks are accompanied by large weirs, so keep a sharp lookout for the signs which direct you safely into the locks.

3 When the river level rises after prolonged heavy rain, the flood gates will be closed. Pleasure craft should stay put until they are advised by a lock keeper that it is safe to proceed.

4 This is a commercial waterway, used by 600-tonne tankers and large sand carrying barges. Keep a lookout for them, and give them a clear passage. Moor carefully, using bollards or fixed rings rather than mooring stakes, since the wash from these craft can be substantial.

Boatyards

Ⓑ **Clarence Dock Leeds** (01977 554351). Beside the Royal Armouries Museum. 🏠 🚽 ⚓ Overnight mooring, long-term mooring, pump out, showers, toilets, disabled facilities.

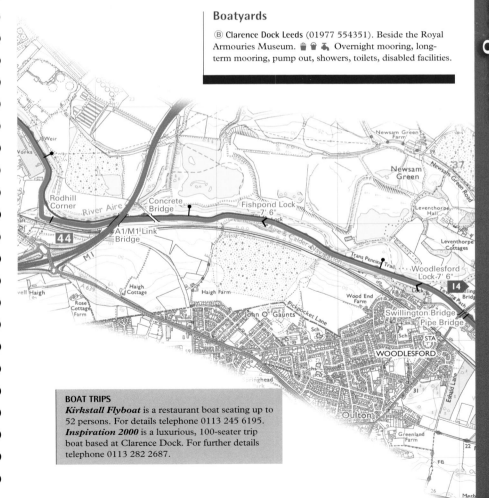

BOAT TRIPS
Kirkstall Flyboat is a restaurant boat seating up to 52 persons. For details telephone 0113 245 6195.
Inspiration 2000 is a luxurious, 100-seater trip boat based at Clarence Dock. For further details telephone 0113 282 2687.

● Leeds

W. Yorks. All services. A vast industrial city that was a wool centre in the Middle Ages and has continued to grow to prosperity under the textile and clothing trades; indeed Marks & Spencer started business here with a stall in the market. Montague Burton also became established in the city, building what was to become, by 1921, the largest clothing factory in the world. However the last few years have brought substantial changes, with old industries being replaced by new, and the atmosphere is one of growth and prosperity. The great town hall in Victoria Square (walk north from Victoria Bridge and turn left at Great George Street) stands as a magnificent monument to Victorian civic pride. It was designed by Cuthbert Brodrick and opened in 1858. Looking at the Corinthian columns on all sides and the clock tower some 255ft high, it is hard to believe that Brodrick was only 29 years old when he submitted his plans. As a measure of this man's self-confidence, note that he also designed the organ, installed in 1859, which itself weighs almost 70 tonnes, has 6,500 pipes and stands 50ft high. The light and airy Corn Exchange (north of Leeds Bridge along Call Lane and now a shopping arcade) built in 1861 is also Brodrick's work. Always the cultural centre of Yorkshire, the city hosts an international concert season and an international piano competition. It has several splendid theatres, including The Grand in Briggate, modelled on La Scala, Milan; the City Varieties, the oldest surviving music hall in the country; and the Leeds Playhouse Repertory Theatre. Also impressive is the way, perhaps unique in the development of northern industrial towns, that contemporary and Victorian buildings stand harmoniously side by side. There are several splendid parks and rich museums, and excellent shopping facilities, including the ornate Victorian Queens and County arcades. Headingley, the home of Yorkshire cricket and a test match venue, attracts an enthusiastic following in the area, and of course the city's association with football and rugby teams is known worldwide. Boaters should try to spend a day here if they possibly can – there are good moorings on the Leeds & Liverpool Canal by Office Lock, or above Leeds Lock. *See also* page 127 (Leeds & Liverpool Canal) for information on Leeds Industrial Museum and Abbey House Museum.

Metro. The area is well served by an excellent, cheap bus and train service which offers a variety of Day Rover tickets. Telephone 0113 245 7676 or visit www.wymetro.com for details.

Tourist Information Centre The Arcade, Leeds City Station, Leeds (0113 242 5242; www.leeds.gov.uk). The usual mine of information concerning places to visit and accommodation. *Open Mon–Sat 09.30–18.00 and Sun 10.00–16.00.*

Henry Moore Institute 74 The Headrow, Leeds (0113 246 7467; www.henry-moore-fdn.co.uk). Walk north from Victoria Bridge. Award winning institute housing four galleries showing temporary sculpture exhibitions of all periods and nationalities. Shop. *Open daily 10.00–17.30 (Wed until 21.00).* Information line 0113 234 3158. Free.

City Art Gallery The Headrow, Leeds (0113 247 8248; www.leeds.gov.uk/artgallery). Fine collections of paintings, watercolours, sculpture and 20th-C British Art. Collections include Victorian paintings, British watercolours, French Post-Impressionist paintings and British sculpture. *Open Mon–Sat 10.00–17.00 (Wed 20.00) and Sun 13.00–17.00.* Disabled facilities. Free.

Leeds–Settle–Carlisle Line From Leeds City Station. The 70 miles from Settle to Carlisle is said to be one of the most memorable rail journeys in the world, so this would make an excellent day trip away from the boat. *Every Sat and Sun, May–Oct* there are free guided walks from trains on the line. Coach tours around the Yorkshire Dales also connect. Details from leaflets at the station or Tourist Information Centre.

Middleton Railway Tunstall Road, Leeds (0113 271 0320; www.middletonrailway.org.uk). Built in 1758 to link Leeds with the Middleton Colliery, this is considered to be the world's oldest railway. It operates at *weekends Easter– end of year* from the industrial suburb of Hunslet, where steam engines were once built. Charge.

Royal Armouries The Waterfront, Leeds (0113 220 1999; www.armouries.org.uk). Beside Leeds Lock with moorings in Clarence Dock, adjacent to the complex. The emphasis is on participation in this massive, interactive museum reputed to be Britain's largest, post-war leisure development. Five themed galleries unfold stories of weapons, battles, tournaments, falconry and the Wild West. See, touch, smell and handle before retiring to watch the skills of an armourer or experience the tranquillity of a Japanese tea garden. *Open daily from 10.00. Closed 24–25 Dec.* Two cafés and a bistro. Full disabled access. Charge.

Thackray Museum Beckett Street, Leeds (0113 244 4343; www.thackraymuseum.org.uk). A hands-on experience covering the history of medicine from Victorian times to the present day. This award winning museum introduces you to Sherlock Bones and his tour of the Giant Gut; allows you to experience surgery without anaesthetics in 'Pain, Pus and Blood' and lets you assist Mrs Hirst with her 12th child. A truly participative establishment. Shop and café. Disabled access. *Open Tue–Sat and B Hol Mon 10.00–17.00. Last admission 15.00 – but allow 3 hours for your visit.* Bus Nos 4, 4C, 22, 42, 50, 50A, 88. Information hotline 0113 245 7084. Charge.

Thwaite Mills Watermill Thwaite Lane, Leeds (0113 249 6453). A canalside flint and china stone-grinding mill built in 1872 and powered by two waterwheels until 1975, when they were washed away, bringing closure a year later. Visitors are able to see the working conditions in the mill, as well as a Marshall engine and various artefacts. *Open daily 10.00–dusk.* Charge.

Tropical World and Roundhay Park Roundhay, Leeds (0113 266 1850; www.leeds.gov.uk). A wide selection of buses from the city centre serve this tropical paradise featuring butterflies, exotic blooms and colourful fish. This is also one of Europe's largest parks with a boating lake, woodland walks, scented gardens (including National Collections), canal gardens and waterfalls. *Open 10.00–dusk daily except Christmas.* Charge.

● **Woodlesford**
W. Yorks. PO, tel, stores, garage, station. Good moorings above the lock and nearby pubs make this a popular stopping place for boaters. There is a very popular bird hide adjacent to the canal.

Pubs and Restaurants

A fine city such as Leeds has many pubs and restaurants. The following is a selection of those fairly close to the navigation.

✕ **Serious Sarnie Company** 'Horbury', 26 Canal Wharf, Leeds (0113 245 6195/07776 067806; www.serioussarnies.com). When a trip boat goes moonlighting it becomes a sandwich bar: in this instance offering more than 30 imaginative fillings (V) on a choice of seven different breads. *Open Mon–Fri 10.00–14.00.*

✕♀ **Hansa's Gujarati Vegetarian Restaurant** 72–74 North Street, Leeds (0113 244 4408; www.hansas.co.uk). Worth seeking out for excellent, home-cooked dishes with an Indian flavour. A unique establishment serving Indian vegetarian cuisine from the State of Gujarat in a split-level restaurant with an elegant, homely atmosphere. *Open L Thur, Fri and Sun and E Mon–Sat 17.30–23.00.* Families warmly welcomed.

✕♀ **Calls Grill** 38 The Calls, Leeds (0113 245 3870). Airy establishment, not limited to its excellent steaks, offering snacks (V) and a children's menu and overlooking the river.

✕♀ **Italian Job** 9 Bridge End, Lower Briggate, Leeds (0113 242 0185). Well-loved Italian favourites (V) and a warm welcome dished up in this busy pizzeria. *L and E (closed Sun).*

● **Grove** Back Row, Leeds (0113 243 9254). South of Victoria Bridge. Small traditional ale house dispensing an excellent selection of real ales (four regulars and four rotating guests) and inexpensive bar snacks (V) *L (not Sat)*. Home-made steak pie and hot beef and onion rolls are specialities. Children welcome *until 21.00*; dogs at all hours. Folk *Fri* and live music *most nights; Sun 14.00–17.00.* Outside seating.

● **Adelphi** Hunslet Road, Leeds (0113 245 6377). South of Leeds Bridge. A superbly restored and very grand Edwardian pub, with lots of etched glass and mahogany. Listed inside and out. Real ale and food (V) *L Mon–Sat.* Children welcome; dogs in taproom only. Outside seating.

● ✕ **Whitelock's** Turk's Head Yard, Briggate, Leeds (0113 245 3950). North of Leeds Bridge. An unspoilt Edwardian pub, one of the first buildings to have electricity. Reputedly the oldest pub in the city (its first licence was granted in 1715) and described by John Betjeman as 'the very heart of Leeds', this hostelry serves up to eight real ales and has a floral-hung beer garden set in an alleyway. Excellent, freshly prepared traditional English food (V) is available *L and E, daily.* Children welcome in restaurant. No electronic machines.

● **Duck & Drake** Kirkgate, Leeds (0113 246 5806). North of Crown Point Bridge, near the church. Simply decorated pub with an open fire and a choice of 15 real ales at weekends (only 13 *during the week*!). Bar snacks available *L only.* Beer garden. Live music *Mon and Thur.* No children.

● **Palace** Kirkgate, Leeds (0113 244 5882). Straightforward, no-frills pub dispensing 12 changing real ales, *open all day.* Food (V) is available *daily 11.30–14.00 and 16.30–19.00.* Children welcome *at mealtimes;* dogs *other than at mealtimes.* Quiz *Mon and Wed.* Outside seating and pub games.

● **Viaduct** 11 Lower Bridgate, Leeds (0113 245 4863). Long, narrow pub featuring a selection of milds together with other real ales. Excellent disabled facilities. This pub is the official home of Leeds United supporters and serves food (V) *L and E, daily.* Children welcome. Pub games and large screen TV. Disco *Fri and Sat.* No-smoking area.

● **Two Pointers** Church Street, Woodlesford (0113 282 3124). Up the hill from the lock. A smart and very friendly village pub serving bar snacks *L and E.* Dogs welcome *until 19.00. Fri* live music, *Sat* 50s/60s night and *Sun* quiz. Patio.

● **White Hart** Church Street, Woodlesford (0113 282 2205). Just past The Two Pointers. A snug and comfy real ale pub.

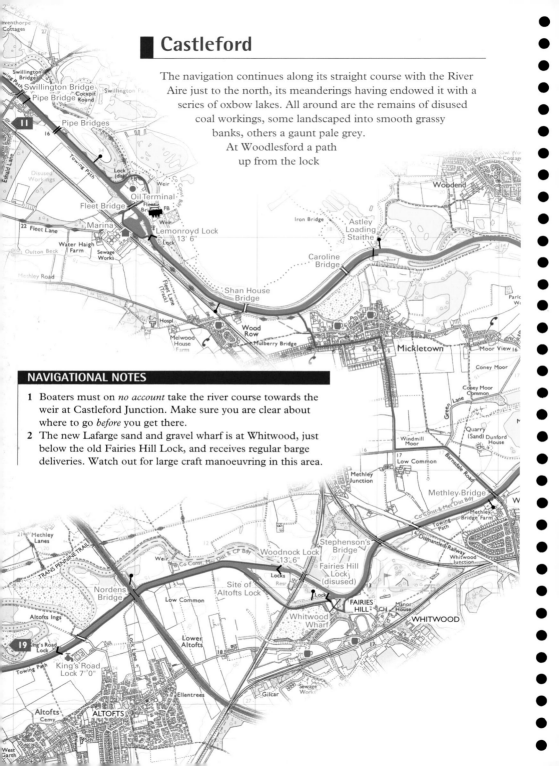

Castleford

The navigation continues along its straight course with the River Aire just to the north, its meanderings having endowed it with a series of oxbow lakes. All around are the remains of disused coal workings, some landscaped into smooth grassy banks, others a gaunt pale grey.

At Woodlesford a path up from the lock

NAVIGATIONAL NOTES

1 Boaters must on *no account* take the river course towards the weir at Castleford Junction. Make sure you are clear about where to go *before* you get there.
2 The new Lafarge sand and gravel wharf is at Whitwood, just below the old Fairies Hill Lock, and receives regular barge deliveries. Watch out for large craft manoeuvring in this area.

leads to *two pubs, a post office, and shops*. There is also a *supermarket and off-licence*. Just before Fleet Bridge an arm branches off to the north. A disused lock here once used to connect with the river. Enclosed by the arm is an oil terminal – notice how the storage tanks have been colonised by house martins. This facility is also visited several times a week by oil tankers so be on the look out for loaded craft manoeuvring above Fleet Bridge. The river by Fleet Lock was the site of a disastrous breach which occurred in March 1988, when the ground separating it from the adjacent St Aidens open-cast mine collapsed and the water poured in. Apparently the river below the breach flowed backwards for half a day, such was the volume of water consumed, and the workforce only just managed to rescue the large cranes. There are visitor and long-term moorings available in the marina above the new Lemonroyd Lock (combining the old Lemonroyd Lock with the now-vanished Kippax Lock). Rejoining the river at Lemonroyd Lock, the mining village of Allerton Bywater appears at the end of the newly constructed section of waterway.

There is a welcome waterside pub here, but make sure you moor securely if you stop, since passing commercial craft cause a considerable wash. There is a waterways 'crossroads' at Castleford. Navigators heading towards Sowerby Bridge should turn right here and must on no account go straight across – since that way leads to the huge Castleford Weir. To the left, through the Flood Lock, are a *sanitary station, showers* and good *moorings*, beyond which lies the route to Sheffield (*see* Book 6), Goole, Hull, York, the River Trent and ultimately the North Sea. The large commercial craft which trade to Fleet and Whitwood emerge from here, so boats travelling downstream on either the rivers Aire or Calder, though not entering the flood lock, must still observe the traffic signals to avoid collision with vessels leaving the lock. Entering the River Calder, navigators will notice that its course here has been straightened, as the oxbow lakes either side will testify. After ducking under a large road bridge and two railway bridges, a path which gives access to two fine pubs at Whitwood can be seen to the south. Your nose will also tell you there is a large sewage works here. Pressing on, the large, deep mechanised Woodnook Lock is reached. This replaced the earlier Fairies and Altofts locks (now disused) to the south. By comparing the sizes of the locks, an impression of the improvements carried out on the navigation during the last 100 years can be gained. Beyond the large motorway bridge is King's Road Lock (also mechanised) and paths from here lead to Altofts, although there is little reason to walk the ½ mile or so, except for supplies.

● **Temple Newsam House and Garden** (0113 264 5535; www.leeds.gov.uk). Walk north from Swillington Bridge, fork left after the river – 2 miles. A superb Tudor/Jacobean house in 900 acres of parkland. Magnificent Georgian and Regency interiors. Walks in park and woods, magnificent displays of roses and rhododendrons in gardens. *House open Easter: Apr–Dec Tue–Sat and B Hol Mon 10.00–17.00, Sun 13.00–17.00 (12.00–16.00 winter).* Charge. *Park and gardens open all year.* Free.

Home Farm Temple Newsam (0113 264 5535; www.leeds.gov.uk). The largest working rare breeds farm in Europe – home to 400 animals. Sheep, pigs, goats, chickens, ducks and largest Vaynol herd in the world. 300-year-old Great Barn and other traditional farm buildings housing a collection of old agricultural tools and machinery. *Open daily 10.00–17.00 (16.00 winter).* Shop and café. Charge.

● **Mickletown**
W. Yorks. PO, tel, stores. Claimed by the locals to be the second largest village in England – it is suggested that Wroxham in Norfolk is the largest – Mickletown has clearly had its problems since the neighbouring colliery closed.

The next-door village of Wood Row is close by, and the *pub, store and PO* there can be easily reached via a path from Caroline Bridge.

● **Allerton Bywater**
W. Yorks. PO, tel, stores. A mining village, but the pit is now closed. Coal was once loaded from wagons onto barges from a small staithe here.

● **Castleford**
W. Yorks. All services. Once the Roman settlement of *Lagentium*, now a busy industrial town which has grown up at this important waterways junction, it is also the birth place of the sculptor Henry Moore. The Waterway Manager's Office can be seen by the Flood Lock, and Allinsons mill is situated by the huge weir – here they produce their popular stoneground flour.

Castleford Museum Carlton Street, Castleford (01977 722085). Victorian Castleford theme exhibition. *Open daily during library opening hours.* Free.

● **Altofts**
W. Yorks. PO, tel, stores. Originally a mining village and now a suburb of Wakefield. There was once a pub by the river, but it is now a private house. There are still two pubs in the village.

WALKING & CYCLING
Currently there is no continuous towpath from Caroline Bridge to Castleford so walkers and cyclists wishing to follow the navigation are presented with two choices:

1 Leave the towpath ½ mile east of Shan Bridge and follow the Trans Pennine Trail signs onto Mickletown Road and thence to the junction of Savile Road and Church Road. Turn left along Savile Road and right along Pinfold Lane at the T junction. At the main road (Barnsdale Road) turn left and follow this road – along the pavement – round a sharp right-hand bend (ignore the left-hand turning here into Micklefield) and then south to Methley Bridge over the Wakefield Branch of the Aire & Calder Canal. Join the towpath here and follow it east into Castlefield. For those following this diversion in reverse (i.e. from Castleford) leave the navigation at Barnsdale Road Bridge and head south, over the river and turn right along Savile Road. Immediately past the roundabout look for a Public Footpath sign leading you back onto the river bank.

2 Follow the directions above to Methley Bridge where, by turning west along the towpath, it is possible to reach Wakefield and, with the assistance of the excellent Metro bus/rail system (0113 245 7676; www.wymetro.com) complete a circular walk/ride that might have commenced in Leeds. N.B. A section of the towpath Methley Bridge to Wakefield is only cyclable with care and at the cyclist's own risk!

3 A third option is to make use of the Trans Pennine Trail throughout its route in the Leeds area. Starting at Crown Point Bridge (*see* page 10) near the city centre, it follows the canal to Mickletown (*see* 1 above) where, by following the excellent waymarking west along a minor road and a disused railway line, it heads into Wakefield making use of a further section of canal (the Aire & Calder Wakefield Branch) at Stanley Ferry. This is part of Euro-route E8 (ultimately running from the west coast of Ireland to Istanbul). For further information (free) and detailed guides (charge) contact the Trans Pennine Trail Officer on 01226 772574 or visit www.transpenninetrail.org.uk.

Pubs and Restaurants

🍺 ✕ **New Bay Horse** Mickletown (01977 553557). Turn right out of Pit Lane, up from Caroline Bridge (do not moor anywhere near the staithe). Family pub and restaurant serving real ale. Food (V) available *L and E (not Sun E)*. Children welcome. Family room, large garden and children's play area. Quiz *Tue*, darts and dominoes.

🍺 **Boat** Boat Lane, Allerton Bywater (01977 552216; www.boatpub.co.uk). An attractive riverside pub where once a ferry operated carrying miners and boat horses across the river, now replaced with a micro-brewery serving their own real ales and guest beers. Food (V) is available *L and E, daily*. Riverside seating. Children's room and outdoor play area. Quiz *Thur and Sun*. Take care when mooring here, as passing commercial craft can create a sizeable wash.

🍺 **Victoria Hotel** Main Street, Allerton Bywater (01977 516438). Friendly, modernised local dispensing real ale and good cheer. Children welcome. Garden. Quiz *Sun*.

🍺 **Old Mill** Castleford (01977 557034). Just south of Castleford Junction, at the Barnsdale Road Bridge. Real ale in a friendly local with two landlords, one the uninvited ghost of the 1928–41 incumbent. Disco and quiz *Fri. PO* and *stores* close by.

🍺 **Griffin** Lock Lane, Castleford (01977 557551). Opposite The Old Mill, this pub also serves real ale. Dogs welcome; no children. Outside seating. Quiz and bingo *Wed*; quiz and open box *Sun*. Try also The Britt, nearby on Lock Lane.

🍺 **Garden House** Castleford (01977 552934). On the south bank of the river. An ideal, comfortable, family pub with food (V) available *L and E, daily*. The Goole packet boat used to leave from outside but now the friendly landlord is more concerned with serving real ale. Children welcome *until 21.00*. Outside seating. Quiz *Mon and Thur*.

🍺 **Bridge Inn** Whitwood (01977 550498). A most interesting pub, newly built but with old bricks and timbers. There is a lofty ceiling over the bar, with more intimate drinking and eating areas off to the sides. Good bar meals – (V) *L and E, daily* – friendly staff and a selection of real ale. Patio, children welcome. B & B.

🍺 ✕ **New Wheatsheaf** Whitwood (01977 553052). Large, brightly decorated traditional pub, where someone clearly takes a great pride in their flower arrangements. Real ales, and a wide range of interesting and appetising food (V) served *L and E* (not *Sun E* in restaurant) in both bar and restaurant – 3-course *Sun L* a speciality. Children welcome, patio. Quiz *Sun*.

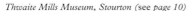

Thwaite Mills Museum, Stourton (see page 10)

Wakefield

Birkwood Lock was for a long time the last mechanised lock when travelling upstream. At Stanley Ferry the canal is diverted over the new aqueduct, which stands alongside the original and was opened in 1981. The original aqueduct was thought to be at risk from the large craft which can now navigate here. There is a British Waterways repair yard and lock gate building workshop immediately before the aqueduct, and a marina with a pub beyond. This has been built in a defunct loading basin beside the splendid, stone wharf office. It was here that empty 'Tom Puddings' were hauled onto railway wagons and, after loading at the nearby colliery, re-launched en route for Goole. After Ramsden's Swing Bridge (*sanitary station, pump out and showers*) the navigation continues in a dead straight line, passing Broadreach Flood Lock and Heath Old Hall before turning west to join the Calder & Hebble at Fall Ing Lock. There are craft moored here by an old loading chute, a *picnic area* and convenient *pub*. Below Wakefield Flood Lock the river is navigable for a short distance towards the weir, beside an impressive new development in the long-abandoned warehouses. Leaving Wakefield you pass under a splendid curving brick railway viaduct known locally as 'the 99 arches'. A careful count will reveal only 95.

Stanley Ferry Aqueduct
It is a good idea to moor at Stanley Ferry Marina and walk to the road bridge for a full view of this fine structure – a trough suspended from a two-pin cast iron arch – built on the same principle as the Sydney Harbour Bridge, which it predates by 100 years. Nearly 7000 tons of Bramley Fall stone and 1000 tons of cast iron were used in its construction. The first boat to pass across it was the *James*, a schooner of 160 tons drawn by three grey horses, on 8 August 1839. The 700 men who worked on it were fed at the nearby public houses, one of which, The Ship, still stands. Designed by George Leather, the strength of the structure was severely tested when, soon after opening, the largest flood for 20 years caused the river below actually to flow into the trough. The towpath is carried on a separate wooden breakwater designed to protect the aqueduct during such floods. The concrete aqueduct was built in 1981, and the original, by its side, is still in water.

NAVIGATIONAL NOTES

1 Take heed of the notices and flood indicator boards at the locks. Pleasure craft should only proceed if the water level is in the *green* or *amber* sectors. Amber indicates that the river is above normal levels and that boaters should proceed with caution to and THROUGH the next lock.
2 Most locks on the Calder & Hebble have a unique type of paddle gear, consisting of a small perforated wheel which is turned using a 'handspike'. These are obtainable from boatyards on the navigation, and from the BW office at Castleford. Or a piece of 3" x 2" hardwood, 3ft long (and planed down to size), will do just as well.
3 When coming downstream (from Sowerby Bridge direction) keep a sharp lookout for the entrance to Wakefield Flood Lock. There is a large weir on the river, a short distance beyond the boatyard, by the bridge.

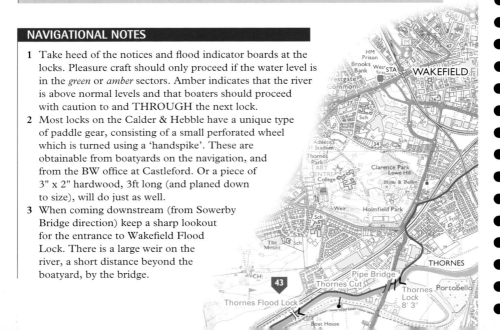

WALKING & CYCLING

1 At Stanley Ferry the Trans Pennine Trail (*see* page 10) joins the towpath and it continues south east of Broadreach Lock over the river footbridge and under the railway arches. Once past the railway those wishing to follow the navigation into Wakefield – and beyond – should bear round to the right and back onto the river bank. In the wooded area, around Heath Old Hall, it may be necessary in the summer to make a slight detour along tracks to avoid the dense vegetation. A slightly longer detour at this point could bring you to the excellent Kings Arms, in the delightful village of Heath itself (*see* page 20).

2 At Wakefield Flood Lock cross over the navigation and head north along Bridge Street to cross the river. Bear left on to Thornes Lane and follow this road along the river bank. Stay on Thornes Lane when it meets Thornes Lane Wharfe and turns away from the river. Go under two railway bridges and turn left at the roundabout, past The Queen's Arms and under a third railway bridge. Turn left down Holmfield Lane (there is a *fish & chip* shop on the corner) and then right past the industrial units along Green End Lane. Rejoin the navigation at Thornes Lock.

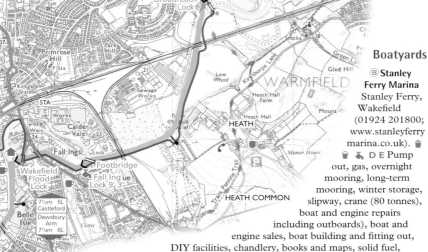

Boatyards

Ⓑ **Stanley Ferry Marina** Stanley Ferry, Wakefield (01924 201800; www.stanleyferry marina.co.uk). D E Pump out, gas, overnight mooring, long-term mooring, winter storage, slipway, crane (80 tonnes), boat and engine repairs including outboards), boat and engine sales, boat building and fitting out, DIY facilities, chandlery, books and maps, solid fuel, groceries, toilets and showers, telephone. *24 hour emergency call out.*

Wakefield

W. Yorks. All services. The city centre is north of the navigation. The regional capital of West Yorkshire, it gained city status in 1888 when the cathedral was granted its charter. Mainly 15th-C Perpendicular in style, the cathedral's 247ft spire is a landmark for miles around. On a much smaller scale, but perhaps of equal interest, is the Chantry Chapel of St Mary, a rare 14th-C example of a bridge chapel, just a short walk north of Fall Ing, by the weir. Industrial pollution has meant that the entire front of the building has had to be replaced twice in the last two centuries: the original now graces the entrance to a boathouse at Kettlethorpe. The city itself is set on a hill, and still contains some quiet streets and dignified Georgian houses, notably those in St John's Square, with its delightful church and handsome council buildings. Wakefield's prosperity was founded on the textile and engineering industries, both of which have taken a battering in recent years. However, the city has been successful in attracting new industry, such as Coca Cola/ Schweppes; and the vast and spectacular Ridings shopping complex has created many new jobs. The Theatre Royal & Opera House (01924 211311; www.wakefieldtheatres.co.uk) provides a lively programme of entertainment, and the Yorkshire Sculpture Park at Bretton Hall (01924 830302; www.ysp.co.uk) – *open daily 10.00–18.00 summer and 10.00–16.00 winter* – displays some important works by Barbara Hepworth and Henry Moore, both local artists.

Tourist Information Centre Town Hall, Wood Street, Wakefield (01924 305000/1; www.visitwakefield. org.uk). North west of the cathedral. *Open Mon–Fri 08.30–17.00 (16.30 Fri) and Sat 09.00–12.00.*

Wakefield Museum Wood Street, Wakefield (01924 305351; www.wakefield.gov.uk). Local history and archaeology, excavations from Sandal Castle, and the Waterton collection of exotic birds and animals. The building, designed in 1820, was originally a music saloon. *Open Mon–Sat 10.30–16.30 and Sun 14.30–16.30.* Free.

Wakefield Art Gallery Wentworth Terrace, Wakefield (01924 305900; www.wakefield.gov.uk). Sculpture by local artists Barbara Hepworth and Henry Moore, plus contemporary paintings, prints and drawings. Also **Elizabethan Gallery** showing a wide range of temporary exhibitions. *Open Mon–Sat 10.30–16.30 and Sun 14.30–16.30.* Free.

Heath Village 2 miles east of Wakefield. A beautifully preserved village with some 18th-C merchants' houses amongst other substantial buildings. Heath Hall is a fine Georgian house by John Carr (1753) with carved woodwork and moulded plaster ceilings. The gas-lit King's Arms pub is a gem (*see* below).

Pubs and Restaurants

🍺 ✕ **Mill House** Ferry Lane, Stanley Ferry (01924 290596). A selection of real ales served in one of the old, converted wharf-side buildings. Carvery food (V) *daily 12.00–21.00 (21.30 Sat).* Children's room and extensive outdoor play area, patio and canalside seating. Adult and children's karaoke *Thur.*

🍺 ✕ **Ship** Stanley Ferry (01924 372420). Close to the marina. Comfortable, family pub, pleasantly decorated. There must have been much merriment here on the day in August 1839 when the new aqueduct opened. Today real ales and an interesting bar and restaurant menu (V) served *L and E daily* contribute more directly to the conviviality. Children welcome. Large garden and outdoor children's play area.

🍺 ✕ **King's Arms** Heath Village (01924 377527). Overlooking the common, originally built as houses in the 18th C and converted into a pub in 1841. A wide choice of real ale is served in an exceptional setting with a gas-lit, wood-panelled bar, a range of different rooms, stone-flagged floors, and full of antiques. Open fire, excellent bar and restaurant food (V) *L and E* – beef in ale pie is a speciality. Children welcome. Two walled gardens and a lawn in front.

🍺 **Ferdnandes Brewery Tap** 5 Avison Yard, Kirkgate, Wakefield (01924 369547). Once a malt store and conditioning room for Beverley Brewery – and a malt kiln before that – this pub resurrects the original brewers name and now dispenses both the present incumbent's own beers and that of guests. Food *L* (V); a dearth of electronic machines; brewery memorabilia and an open fire *in winter* makes this popular hostelry a real ale drinker's dream. *Open all day Fri–Sun and from 17.00 Mon–Thur.*

🍺 **Henry Boon's** Westgate, Wakefield (01924 378126). West of the cathedral, next to the prison. Fine traditional brewery tap for Clark's Brewery, also serving other real ales in an enthusiasts' pub, with live music *Sat.* Outside pavement seating.

✕ 🍺 **Redoubt** 28 Horbury Road, Wakefield (01924 377085). Little changed in 150 years, this heritage pub dispenses real ales *all day, every day.* Pub games, its own cricket and football teams and outside seating. A 'bring your own food' regime operates in lieu of a more local provision. Disabled access.

🍺 **Wagon** 45 Westgate, Wakefield (01924 372478). Near the railway station. A selection of real ales served in this popular, friendly local with outside seating and bar games. Toasted sandwiches are available *all day, every day.* Small garden with play area.

🍺 **Jolly Sailor** 46 Thornes Lane Wharfe, Wakefield (01924 374172). Opposite Wakefield Flood Lock. Traditional pub with a friendly atmosphere serving real ales and inexpensive bar food (including a 99p breakfast) *L (not Sun).* Children welcome. Garden. Pub games. Varied *Sat* night entertainment. Wakefield Folk Group play *Sun afternoons.*

■ BRIDGEWATER CANAL

Bridgewater Canal Introduction

MAXIMUM DIMENSIONS
Length: 70'
Beam: 14' 9"
Headroom: 8'
Draught: 2' 6"

LICENCES
Manchester Ship Canal Company, Land
Planning, Peel Dome, The Trafford Centre,
Manchester M17 1PL.
Enquiries: 0161 629 8266.

All craft using the canal must be licensed.
They must also be insured against third party
risks which should include the cost of salvage
and removal of wreck. Any boat holding a
British Waterways canal and river licence

may cruise on the Bridgewater Canal for
seven consecutive days free of charge.

MILEAGE
PRESTON BROOK to:
Lymm: 10 1/2 miles
Waters Meeting, junction with
Leigh Branch: 22 miles
CASTLEFIELD JUNCTION, start of
Rochdale Canal: 23 1/2 miles
No locks
DUCIE STREET JUNCTION, start of
Ashton Canal: 25 miles (Rochdale Canal,
9 locks)
Preston Brook to Runcorn: 4 3/4 miles, no
locks
Leigh Branch: 10 3/4 miles, no locks

The Bridgewater Canal received Royal Assent on 23 March 1759, four years after
the Sankey Brook, or St Helens, Canal and 18 years after the Newry Canal (once
known as Black Pig's Dyke), which linked Lough Neagh to the sea below Newry, in
Northern Ireland, and was probably the first 'modern' canal in the British Isles. The
Bridgewater was built by Francis Egerton, third Duke of Bridgewater, to enable coal
from his mines at Worsley to be transported to Manchester and sold cheaply. His
agent was John Gilbert and his engineer was James Brindley, who designed a lockless
contour canal which crossed the River Irwell on a stone aqueduct – a revolutionary
concept and one that was ridiculed by many sceptics. However, the line was open to
Castlefield by the end of 1765.

While the canal was under construction, there began the excavation of a remarkable
system of underground canals to serve the Duke's mines, reached through two
entrances at Worsley Delph. Eventually 46 miles of underground canal were built,
some on different levels and linked by an ingenious inclined plane built along a fault
in the sandstone. The craft used in the mines were known as 'starvationers', double-
ended tub boats which could carry up to 12 tons of coal. This whole system
remained in use until the late 19th C.

In 1762 the Duke received sanction to extend his canal to the Liverpool tideway at
Runcorn – this was later amended in order to connect with the new Trent & Mersey
Canal at Preston Brook. The route between Liverpool and Manchester was opened
in 1776, although Brindley did not live to see its completion. In 1795 the Duke, then
60 years old, received the Royal Assent for the final part of the network, which linked
Worsley to the Leeds & Liverpool Canal at Leigh.

The coming of the railways did not initially affect the prosperity of the canal. In 1872 the
newly formed Bridgewater Navigation Company purchased the canal for £1,120,000,
and they in turn sold it to the Manchester Ship Canal Company in 1885. The building
of the new Ship Canal meant that Brindley's original stone aqueduct over the River
Irwell was replaced. Its successor, the Barton Swing Aqueduct, was no less outstanding
than the original, being a steel trough closed by gates at each end, pivoting on an island
in the Ship Canal. The moving structure weighs 1450 tons, including 800 tons of water.
The Bridgewater Canal is a tribute to its builders in that it continued to carry
commercial traffic until 1974 – indeed its wide gauge, lock-free course and frequent
use of aqueducts makes many later canals seem retrograde.

Preston Brook

Although the main line of the Bridgewater once locked down to the Mersey in Runcorn, this is now a dead end, with the locks being closed in 1966. It does, however, still make an interesting diversion – there is a *supermarket* and *PO* south of bridge 74. What is now the main canal route to Manchester bears to the right immediately after the big M56 motorway bridge, and its direct course to the south of the Mersey affords good views of the Manchester Ship Canal. The canal frontage at Moore is attractive, with moored boats, a *PO, shop and off-licence*, and a *telephone box* right by the canal.

Boatyards

Ⓑ **Claymoore Navigation** The Wharf, Preston Brook (01928 717273; www.claymoore.co.uk). 🛉 🕭 D Pump out, gas, narrowboat and day-hire craft, overnight mooring, boat repairs, engine sales and repairs, toilets, books, maps and gifts, laundrette. *Emergency call out service.*

Ⓑ **Preston Brook Marina** Preston Brook (01928

719081; beverley@bromiley.freeserve.co.uk). 🛉 🕭 🕭 Gas, long-term mooring, slipway, boat sales, toilets, showers, solid fuel.

Ⓑ **Boat and Butty Company** Ockleston's Wharf, Ringway Road, Runcorn (01928 569069/733522 or 07976 303696). 🛉 🕭 🕭 Pump out, gas (next door), long-term mooring, winter storage, DIY facilities.

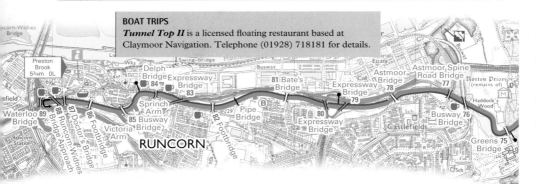

BOAT TRIPS
Tunnel Top II is a licensed floating restaurant based at Claymoor Navigation. Telephone (01928) 718181 for details.

● **Preston Brook Tunnel**
1239yds long and forbidden to unpowered craft. *A notice indicates when you may enter – see page 186.*

● **Preston Brook**
Ches. *PO, tel, stores.* A village which grew to serve the canal, where goods were transshipped from wide beam craft of the north west to narrowboats of the Midlands. Unfortunately, little remains as evidence of this activity, and the M56 dominates.
Norton Priory (01928 569895). Access from mooring north east of bridge 75. Only the undercroft survives from the 11th C. A recorded commentary describes points of interest. Pleasant woodland and sculpture gardens. *Open Apr–Oct, Mon–Fri 12.00–17.00, Sat, Sun and public holidays 12.00–18.00; Nov–Mar, daily 12.00–16.00.* Charge.

● **Runcorn**
Ches. *All services.* The old town is to be found down by the docks, where the elegant curved 1092ft single span of the steel road bridge (built 1961), with the railway beside, leaps over the Ship Canal and the Mersey. The massive flight of 10 double locks which connected the Bridgewater Canal to the Mersey was abandoned in 1966 and filled in, much to the dismay of industrial archaeologists and canal

enthusiasts. Since 1964 Runcorn has been a 'new town', its rapid growth being carefully planned.
Runcorn Tourist Information Centre 6 Church Street (01928 576776, tourist.info@halton-borough. gov.uk). *Open Mon–Thur 08.45–17.15, Fri 08.45–16.30, Sat 10.00–12.30.*

● **Daresbury**
Ches. *Tel, stores.* Half-a-mile up the road from Keckwick Bridge, this was the birthplace of Charles Lutwidge Dodgson, better known as Lewis Carroll. The church of All Saints has a pretty Lewis Carroll memorial window in the Daniell Chapel, where he is shown with characters from *Alice in Wonderland:* the Dormouse, the Mad Hatter and the Cheshire Cat. This window was designed by Geoffrey Webb, and was dedicated in 1934. The original church on this site dates from the 12thC, and was a daughter house of nearby Norton Priory (*see* above). The present tower dates from around 1550, with the rest of the church being rebuilt in the 1870s. The fine oak pulpit, dating from 1625, and the rood screen incorporated into the panelling behind the altar, are both worth a look. *The church is open most afternoons.*

Pubs and Restaurants

🍺 **Ring O' Bells** Old Chester Road, Daresbury (01925 740256). There has been an ale house here since 1641, although this building dates from 1841. The adjoining stables are older than the pub: to the other side the old Petty Sessions room has been incorporated. Pleasantly busy, with a relaxed atmosphere and open fires. Real ale, and good food, including fresh fish specials (V) *12.00–22.00 (21.30 Sun)*. Children are welcome.

🍺 **Red Lion** Runcorn Road, Moore (01925 740205; www.the-red-lion-moore.co.uk). A friendly and traditional pub just a few minutes' walk west of bridge 7. Real ale, and meals, with an excellent choice (V) *L and E*. Children are welcome in the tap room. Quiz on *Tue*. Garden.

There are plenty of pubs in Runcorn, including:

🍺 **Grapes Inn** (01928 575091). Between bridges 82 and 83. Families are welcome in this pub, which has a bowling green in the garden.

🍺 **Waterloo** 88 High Street (01928 772276; pat@waterloohotel.fsnet.co.uk). Between bridges 88 and 89. A Victorian pub with a canal boat theme in the bar. Patio garden. Families welcome. Karaoke *Thur* and *Sat*. B & B.

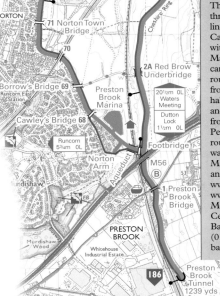

WALKING & CYCLING
The towpath is in good condition throughout. The towpath on the main line forms part of the Cheshire Ring Canal Walk, which makes a circuit with the Ashton, Peak Forest, Macclesfield and Trent & Mersey canals. Leaflets giving details of cycle routes in Runcorn can be obtained from transport.co-ordination@ halton-borough.gov.uk. A Cyclists Map and Guide to Runcorn can be obtained from www.cycling.org.uk. The Trans Pennine Trail is a 350-mile national route which crosses Runcorn on its way from Liverpool to Warrington. Maps and an Official Accommodation and Visitor Guide are available from www.transpenninetrail.org.uk, www.sustrans.gov.uk or Barnsley Metropolitan Borough Council, Central Offices, Kendray Street, Barnsley, South Yorkshire, S70 2TN (01226 772574; transpenninetrail@ barnsley.gov.uk).

Stockton Heath

A short rural stretch is interrupted by the estate village of Higher Walton, which can be seen among trees, and this is followed by a secluded tree-lined length in a shallow cutting before the outskirts of Stockton Heath are approached. There follows a pleasant example of urban canal, busy

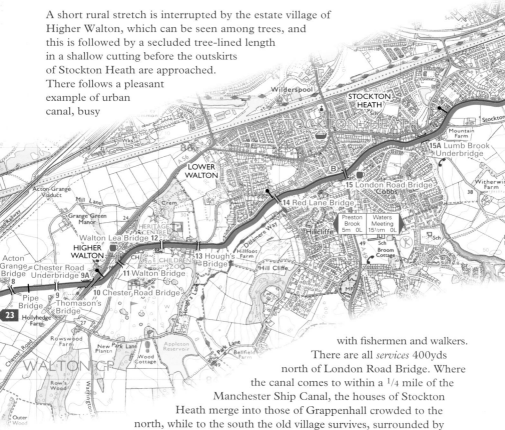

with fishermen and walkers. There are all *services* 400yds north of London Road Bridge. Where the canal comes to within a 1/4 mile of the Manchester Ship Canal, the houses of Stockton Heath merge into those of Grappenhall crowded to the north, while to the south the old village survives, surrounded by open country. The canal makes a dog-leg turn past Thelwall and then proceeds under the M6 motorway south of the vast Thelwall Viaduct, which climbs laboriously over the Ship Canal. *Coal* and *logs* are sold canalside near Thelwall Underbridge.

Boatyards

Ⓑ **Thorn Marine** London Bridge, Stockton Heath (01925 265129; www.thornemarine.co.uk). ☏ ⚓ D Pump out, gas, day-boat and short breaks hire, engine sales, boat and engine repairs, chandlery, toilets, showers, books, maps and gifts, solid fuels. Public telephone and shopping centre *nearby*.

● **Higher Walton**
Ches. PO, tel, stores. A pretty, late-Victorian estate village among trees.
Walton Hall Higher Walton (01925 601617; waltonhall@warrington.gov.uk). Twenty acres of parkland and gardens *open from dawn to dusk*. Facilities include children's zoo, outdoor games, heritage centre, play area, café and Ranger Service organising activities for the public and groups (telephone for details). Charge for facilities only.

● **Stockton Heath**
Ches. PO, tel, stores. Shops and services north of London Bridge. An outer suburb of Warrington, England's centre for vodka distilling and a useful place for supplies.

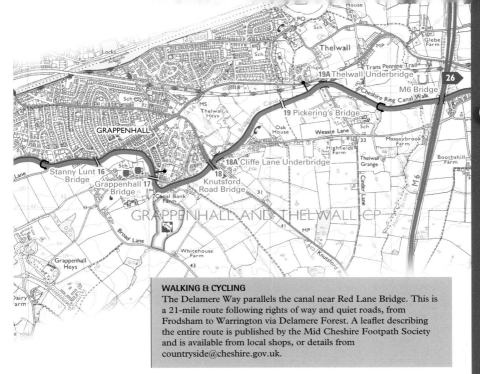

WALKING & CYCLING
The Delamere Way parallels the canal near Red Lane Bridge. This is
a 21-mile route following rights of way and quiet roads, from
Frodsham to Warrington via Delamere Forest. A leaflet describing
the entire route is published by the Mid Cheshire Footpath Society
and is available from local shops, or details from
countryside@cheshire.gov.uk.

Stockton Quay Bridge 15. The terminus of the
canal from 1771 to 1776, before the Duke of
Bridgewater completed his route from
Manchester to Runcorn, and consequently a
major transshipment point with stables, yards,
wharves, warehouses and a canal company
office. Passenger packet boat services also ran
from here from 1771 to the mid 1880s, one of
the craft being the renowned *Duchess-Countess*.

● **Grappenhall**
Ches. PO, tel, stores. A fine group of buildings
on cobbled streets survive around the church
of St Wilfred, where the village stocks remain.
There are two excellent pubs, which makes a
stop here very worthwhile.

● **Thelwall**
Ches. PO, tel, stores. A short walk north from
Thelwall Underbridge will bring you to 'The
Penny Ferry' where, for a minimal charge,
you can be carried across the Ship Canal (*see
also* Pubs and Restaurants).

Pubs and Restaurants

● ✕ **Walton Arms** Chester Road, Higher
Walton (01925 262659). Real ale in a
comfortable 'Country Carvery'. Traditional
food (V) *all day, every day.* Children
welcome if eating. Outside seating.

● **London Bridge** Stockton Heath. By bridge
15. A homely and welcoming pub with a
canalside terrace, offering real ale and food.

● ✕ **Rams Head** Church Lane, Grappenhall
(01925 262814). A comfortable old-fashioned
pub on a cobbled street in a conservation
village, where *Sherlock Holmes* was filmed. À la
carte meals (V) are served in the restaurant *L*
and E Mon–Sat, and 12.00–20.00 Sun. Outside
seating. B & B.

● **Parr Arms** Church Lane, Grappenhall
(01925 267393). A comfortable and homely
pub on the cobbled street, right beside the
church, serving real ale. Good food (V) *L and
E.* Children welcome *until 20.30.* Outside
seating.

● **Penny Ferry Inn** 271 Latchford Lane,
Latchford, Warrington (01925 638487). You
can have a snack and a pint here while you
wait for the ferry. Children are welcome, and
there is a garden and a play park next door.

Lymm

There are fine views of the distant Pennines to the north before the canal makes a very pleasing passage through the heart of Lymm, where the streets come right down to the water's edge. There are

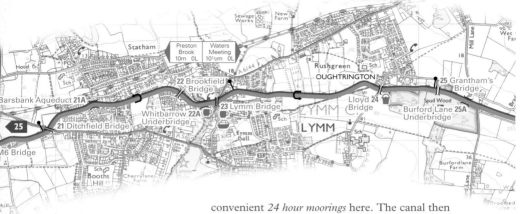

convenient *24 hour moorings* here. The canal then passes the village of Oughtrington to the north and a row of smart new houses to the south before entering surroundings which are surprisingly rural. Rows of moored boats, some in an advanced state of decay, announce the presence of two useful boatyards and a pub. The fields then gently fall away into the valley of the River Bollin, which the Bridgewater crosses on a large embankment, with fine views of the Manchester Ship Canal and Dunham Park. Dunham Underbridge is a new concrete and steel construction, built to replace the original stone trough which breached disastrously in August 1971 and resulted in a two-year closure and repairs amounting to £250,000 at the time. There are good moorings by Dunham Town Bridge.

● **Lymm**
Ches. PO, tel, stores, banks, fish & chips, laundrette.
The 17th-C Lymm Cross stands just a few yards from the canal in the centre of this hilly and attractive little town. The dam at the back of the town was built to carry the turnpike road over a sharp ravine, thus creating a pleasant lake in the process.

● **Oughtrington**
Ches. PO, tel, stores. A good place for supplies.

● **Bollington**
Ches. A compact and attractive village, with a fine old pub and a converted mill.
Dunham Massey Hall NT Altrincham (0161 941 1025; www.nationaltrust.org.uk). Once the seat of the Earl of Stamford, this beautiful 18th-C house by John Norris stands in a wooded and well-stocked deer park, landscaped by George Booth, the Second Earl of Warrington, and now considered to be one of the north west's great plantsman's gardens. A sumptuous interior contains collections of Huguenot silver,

paintings and walnut furniture. There is also an 18th-C orangery, an Elizabethan mount and a well-house. Concerts are staged in the gallery; exhibitions, fairs and services are held in the house and chapel; and there is a short programme of interesting conducted walks. Access is via Bollington, over the footbridge near the Swan with Two Nicks pub. *House open late Mar–Oct, Sat–Wed 11.00–17.00 (Oct 12.00–16.00); garden open Apr–Oct, daily 11.00–17.30.* Admission charge. Restaurant and shop.

● **Dunham Town**
Gt Manchester. PO, tel, stores. A small, scattered, farming village with a pub.

WALKING & CYCLING
From Lymm Dam it is possible to access an excellent footpath network, details from www.warrington.gov.uk.

Bridgewater Canal Lymm

Boatyards

Ⓑ **Hesford Marine** Warrington Lane, Lymm (01925 754639). ♿ D Gas, long-term mooring, winter storage, slipway, crane (16 ton), dry dock, boat building, boat sales and repairs, engine repairs, chandlery, toilets, books, maps and gifts, solid fuel, DIY facilities.

Ⓑ **Lymm Marina Boat Sales** Warrington Lane, Lymm (01925 752945 or 07798 752945;

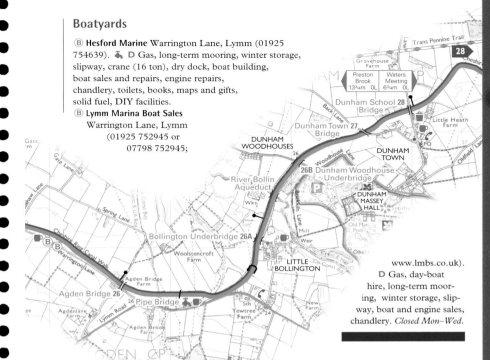

www.lmbs.co.uk). D Gas, day-boat hire, long-term mooring, winter storage, slipway, boat and engine sales, chandlery. *Closed Mon–Wed.*

Pubs and Restaurants

Golden Fleece 41 The Cross, Lymm (01925 755538). By bridge 23. A picturesque canal-side pub, serving real ale. Food (V) is available *Mon–Fri 12.00–16.00, Sat and Sun 12.00–18.00.* Children welcome *until 20.00,* garden with swings. Quiz night *Thur.*

Bull's Head 30a The Cross, Lymm (01925 752831). By bridge 23. A cosy traditional village local serving real ale. Children are welcome *during the day.* Small courtyard.

Barn Owl Inn ✕ Agden Wharf, Warrington Lane (01925 752020). Between bridges 25 and 26. A friendly pub in a converted boatyard building, with fine views and serving a variety of real ales. Food (V) *L and E, daily.* Children welcome, canalside garden. Live music *Sat.* You can call for a ferry from the towpath side.

Ye Olde No. 3 Lymm Road, Little Bollington. Near Bollington Underbridge. An attractive former coaching inn with no less than three ghosts, which now has a selection of special nights, including live music. Bar meals (V) *Mon–Fri L, Sat 12.00–21.30, Sun L and E.* Canalside garden. Children welcome for meals.

Swan With Two Nicks ✕ Park Lane, Little Bollington (0161 928 2914). By Bollington Underbridge (26A), and just a few minutes' walk into the village. A very fine, comfortable and cosy pub with a friendly atmosphere, serving real ale. Extensive menu (V) for upmarket bar food and à la carte *Mon–Sat L and E, and Sun all day.* The name of the pub harks back to times when swans were taken as food: unmarked birds belonged to the monarch, who could dispense them at will. The nicks indicated ownership. It is all very similar to 'Swan Upping' on the River Thames, a ceremony which still continues today. Collections of key rings, bottles and bottle openers. Large garden. Children welcome.

Axe and Cleaver Hotel School Lane, Dunham Town (0161 928 3391). Village pub with log fires, candles and traditional decor, serving real ale and food (V) *all day, every day.* Family room, garden with play area and bouncy castle. Regular club meetings take place here including Harley Davidson, MG, Triumph and Stag owners. Food theme nights *Sep–Dec.*

Sale

Beyond Seamons Moss Bridge buildings close in upon the canal, and the countryside rapidly disappears from view. Among the many industrial buildings, both old and new, stands the superb Victorian Linotype Factory, dated 1897, where metal printing type was manufactured. The Metrolink tramway closes in from the south east and escorts the canal all the way through Sale and on into Stretford – as the trams pass by you can enjoy a more relaxing 3mph. There is a handy canalside pub before the waterway is crossed by the M63 motorway, which then crosses the River Mersey. A large expanse of graves opposite the Watch House Cruising Club heralds the entrance to Stretford. *PO, stores, fish & chips* are to be found south of Seamons Moss Bridge.

Pubs and Restaurants

Bay Malton Seamons Road, Dunham Massey (0161 928 0655). By Seamons Moss Bridge, no 29. A friendly community pub, offering real ale and food (V) *L and E*. Children welcome *until 20.00*. The garden has a new patio area, with a barbecue and outside heating. Live music and karaoke *Fri*.

Old Packet House Navigation Road, Broadheath, Altrincham (0161 929 1331). North of bridge 30. A fine old inn dating from the 1770s, when it was a staging post for the Bridgewater packet boat. It is a warm and friendly place, with open fires, dark panelling and exposed brickwork. Real ales are served and good food (V) is available *L and E (not Sun or Mon E)*. Children are welcome, and there is an enclosed garden for sunny days. Karaoke *Fri*, 60s and 70s music *Sun*.

King's Ransome Sale (0161 969 6006). By bridge 35. A new pub in fine converted canalside brick buildings, which were at one time part of a coal yard. They extend under the railway, so the pub is larger than you might think. Real ale is served, and food is available *L and E (not Sun E)*. They are particularly proud of their roast meat carvery *Sun L*. Children over ten years are welcome if eating. Live music *Thur*, and a magician performs on *Sun*. Fine selection of malt whiskies, and canalside seating on a floating pontoon.

Bridge Inn Dane Road, Sale (0161 969 7536). By bridge 36A. Comfortable canalside pub offering an ever-changing range of real ales, along with bar meals (V) *L and E, daily*. Children welcome. Garden with children's play area. Mooring. Live music *Sat*, quiz and disco *Mon*.

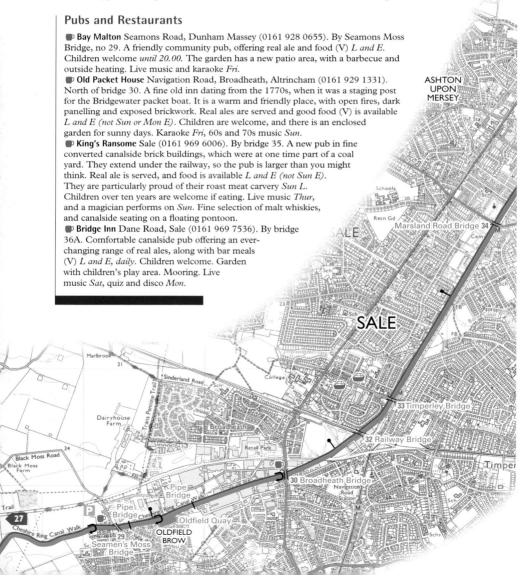

STRETFORD

(map labels)

30
B
M
38 Edge Lane Bridge
Sch
94
Watch House C.C.
Cut Hole
Aqueduct P
Flood
Gates
Hawthorn Road
23
Barfoot Aqueduct
37 M60 Motorway
Crossford
Bridge
Sale
Water Park
93
P
36 Whites
Bridge
Sale Ees
M
P
2m 0L
Waters
Meeting
Preston
Brook
18½m 0L
Allot
Gdns
M 35 Sale Bridge
Sch
Offices
Brooklands
FB

Boatyards

B **Egerton Narrowboats** Edge Boatyard, Edge Lane, Stretford (0161 864 1066; www. egertonnarrowboats. co.uk). ☎ 🛒 ⚓ D Pump out, gas, long-term mooring, winter storage, crane, boat and engine repairs, toilets.

● **Altrincham**

Gt Manchester. PO. A few black and white half-timbered buildings remain in the market square of what was once a small market town. Later in the 18th C it became a textile manufacturing centre, and is now, inevitably, a dormitory town for Manchester.

● **Sale**

Gt Manchester. All services. A residential suburb of Manchester, transformed from a farming community by the building in 1849 of the Altrincham to Manchester Railway – hence most of its buildings are Victorian or later. St Martin's Church is, however, 18th-C and has a hammerbeam roof. The clock tower of the town hall, built in 1914, is a prominent landmark. Look for the plaque in the wall commemorating the work of James Prescott Joule, who was born in Salford and calculated the mathematical relationship between heat and electrical energy. The northern part of Sale merges without boundary into Ashton upon Mersey, which is unremarkable except as the birthplace of Stanley Houghton (1881–1913) who wrote *The Dear Departed* in 1908 and *Hindle Wakes* in 1912.

ARTERIES OF INDUSTRY

A growing economy demands transport and power. The Romans recognised these needs and built the Caer-dyke, a part of which still survives as the Fossdyke Navigation, to the west of Lincoln. They realised a horse can pull only 2 tons on a good road, but up to 100 tons on a waterway.

Edward the Confessor ordered improvements on the Thames, Severn, Trent and Yorkshire Ouse, and it was about this time that an artificial cut, a revolutionary idea at the time, was made to improve navigation on the Itchen. The development of the 'flash' lock, where a weir was used to build up a head of water which was then released to propel craft over an obstruction, was eventually superseded by the 'pound' lock, still in use today.

But it was the Newry Canal, the Sankey Brook and the Bridgewater Canal, which was built to serve the Duke's mines at Worsley and was still in commercial use until the 1970s, which heralded the start of the Canal Age.

At Waters Meeting, marked with a fine vortex sculpture, the original main line of the canal is joined – to the north west is Barton, Leigh and the connection with the Leeds & Liverpool Canal; to the east is the centre of Manchester and the Rochdale Canal, which once again crosses the hills to Rochdale, having recently been restored. The Bridgewater's route is now hemmed in by factory walls and fences, passing close to Manchester United football ground, where the new stand of this famous club towers above the canal, and the magnificent Salford Quays. Old Trafford cricket ground, the home of Lancashire Cricket Club and a Test Match venue, is a little further south. Near bridge 95 there is a fine mural, painted in 1993 by Walter Kershaw, depicting transport and industry. More empty docks are passed following the well-painted Throstle Nest Footbridge. The Manchester Ship Canal is now very close – indeed just across the towpath – with good views of the City Park buildings and the distant city centre. The new Metrolink towers over the waterway, before crossing high above Pomona Lock – the connection with the Ship Canal. Have a look on the towpath side for the circular overflow weir by bridge 97, and notice the disused basins beyond the towpath. These are followed by a railway bridge, more overgrown basins and the remains of the Hulme Lock Branch – the original junction with the Ship Canal. The excitingly restored Castlefield Junction is then reached. It is well worth stopping here to explore the basins under the railway bridge, and to visit the pubs and restaurants. Moor on the stretch below Grocers Warehouse (*laundrette* facilities are available at the YHA on the Staffordshire Arm). The first of the nine wide locks of the Rochdale Canal is right beside the restored Merchants' Warehouse. The gear is anti-vandal locked, so you will need to use the British Waterways key. The canal now passes between the backs of tall buildings and beneath elaborate railway arches, all of which have a certain faded grandeur. Tantalising glimpses of Victorian buildings invite exploration, but be wary of mooring away from Castlefield. You then pass the gay village, adjacent to Chorlton Street Lock, before finally the canal crawls under an 18-storey office block where you will find the top lock amidst concrete pillars. Ahead lies the Rochdale Canal (*see* page 158). Sharp right and left turns bring you to the start of the Ashton Canal, and the climb to Fairfield Junction (*see* page 154).

Boatyards

Ⓑ **Egerton Narrowboats** The Arches Boatyard, Potato Wharf, Castlefield (0161 864 1066; www.egertonnarrowboats.co.uk). 🚽 🚽 🔧 **D** Pump out, gas, overnight mooring by arrangement – telephone in advance, long-term mooring.

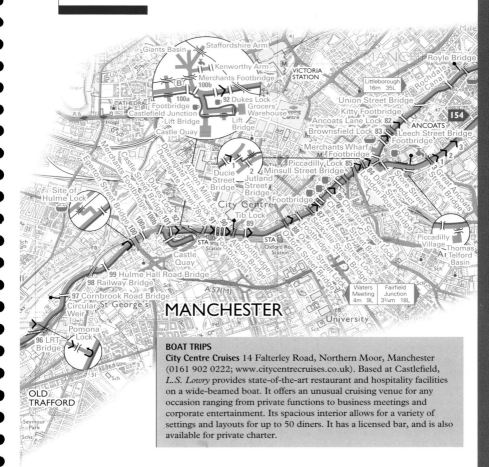

BOAT TRIPS
City Centre Cruises 14 Falterley Road, Northern Moor, Manchester (0161 902 0222; www.citycentrecruises.co.uk). Based at Castlefield, *L.S. Lowry* provides state-of-the-art restaurant and hospitality facilities on a wide-beamed boat. It offers an unusual cruising venue for any occasion ranging from private functions to business meetings and corporate entertainment. Its spacious interior allows for a variety of settings and layouts for up to 50 diners. It has a licensed bar, and is also available for private charter.

● **Manchester**
All services. One of Britain's finest Victorian cities, a monument to 19th-C commerce and the textile boom, its size increasing remorselessly with the building of the canals, and later railways. Unfortunately virtually no early buildings survived the city's rapid growth, although there is an incredible wealth

of Victorian architecture surviving, in spite of redevelopment. The town hall and surrounding streets are a particularly rich area (north of Oxford Street Bridge). St Peter's Square, by the town hall, was the site of the 'Peterloo Massacre' in 1819, when a meeting demanding political reform was brutally dispersed by troops carrying drawn sabres. Eleven people were killed and many more were injured. The Free Trade Hall, once the home of the Hallé Orchestra, is a little further along the road. Built in 1856, it was badly damaged in World War II, but was subsequently re-built to its original Palladian design. There is theatre, ballet and cinema, art galleries, and a wealth of interesting buildings, Victorian shopping arcades, many pubs with a choice of good beer and a variety of restaurants just a short walk from the canal. Sporting facilities are excellent, partly as a consequence of Manchester being the venue for the 2002 Commonwealth Games. The new developments at Salford Quays, on the Manchester Ship Canal, are quite breathtaking.

Museum of Science and Industry Liverpool Road, off Deansgate (0161 832 2244; www.msim.org.uk). Located on the site of the world's first passenger railway station, this exciting hands-on museum has 14 galleries covering everything from steam to space, transport to textiles, and includes a working steam train, a

NAVIGATIONAL NOTES

MANCHESTER SHIP CANAL

Harbour Master, Queen Elizabeth II Dock, Eastham, Wirral (0151 327 1461). The ship canal currently carries an increasing annual tonnage of approximately 2,500 vessel movements per year. A great deal of it is hazardous, petro-chemical traffic and therefore a no smoking régime is enforced. The canal company is happy to allow pleasure boats use on the understanding that certain conditions are adhered to. It is not a navigation for the novice boater and should be viewed as a transit corridor for the experienced boat owner (not hire boater) to access the River Weaver, the River Mersey and the Shropshire Union Canal. In essence the company's requirements are as follows:

1   The boat must carry £1 million third party insurance cover.
2   The boat is subject to an annual Certificate of Seaworthiness (not required for the passage from Pomona Lock *east* to Hunts Bank).
3   The appropriate fee is paid for each lock used, plus a fixed charge per passage.
4   The boater must contact the harbourmaster in advance of passage to obtain copies of:
    a) Pleasure Craft Transit Notes;
    b) Port of Manchester Navigation By-laws.
    At this juncture boaters can discuss appropriate times of arrival and departure to coincide with scheduled shipping movements.
5   At all times the boater is required to act in a responsible manner and be aware that this is a *daytime* transit route only, with no lay-by facilities. Boaters should familiarise themselves with the geography of the canal before setting out.
6   VHF radio equipment is desirable (the Manchester Ship Canal Company call on channel 14 and operate on channels 14 and 20) and if not available a mobile phone should be considered essential. (Eastham VTS – 0151 327 1242; Latchford Locks – 01925 635249).

The above synopsis is a brief note of the essential requirements and should be read in conjunction with **The Transit Notes** and **Navigation Bylaws** referred to in 4 above. Also available from the MSC at Peel Dome are notes for the transit of Pomona Lock and 'The Upper Reach', for which a Certificate of Seaworthiness is NOT required.

Weston Marsh Lock Access to the River Weaver via Weston Marsh Lock is during the following duty hours and only after prior notice to BW at Northwich (01606 723900): *Mon–Thur 08.00–16.00, Fri 08.00–15.00.* The lock may be available on some summer weekends *(end of May B Hol–Sep)*. Contact BW for further details. VHF channel for the River Weaver is 74.

Ellesmere Port Bottom Lock Entry into the Manchester Ship Canal from the Shropshire Union is restricted by a swing bridge over the first lock (adjacent to the Holiday Inn) which is not under the control of BW. Boaters wishing to enter the canal must first contact Ellesmere Port & Neston Borough Council (0151 356 6433) to make arrangements for the bridge to be swung. Any difficulties in obtaining assistance should be referred to the BW Chester office on 01244 390372.

reconstructed Victorian sewer (complete with smells!) and an interactive science centre. *Open daily 10.00–17.00.* Free. Coffee shop.
Granada Studios Water Street, close to the Museum of Science and Industry (0161 833 0880). An extremely popular attraction, where you can visit Coronation Street, 'Baker Street', '10 Downing Street', The Giants Room, 3D shows, Motion Master cinema and many other highlights. Restaurants and shops. Disabled facilities. *Opening times vary: open daily Jul–Aug, plus most days during the summer season; open less often during the winter. You are advised to telephone for details. Admission for tours 09.45–15.00, closes at 17.00.* Charge.
Lowry Centre Pier 8, Salford Quays (0161 876 2020; www.manchester.com/java/guidebook/museums/lowry/home). On the promontory between Huron Basin and the Ship Canal. A gallery depicting the life and works (over 350) of the Salford artist L. S. Lowry, along with theatre, opera, ballet, cabaret, comedy, jazz and a children's gallery, housed in an exciting new waterside building by Michael Wilford & Partners. *Gallery usually open 11.00–17.00 but it can vary, so telephone to confirm.*
Imperial War Museum North Trafford Wharf Road, Trafford Park (0161 836 4000; www.iwm.org.uk/north). Right beside the Ship Canal, in a stunning new building by Daniel Libeskind, clad in shimmering aluminium and representing a world shattered by war. Visitors enter through the 55-metres-high air shaft, giving fine views over the city. Exhibitions

depict weapons, aircraft, the experience of war, science and war, interactive collections and a spectacular audio-visual display. *Open daily 10.00–18.00.* Free.
Metrolink The new electric 'supertram'. G-Mex is a station close to the canal, near to the second lock, if you fancy a ride. Information on 0161 205 2000.
Tourist Information Centre Town Hall Extension, Lloyd Street, St Peter's Square, Manchester (0161 234 3157; www.manchester.gov.uk). To the north of Oxford Street Bridge. *Open 10.00–17.30 (Suns and B Hols 16.30).*
● **Manchester Ship Canal**
The Harbour Master, Manchester Ship Canal Company, Eastham Locks, Queen Elizabeth II Dock, Eastham (0151 327 1461). The canal was opened in 1894 at a cost of £15½ million and carries ships up to 15,000 tons displacement. It is 36 miles long and connects the tidal Mersey at Eastham to Manchester. The Weaver Navigation, the Bridgewater Canal and the Shropshire Union Canal connect with it. All craft using the canal must be licensed. They must also be insured against third party risks which should include the cost of salvage and removal of wreck. There is a charge for the use of Pomona Lock, and advance notice is required – telephone 0161 629 8266. Any boat holding a British Waterways canal and river licence may cruise on the Bridgewater Canal for seven consecutive days free of charge.

Pubs and Restaurants

There are many fine pubs in Manchester. Those close to the canal include:
● **Dukes '92** Castle Street (0161 839 8646). Serving real ale, this modern bar was once a stable for the nearby Merchant's Warehouse. Food, cheese and paté *all day.* Outside seating. Children welcome. Gallery of prints upstairs. DJ *Fri and Sat.*
● **Jacksons Wharf** Opposite Dukes '92 (0161 819 5317). This large and smart bar overlooks Castlefield, and has plenty of outside seating. Food (V) is available *all day, every day.* Children welcome. A DJ entertains *each Fri and Sat.*
● ✕ **New Union** Princess Street (0161 228 1492). Towpath side by Princess Street Lock. A comfortable pub in the gay village serving real ale, and sandwiches *L (not Sun).* Drag queens perform *Tue and Sun,* karaoke *Thur.*
● **Rembrandt Hotel** 33 Sackville Street (0161 236 1311; rembrandthotel@aol.com). Towpath side between the Princess and Chorlton Street locks. A friendly hotel in the

centre of the gay village, and serving real ale. Food (V) is available *L and E (not Tue).* Canalside seating. Children over 12 welcome upstairs. B & B.
● **Churchills** 37 Chorlton Street (0161 236 5529). Towpath side by Chorlton Street Lock. A recently refurbished traditional pub one side, with a café/bar on the other. Full disabled facilities, and clean air award winners. Meals (V) are available *all day, every day.* Children welcome, plenty of outside seating. DJ and karaoke *nightly,* and live music *Wed.* Mooring.
● **Jolly Angler** Ducie Street, Manchester (0161 236 5307). Near the junction. A small, plain and very friendly pub visited every few months by Mike Harding, the folk singer, and offering real ale and snacks *at all times* (or you can eat your own sandwiches!). Café nearby. Regular Irish music sessions *Thur and Sat,* folk on *Sun* and ad hoc sessions whenever enough customers are willing. Children welcome. Moorings nearby, but don't leave your boat here overnight.

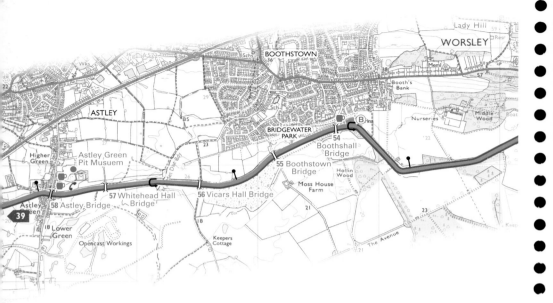

Worsley

This is a surprisingly interesting section of waterway, well worth visiting for its own sake and a useful link with the Leeds & Liverpool Canal. What was the original line of the canal leaves Waters Meeting through the vast Trafford Park Industrial Estate to cross the Manchester Ship Canal on the impressive Barton Swing Aqueduct, after passing an incongruous landscaped pagoda. Curving through the suburbs of Salford and the leafy expanse of Broadoak Park, the navigation reaches the village of Worsley and what was the entrance to the underground mines which provided its *raison d'être*. It is well worth stopping to take a look around the Delph, to see at first hand what brought about the canals' construction. You will also notice that dissolved iron ore colours the canal bright ochre around here – a scheme has been proposed to clean the water, although many locals have now formed an attachment to its unnatural colour! After Worsley the M60 motorway and its attendant slip roads cross the canal. The Bridgewater then heads west through open country now only hinting at its industrial past, thanks to a vast clearing-up operation. There is, however, more solid evidence of the area's mining connections at Astley, where it's worth stopping for a short while to visit the Colliery Museum.

Boatyards

ⓑ **Worsley Dry Docks** The Boatyard, Worsley (0161 793 6767). By bridge 51. Moorings, some chandlery and dry dock.

ⓑ **Bridgewater Marina** Boothstown Basin, 14 Quayside Close, Worsley (0161 702 8622). By bridge 54. 🛉 🛉 🕹 D Pump out, gas, day-boat hire, overnight and long-term mooring, winter storage, boat sales and repairs, engine repairs, chandlery, toilets, showers, books, maps and gifts, laundrette, solid fuel, DIY facilities. *Emergency call out.*

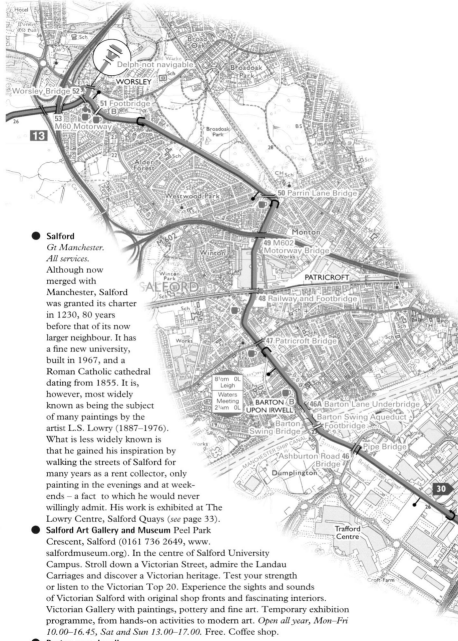

Salford
Gt Manchester.
All services.
Although now
merged with
Manchester, Salford
was granted its charter
in 1230, 80 years
before that of its now
larger neighbour. It has
a fine new university,
built in 1967, and a
Roman Catholic cathedral
dating from 1855. It is,
however, most widely
known as being the subject
of many paintings by the
artist L.S. Lowry (1887–1976).
What is less widely known is
that he gained his inspiration by
walking the streets of Salford for
many years as a rent collector, only
painting in the evenings and at weekends – a fact to which he would never
willingly admit. His work is exhibited at The
Lowry Centre, Salford Quays (*see page 33*).

Salford Art Gallery and Museum Peel Park
Crescent, Salford (0161 736 2649, www.
salfordmuseum.org). In the centre of Salford University
Campus. Stroll down a Victorian Street, admire the Landau
Carriages and discover a Victorian heritage. Test your strength
or listen to the Victorian Top 20. Experience the sights and sounds
of Victorian Salford with original shop fronts and fascinating interiors.
Victorian Gallery with paintings, pottery and fine art. Temporary exhibition
programme, from hands-on activities to modern art. *Open all year, Mon–Fri*
10.00–16.45, Sat and Sun 13.00–17.00. Free. Coffee shop.

Barton upon Irwell
Gt Manchester. Tel, stores, garage. In an interesting position overlooking the two canals. The richly
decorated Catholic Church of the City of Mary Immaculate is by Pugin, 1867, and is considered
to be one of his best works. Indeed the architect can be found featured in a painting on the south
wall of the chancel.

● **Barton Aqueduct**

One of the wonders of the waterways, it carries the Bridgewater Canal over the Manchester Ship Canal. Designed by Sir Edward Leader Williams, it was built in the early 1890s in a bold style comparable to contemporary railway engineering. Gates seal off the 235ft-long 1450-ton section that swings at right angles to the Ship Canal over a central island. It replaced Brindley's earlier aqueduct, built in 1761 and which carried the canal in a trough over 660ft long and 39ft above the Irwell, truly a wonder in its day. The aqueduct operates *summer, Mon–Thur 09.15–18.30, Fri–Sun 09.15–20.30; winter, daily 09.15–16.30.* The aqueduct is usually *closed for maintenance during the last two weeks of September* – telephone 0161 888 8266 for details.

● **Patricroft**

Gt Manchester. All services. Here are the Bridgewater Mills, established in 1836 by Nasmyth, who invented the steam hammer.

● **Eccles**

Gt Manchester. All services. The town peaked as a cotton and silk weaving centre between 1870–90, and little has happened since, although its name will always be remembered in connection with the famous cakes – round pastry filled with currants. The Church of St Mary has its origins in the 10th C, although the present sandstone building dates from the late 15th C.

Monks Hall Museum Wellington Road. Contains an important collection of Nasmyth machine tools and relics. *Closed Sun.*

● **Worsley**

Gt Manchester. PO, tel, stores, garage. An attractive estate village dating from the 18th–19th C, and widely recognised as the place which triggered the 'canal age', in spite of the fact that the Bridgewater was not the first modern canal in the British Isles. Coal had been mined in Worsley since the 14th C, originally from the surface, and later by sinking shafts. It is thought that a drainage sough, common in underground workings, may have provided the germ of the idea for an underground canal network which could be used to bring the coal out. John Gilbert, the Duke of Bridgewater's agent, probably designed the system, which included an inclined plane on a 1 in 4 gradient 453ft long and 60ft wide. Work started at the same time on the building of the canal to Manchester, and eventually 46 miles of tunnels were hewn out. A particular kind of simple double-ended tub boat was used underground, called a 'starvationer'. These carried up to 12 tons of coal. The old canal basin at Worsley Delph, with its entrance tunnels to the mines, is still intact, and information boards help to explain its workings. On the canal, look out for the Boathouse, built by Lord Ellesmere to house the royal barge, prepared for Queen Victoria's visit in 1851, and Duke's Wharf, an old oil store. Close by is Worsley Old Hall, the half-timbered Court House and The Old Reading Room, which was originally a nailers shop, shown on a plan of 1785 and painted on a Wedgwood dinner service presented to Queen Catherine II of Russia. The church, by George Gilbert Scott, 1846, has a spire decorated with crockets and gargoyles – inside there is a rich collection of monuments to the Dukes of Bridgewater.

● **Astley Green**

Gt Manchester. Tel, stores. Canalside mining village dominated by a gaunt red-brick Victorian church. **Astley Green Colliery Museum** Higher Green Lane, Astley (01942 828121; www.astleygreen. freeservers.com). To the north of the canal, perched on the edge of Chat Moss. The colliery was originally owned by the Pilkington Colliery Company, a branch of the Clifton and Kearsley Coal Company, which commenced the sinking of the first of two shafts in 1908. There are various pit relics to explore, plus a superb engine house containing a 3,300 HP twin tandem compound engine by Yates & Thom of Blackburn. This once wound the 8 ton lift which transported the miners to their work 873yds underground, at a maximum speed of 82ft per second (55mph!). Astley Green Colliery is situated in an area that was once full of collieries, but over the years they have all been closed, and demolished. There is now only one headgear and engine house left in Lancashire – this one, which ceased commercial activity in 1970. Being restored by the Red Rose Steam Society, it remains as a valuable reminder of life and work in this area in the recent past. *Open Sun 12.00–17.00, Tue and Thur 13.00–17.00. The site can also be visited at any other time by prior arrangement by school parties and groups.* No fixed charge, just give as you wish.

CHAT MOSS DESCRIBED

From hence [Warrington], on the road to Manchester, we passed the great bog or waste called Chatmos, the first of that kind that we see in England, from any of the south parts hither. It extends on the left-hand of the road for five or six miles east and west, and they told us it was, in some places, seven or eight miles from north to south. The nature of these mosses, for we found there are many of them in this country, is this, and you will take this for a description of all the rest. The surface, at a distance, looks black and dirty, and is indeed frightful to think of, for it will bear neither horse or man, unless in an exceedingly dry season, and then not so as to be passable, or that any one should travel over them. What nature meant by such a useless production, 'tis hard to imagine; but the land is entirely waste, except for the poor cottager's fuel, and the quantity used for that is very small.

Daniel Defoe, around 1720.

*Throstle Nest Bridge, Old Trafford, Manchester (*see *page 30)*

(see *page 30)*

WALKING & CYCLING
Broadoak Park, to the north of Parrin Lane Bridge (50), contains some pleasant paths, suitable for a short walk. Bridgewater Park, Boothstown, has a few paths which can be enjoyed, while to the south of the canal is an area known as Chat Moss, a surprisingly remote area about 7,000 years old, and which was not reclaimed until the late 18th C. Close to the canal it consists mainly of reclaimed open-cast mine workings. A path from bridge 56 gives restricted access.

Pubs and Restaurants

Packet House Liverpool Road, Eccles (0161 789 0047). By bridge 47. A corner pub serving real ale. Children welcome, garden with swings.

Wellington Church Street, Eccles. Between bridges 48 and 47. A local pub.

✗ **Barge Inn** (0161 788 8788). By bridge 50. A cosy real ale pub offering food (V) *L and E, daily.* Children welcome *until 19.30,* and a large garden. Quiz on *Thur,* DJ *Fri.*

Barton Arms Stablefold (0161 794 9373). Real ale is served in this traditional bar, along with food (V) *available 12.00–20.00, daily.* Quiz nights and other games are featured.

Bridgewater Hotel 23 Barton Road, Worsley (0161 794 0589). By bridge 51. Large comfortable pub serving real ale and food (V) *11.00–21.30, daily.* Children welcome if eating. Outside seating. DJ performs *Fri–Sun.* Nearby 🛏 ♿ .

✗ ☿ **Tung Fong** Worsley Road, Worsley (0161 794 5331). Smart Chinese restaurant, with interesting decor. *Open E.*

Millers 2 Quayside Close, Boothstown, Manchester (0161 702 6251). By bridge 54. A newly renovated pub with modern decor in a lovely spot overlooking open country and the canal, on the corner of the Bridgewater Park Nature Reserve. It serves real ale, bar meals (V) and snacks *all day, every day.* Children welcome, and there is a separate family dining area. Play area, canalside seating, mooring.

Old Boathouse Inn 164 Higher Green Lane, Astley, Tyldesley (01942 883300; www.the-oldboathouse.co.uk). By bridge 58. A comfortable canalside pub with a games room and a garden, serving real ale and food (V) *L and E, daily.* Children welcome, mooring. Handy for the Colliery Museum. Karaoke and various artistes *Sat.*

Ross' Arms 130 Higher Green Lane, Astley, Tyldesley (01942 874405). A 'food-led' pub which serves a range of real ales, plus meals (V) *L and E, daily.* Children welcome *until 21.00,* large garden and conservatory. Karaoke *Fri,* live singer *Sat.*

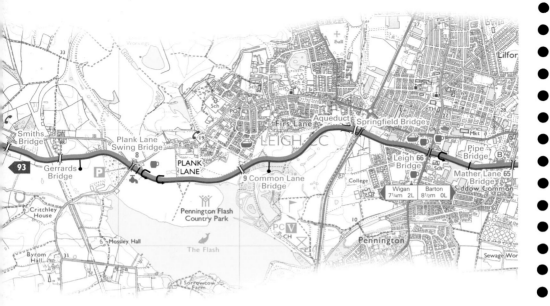

Leigh

After the excitement and interest of Barton, Worsley and Astley Green, the canal now passes through pleasant open land towards the mill town of Leigh, where it transforms into the Leeds & Liverpool Canal, continuing the route to Wigan. Raised canal banks reveal past problems of subsidence in this area, caused by old mine workings. At Leigh the canal passes a sturdy warehouse by bridge 66 before it becomes the Leeds & Liverpool – the familiar stop plank cranes of the Bridgewater finish here, and signs announce you are back in British Waterways territory. Wigan is 7¹/4 miles away (*see* page 93).

Pubs and Restaurants

Bull's Head Butts Bridge (64), Leigh (01942 671621). Towpath-side local. Garden. Children welcome.

Wheatsheaf Hotel 298 Chapel Street, Leigh (01942 709132). A sociable canalside pub on the corner of Warrington Road, serving real ale. There is a new conservatory, and children are welcome. Live entertainment and karaoke *Sat and Sun*. B & B and shower facilities.

Moonraker Hotel 79 King Street, Leigh (01942 740747). A friendly no frills pub with a garden. Children welcome *until 20.00*.

Ellesmere Hotel 20 St Helen's Road, Leigh (01942 703445). A friendly pub, showing live sport on TV. You can bring your children here, and there is entertainment *Fri–Sun*.

Waterside Inn Twist Lane, Leigh (01942 605005). This pub is contained within very handsome grade II listed canalside buildings, one a two-storey stone warehouse dated 1821, the other a brick warehouse dated 1894. A distinctive wooden tower adjoins. Real ale is served, and food (V) is available *L and E, daily*. Their menu is arranged in conjunction with 'Slimming World'. Children aged ten and over welcome if you are eating. Live music *Thur and Sun*, disco *Sat*. *Twice a month* they have food theme evenings – Chinese and Italian for example, and in *Jan,* for Burns Night, haggis and neaps.

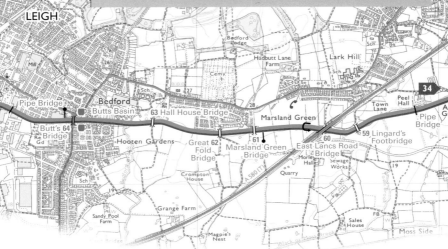

WALKING & CYCLING

Pennington Flash is a 200ha Country Park, centred on a 70ha lake or 'flash', with a variety of well-maintained paths suitable for both walkers and cyclists. Over 230 bird species have been recorded in the park, and there is a wide variety of butterflies, dragonflies and damselflies. There is a small Information Centre.

● **Leigh**

Gt Manchester. All services. Once the archetypal mill town, most of the tall buildings and chimneys have now been demolished to be replaced with ubiquitous new developments. However, in the market place you can see the fine Edwardian baroque town hall, built 1904–7, facing the battlemented church of St Mary.

Boatyards

Ⓑ **Lorenz Canal Services** Bedford Basin, Henry Street, Leigh (01942 679690). Ⓓ Gas, overnight mooring *summer only*, long-term mooring, boat and engine repairs.

A VISIT TO THE MINES AT WORSLEY

'Arrived at Worsley, passing athwart the river Irwell, over which the canal runs, being raised on arches not less than fifty feet in height above that stream. Sent compliments to Mr Gilbert, the steward, asking the favour of seeing the duke's underground works, which was granted, and we stepped into the boat, passing into an archway partly of brick and partly cut through the stone, of about three and a half feet high; we received at entering six lighted candles. This archway, called a funnel, runs into the body of the mountain almost in a direct line three thousand feet, its medium depth beneath the surface about eighty feet; we were half an hour passing that distance. Here begins the first underground road to the pits, ascending to the wagon road, so called, about four feet above the water, being a highway for wagons, containing about a ton weight of the form of a mill-hopper, running on wheels, to convey the coals to the boats.

Arrived at the coal mine, which appearing about five feet through the roof, was supported by many posts, the area being about twenty feet square and the height scarce four. A hundred men are daily employed, and each turns out a ton a day; the miners' wages two shillings, and the laborers' about one shilling.'

Samuel Curwen, *Journal and Letters*, 7 June 1777.

CALDER & HEBBLE NAVIGATION

CALDER & HEBBLE NAVIGATION

Wakefield to Broad Cut
Length: 120'
Beam: 17'
Headroom: 12'

Broad Cut to Sowerby Bridge
Length: 57' 6" (or 60' narrowboat)
Beam: 14'
Headroom: 9' 6"

HUDDERSFIELD BROAD CANAL
Length: 57' 6" (or 60' narrowboat)
Beam: 14'
Headroom: 9' 6"

MANAGER
01977 554351;
enquiries.castleford@britishwaterways.co.uk

MILEAGE
WAKEFIELD to
Cooper Bridge: 13 miles, 13 locks
Sowerby Bridge: 23¹/₂ miles, 27 locks including
Fall Ing
Huddersfield Broad Canal: 3³/₄ miles, 9 locks

SAFETY NOTES
Where locks give access onto river sections of the navigation, river level gauge boards are located at each lock chamber indicating conditions as follows:

Green band – Normal river levels safe for navigation.

Amber band – River levels are above normal. If you wish to navigate the river section you are advised to proceed on to and through the next lock.

Red band – Flood conditions unsafe for navigation. Lock closed.

In an emergency telephone the manager's office or out of office hours telephone 0800 47 999 47. Mobile phone users telephone 01384 215785.

The construction of the Aire & Calder resulted in pressure to improve the Calder above Wakefield. After much opposition, the Calder & Hebble was built, with boats finally reaching Sowerby Bridge in the 1770s. The first survey had been made in 1740 and the Bill to implement it defeated by partisan landowners and millers. Sixteen years later John Smeaton produced a survey that was more acceptable and a Bill was finally passed in 1758. Construction was slow and conflict amongst the overseeing commissioners was rife. In 1765 Brindley was called upon to advise and Smeaton was dismissed. Three years later the position was reversed after serious flooding had damaged the recently completed navigation at Salterhebble. Further monies were raised to fund repairs and the waterway finally re-opened throughout. Never as successful as the Aire & Calder, it did, however, benefit from trade coming in from the Huddersfield Broad Canal and later, in 1811, from the Huddersfield Narrow. Commercial traffic ended in 1981, when the last coal barges unloaded at Thornhill Power Station. Becoming increasingly popular and yet still uncrowded, this waterway has much to offer, with great industrial interest and, in many places, considerable charm. The Huddersfield Broad Canal was built to serve the rapidly expanding woollen industry of the 18th C. Completed in 1780, and costing £12,000, the waterway gave local textile manufacturers access to markets throughout Yorkshire as well as coal to feed the steam-driven mills. Despite the inevitable amalgamation with the competing railway company (the London and North Western Railway in 1847) the waterway remained a profitable concern until the late 1940s. It was conceived as a broad gauge canal to accommodate square-rigged, sailing keels or 'Yorkshire craft' – 58' 0" in length and 14' 0" beam. Due to the navigation's low bridges these had to be de-rigged at Cooper Bridge and bow hauled the remaining 3³/₄ miles. The Huddersfield Narrow

Canal, completed some 30 years later, was built as a narrow gauge waterway unable to accept traffic from the Broad Canal; consequently warehousing and transshipment facilities were developed at Aspley Basin. The problem was partially overcome with the introduction of the West Riding narrowboat: a specially shortened craft able to negotiate locks on both systems.

WALKING & CYCLING

The Calder & Hebble, as its name suggests, is largely a river navigation and it incorporates a series of lock cuts where weirs have been constructed to maintain a navigable depth. This approach, whilst excellent for boaters, can pose problems for those following the waterway along the towpath. These problems are twofold: erosion of the river bank during times of flood and the need to cross the river at either the head or tail of a lock cut in order to remain with the navigation. When boats relied upon horse power, before the invention of the internal combustion engine, both towpaths and horse bridges were maintained in a usable condition. Subsequently both have suffered from the ravages of time and the vagaries of flood – hence the need to come up with some 'creative alternatives' as detailed below.

1 At Thornes Flood Lock (*see* page 43) follow the river south west and under the motorway bridge. Strike off west across the mown sward through the clumps of trees at almost any point before reaching Broad Cut Low Lock and head west to meet the railway line where it intersects the north bank of the river. The bridge here incorporates an enclosed walkway accessible to walkers and cyclists and, in conjunction with a lane running south, returns you to Broad Cut beside the Navigation pub.
2 At Ledgard Bridge 17 (*see* page 44) cross over the navigation, go under the railway and over the river and turn right. At Chadwick Lane fork right and go through the industrial estate with Ledgard Boats on your right. Pass Central Garage on the left and as the road swings left, take the stone path on the right back towards the river, to the left of the PFS Factory Unit.
3 Due to severe bank erosion, only a small section of the towpath between Cooper Bridge and Brighouse (*see* page 46) remains, therefore walkers and cyclists should leave the navigation at Cooper Bridge, briefly heading south west along the A6107, before turning right at the garage along Lower Quarry Road. Cross the railway bridge and fork right down a track under the line signposted to Bradley Hall Farm. Just before the farm turn right and rejoin the waterway at bridge 11, below Kirklees Top Lock.

*Sowerby Bridge Basin (*see *page 48)*

Horbury Bridge

At Thornes Lock only one of the two chambers is now in use – you will need a Calder & Hebble handspike to operate this, and subsequent locks. Here the navigation enters a short cut and rejoins the River Calder at Thornes Flood Lock, before passing under the M1 motorway. Ahead is the tall spike of Elmley Moor television transmitter. The beautifully kept Broad Cut Low Lock marks the start of a 5-mile-long canal section with 8 locks. There was regular trade on this stretch until 1981, when West Country barges took coal from the British Oak Colliery to Thornhill Power Station. Remains of loading staithes can be seen opposite the Navigation Inn. There are good moorings at Horbury Bridge, and a *post office* and *farm shop* are close by. A short arm here used to connect with the river and this has now become an attractive long-term mooring with *showers* and the usual *facilities*. Beyond the bridge a tree-lined cutting leads to Figure of Three Locks. There are two locks on the navigation with another now disused which used to connect with the river. Is it this, or the fact that the river here makes the shape of a '3', which gives these locks their unusual name? Experts seem unable to agree. The towpath from Broad Cut to Dewsbury is good, having been improved in 1986–7. After Mill Bank look out for a milestone marked 'from FALL ING 7 miles' on the towpath side, by the next bridge. Thornhill Double Locks mark the junction with the Dewsbury Arm, which branches off to Savile Town Basin. This is a worth-while diversion to discover Dewsbury's best-kept secret: namely, the whereabouts of the Sunset Cider

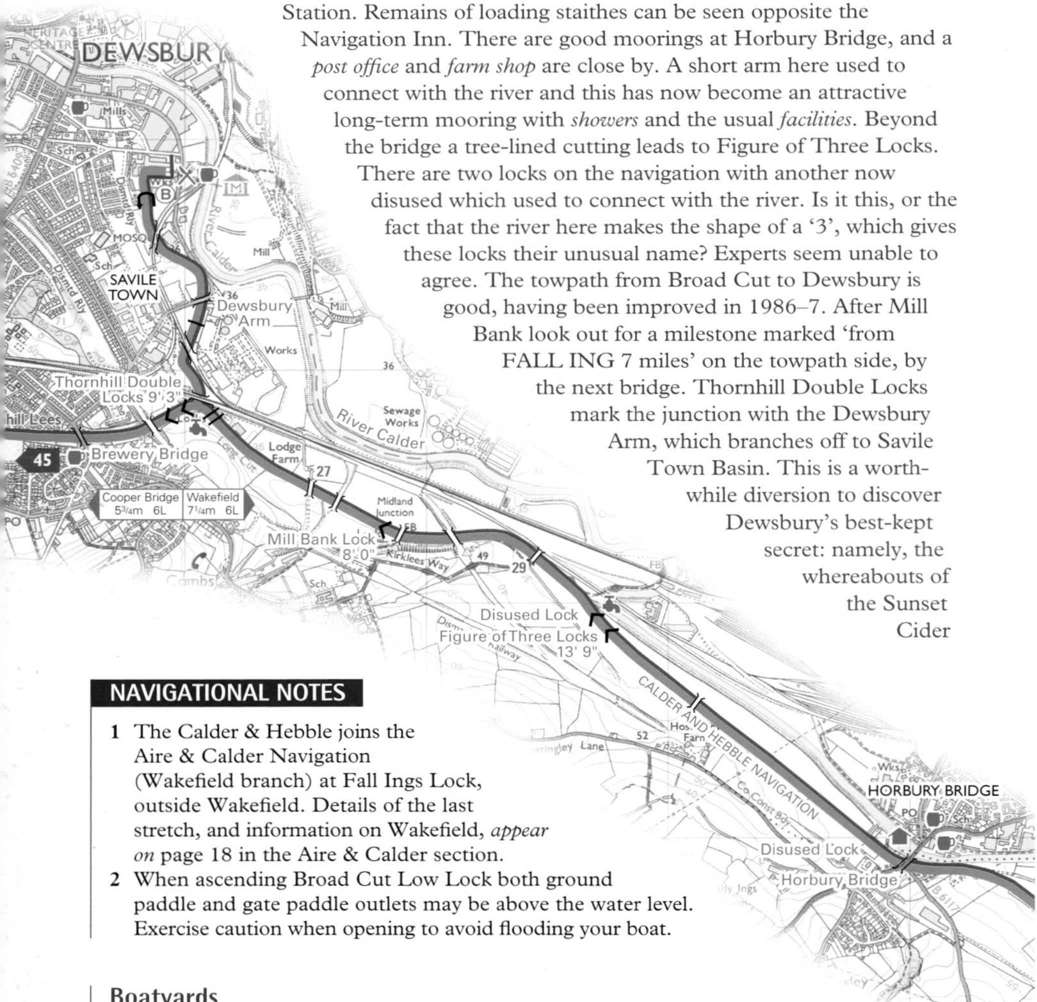

NAVIGATIONAL NOTES

1 The Calder & Hebble joins the Aire & Calder Navigation (Wakefield branch) at Fall Ings Lock, outside Wakefield. Details of the last stretch, and information on Wakefield, *appear on page 18 in the Aire & Calder section.*
2 When ascending Broad Cut Low Lock both ground paddle and gate paddle outlets may be above the water level. Exercise caution when opening to avoid flooding your boat.

Boatyards

Ⓑ **Robinson's Hire Cruisers** Savile Town Wharf, Dewsbury (01924 467976). 🚿 🚿 ♿ D E Gas, pump out, overnight mooring, long-term moor-ing, slipway, winter storage, boat build-ing, boat and engine repairs, boat sales, crane, books and maps, showers, laundry, toilets, telephone.

& Wine Company and their regular exploits (*see* below). Climbing Thornhill Double Locks (good *moorings* here) the navigation enters a deep, secluded cutting spanned by tall bridges.

Pubs and Restaurants

 Navigation Calder Grove (01924 274361). Broad Cut Top Lock, by the railway viaduct. A well-placed canalside pub serving real ales and inexpensive bar snacks and meals (V) *all day, every day.* Children welcome; dogs outside only. Children's room and indoor ball pool. Massive garden and play area. Entertainment most nights including karaoke and quiz. Good moorings here; *PO and fish & chips just a short distance to the south.*

Bingley Arms 221 Bridge Road, Horbury Bridge, Wakefield (01924 281331). A warm friendly establishment in another fine-looking pub serving real ales and food *L (not Mon).* Children and dogs welcome. Garden with swings. Regular quiz and karaoke. Pub games and pool.

Ship Inn 201 Bridge Road, Horbury Bridge, Wakefield (01924 272795). Comfy local with a restaurant serving real ale. Excellent value food (V) *L (not Mon).* Children welcome if kept under strict control; dogs in bar only. Garden, children's play area and barbecue. Quiz *Sun and Tue*; karaoke *Thur and Sat.*

Leggers' Inn Savile Town Wharf, Dewsbury

(01924 502846). A tantalising array of real ales from their own 'Canal' range, brewed in the cellar below the pub and supplemented by an ever-changing selection of guest beers. Inexpensive bar snacks available from breakfast onwards. Children welcome *until 21.00.* Outside seating and pub games. *Open all day.*

✗ **Marina Café** Savile Town Wharf, Mill Street East, Dewsbury (01924 488724). Good honest café fare – large portions, low prices and a wide selection including a range of salads (V). Takeaway or eat in. *Open Mon–Fri 07.30–14.30 and Sat 07.30–12.00.*

✗ **Agra** Warren Street, Savile Town, Dewsbury (01924 467365). Turn left out of the basin, left again, over the bridge and bear left. Superb inexpensive Asian takeaway. Pizzas. Free delivery. *Open Mon–Thur and Sun to 23.30, Fri and Sat to 00.30. PO and grocers close by.*

Nelson Slaithwaite Road, Dewsbury (01924 461685). Scramble up the bank at Brewery Bridge. Real ales served in a pub atop the canal. Children welcome. Outside seating and games room. Quiz *Thur and Sun.*

● **Horbury**
W. Yorks. PO, tel, stores, takeaway. A small town up a steep hill from the bridge. The hymn 'Onward Christian Soldiers' was written and first sung here by the Reverend S. Baring-Gould as a marching song for children.
National Coal Mining Museum for England Caphouse Colliery, New Road, Overton, Wakefield (01924 848806; www.ncm.org.uk). On the A642, 2 miles south west of Horbury Bridge (bus service) and accessible by bus 263 from Huddersfield and Wakefield. Go 450ft underground to visit old- and new-style coalfaces. Audio visual show, cafe, shop, picnic area. Wear warm clothes; not suitable for children under 5. *Open daily 10.00–17.00.* Charge.

● **Dewsbury**
W. Yorks. All services, station. The compact and attractive town centre is 1 mile away from Savile Town Basin.
Dewsbury Arm Extending for ³/₄ mile to Savile Town Basin.

BOAT TRIPS
Calder Lady Trips from Savile Town Basin to Horbury in this restaurant boat with a bar. Contact Robinson's Hire Cruisers, Dewsbury (01924 467976).

Cooper Bridge

Before long the deep cutting gives way to an open industrial wasteland (for which there are large-scale redevelopment plans) around the site of Thornhill Power Station, where barges once used to unload coal. Between Thornhill Flood Lock and Greenwood Lock a short, wide, river section intervenes before the navigation enters another artificial channel to the south of Mirfield. Landscaping and pretty waterside gardens make this a pleasant spot. At Greenwood Flood Gates the river is briefly rejoined on a sweeping

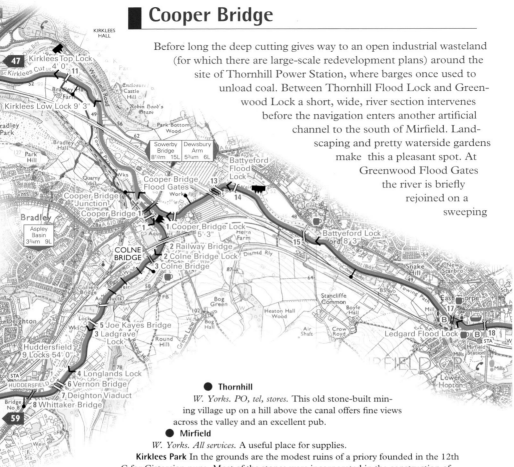

● **Thornhill**
W. Yorks. PO, tel, stores. This old stone-built mining village up on a hill above the canal offers fine views across the valley and an excellent pub.

● **Mirfield**
W. Yorks. All services. A useful place for supplies.

Kirklees Park In the grounds are the modest ruins of a priory founded in the 12th C for Cistercian nuns. Most of the stones were incorporated in the construction of Kirklees Hall during the late 16th C. It is believed that Robin Hood died whilst at the priory but before so doing he shot two arrows from the window to mark his burial place. One landed in the River Calder and floated away, the other landed in the grounds of the park. A tablet marks the spot thought to be his grave.

Boatyards

ⓑ **Ledgard Bridge Boat Company** 29A Butt End Mills, Chadwick Fold Lane, Lower Hopton, Mirfield (01924 491441/07850 249449). Gas, boat sales and repairs, engine repairs, boat building and alterations, chandlery, boat fitting out, craning wharf.

ⓑ **Mirfield Boatyard** 10 Station Road, Mirfield (01924 492007). Below Shepley Bridge Flood Lock. **D** Gas, pump out, long-term mooring,

winter storage, toilets and showers, laundrette, DIY facilities, solid fuel.

ⓑ **Shepley Bridge Marina** Huddersfield Road, Mirfield (01924 491872; www.shipleybridgemarina. com). 🛏 🛒 🔧 **D E** Pump out, gas, narrowboat hire, overnight mooring, long-term mooring, winter storage, slipway, boat sales, engine repairs, chandlery, books, maps and gifts, toilets, dry dock, wet dock, coffee shop.

bend, before the navigation enters another artificial cut. The towpath is generally good on the canal sections, less so, or indeed non-existent, on the river sections (*see* note on page 41). At Battyeford there is a short canal section which rejoins the river opposite a large sewage works. A fine display of roses suggests they are not short of fertilizer! Cooper Bridge marks the junction of the Calder & Hebble with the Huddersfield Broad Canal (*see* page 58), which branches off to the south below the flood gates, overlooked by the tall chimney of Bottomley & Sons. Kirklees Park lies on a hillside to the north before the navigation passes under the M62 motorway.

NAVIGATIONAL NOTES

1 When coming downstream, look out for the entrance to Ledgard Bridge Flood Lock. A large weir awaits those who miss it. This warning applies equally to boaters leaving Shepley Bridge Lock and approaching Greenwood Flood Gates.
2 There are landing stages below the locks which you can use, as well as ladders in virtually all the locks.

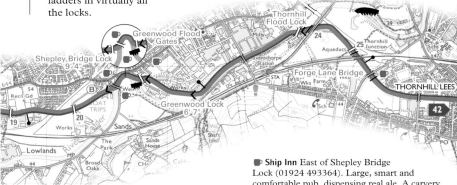

Pubs and Restaurants

🍺 **Perseverance** Forge Lane, Thornhill Lees, Dewsbury (01924 463447). Spacious, airy, newly refurbished pub serving real ale and home-cooked food (V) *12.00–19.00 daily*. Children welcome as are dogs outside. Pool. Secure children's play area; canalside garden. Moorings.

🍺 **Savile Arms** Church Lane, Thornhill (01924 463738). North of Thornhill Lees. A genuine old village local that rather surprisingly shares consecrated ground with the nearby church, hence its other name – Church House. It dispenses an excellent range of real ales and totally eschews noisy machines. Pub games and outside seating. *Open Mon-Fri eves and Sat and Sun lunchtimes and eves.*

🍺 **Bull's Head** Huddersfield Road, Ravensthorpe, Dewsbury (01924 496920). 300yds from Greenwood Flood Lock. Bar meals (V) *L and E* and a selection of real ales served in this pub set in 2 acres of parkland. Children welcome *until 20.00. Sat* karaoke or disco.

🍺 **Ship Inn** East of Shepley Bridge Lock (01924 493364). Large, smart and comfortable pub dispensing real ale. A carvery restaurant serves food (V) *all day until 21.00, every day.* Children welcome. Garden, indoor and outdoor play area.

🍺 **Swan Inn** Huddersfield Road, Mirfield (01924 492054). Above Shepley Bridge Lock. Smart real ale pub with a roadside patio. Bar food (V) *L, Mon-Fri.* Karaoke *Thur-Sat.*

🍺 **Navigation Tavern** Station Road, Mirfield (01924 492476). Canalside near Shepley Bridge Flood Lock. Garden and limited moorings.

🍺 ✕ **Railway** 212 Huddersfield Road, Mirfield (01924 480868; www.railwaymirfield.com). North of bridge 17. A selection of real ales together with two guests in a large pub serving food (V) *L and E (until 21.30)*. Children over 12 allowed if eating. Outside seating. *Open all day Mon-Sat.* Pub games and disabled access. Quiz *Tue.*

🍺 **Peartree Inn** 259 Huddersfield Road, Battyeford (01924 493079). Near Battyeford Lock. Riverside pub (complete with cellar-based ghost) serving real ales and home-made food (V) *Mon-Sat L and E and Sun 12.00–17.00.* Children's play area. Large beer garden overlooking the navigation. *Fortnightly Thur* quiz. Moorings.

Brighouse

Leaving the river the navigation enters an artificial cut on its approach to Brighouse, completely enclosed by factories. There are good *moorings* between the two Brighouse Locks, and the passage through the town is pleasant, with gardens, seats and willow trees. At Brookfoot Lock there is evidence of a connection with the river giving some idea of how the navigation has evolved as canalised sections were progressively constructed.

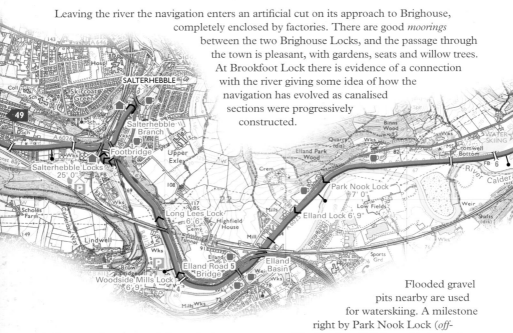

Flooded gravel pits nearby are used for waterskiing. A milestone right by Park Nook Lock (*off-licence and grocers nearby*) reveals that you are now 18 miles from Fall Ing, with just a short distance to travel to Sowerby Bridge. Elland Basin, with its tastefully restored buildings and gardens, is worth more than a fleeting glance, however, and makes a good stopping place en route. There are several pubs close by. Have a look at the fine converted warehouse with its covered dock, before pressing on to the three superbly kept and picturesque Salterhebble Locks. The bottom lock here has an electrically-powered guillotine gate operated with a Watermate key. This was installed when the road was widened in the 1930s. The towpath passes separately through its own narrow tunnel. Immediately after this first lock the canal passes over a small aqueduct before climbing the top two. To the right is the Salterhebble Branch (where the old Salterhebble Basin has been restored providing visitor and long-term *moorings* and a range of boater *facilities*), to the left the route to Sowerby Bridge. The towpath improves above Brighouse.

BOAT TRIPS
M.V. Waylon featured as *Sally H* in the TV series *Stay Lucky,* and is available for both short and long trips for up to 12 passengers throughout the north eastern waterways. A converted working boat providing a flexible and participative, self-catering, cruising itinerary at very reasonable rates. An imaginative concept that introduces families and small parties to the waterways. For further details contact Mr Richardson at Brighouse Canal Basin on 01484 713424.

Boatyards

Ⓑ **Sagar Marine** Victoria Works, Wharfe Street, Brighouse (01484 714541; www.sagarmarine.com). Ⓓ Pump out, boat building, boat fitting out.

Ⓑ **Tayberg Steel Boats** Brookfoot Mills, Elland Road, Brighouse (01484 400221) Boat building, boat repairs and alterations.

● **Brighouse**
W. Yorks. All services, station. A woollen textile producing village transformed into an important canal port with the building of the Calder & Hebble Navigation. In the 19th C silk and cotton were also spun here. Now there seems to be plenty of thriving new industry. The canal bisects the town, passing very close to the market place. A large Victorian church at the top of the hill is surrounded by trees and flowers.

Smith Art Gallery Halifax Road, Brighouse (01484 719222). Permanent display of 19th-C art works and touring exhibitions. *Open Mon, Tue, Thur and Fri 10.00– 18.00 and Sat 10.00–16.00. Free.*

● **Elland**
W. Yorks. PO, tel, stores, bank. Elland has an enviable position on the steep south side of the Calder Valley, its narrow streets discourage through traffic, and its handsome church and terraces of stone houses give an air of tranquillity. The well-restored canal basin makes an excellent stopping point.

WALKING & CYCLING
At Anchor Pit Flood Lock follow the track around the outside of the river bend and join the straight road running north west through the industrial estate. Turn left at the T junction with Calder Street and right at its junction with Birds Royd Lane. At the junction with Huddersfield Road again turn right and rejoin the navigation at bridge 10.

Pubs and Restaurants

🍺 **Prince of Wales** Betnal Street, Brighouse (01484 400718). North of bridge 10. A handsome black and white half-timbered pub rebuilt in 1926 with timber from *HMS Donegal*, a wooden battleship launched in 1858. The Tudor-style interior is compromised by two TVs, a juke box and a battery of fruit machines. Real ales are served and children are welcome. *Sat* discos and outside seating.

✕ 🍷 **Prego** Huddersfield Road, Brighouse (01484 715566). Beside bridge 10. Italian and continental cuisine (V) served in a sophisticated contemporary setting. *Open daily L and E (not Sat L).* Children welcome.

🍺 **Red Rooster** 123 Elland Road, Brookfoot (01484 713737). North of Brookfoot Lock. Real ale enthusiasts' pub, with a real fire as well – always between seven and ten cask ales available. Also a selection of fruit wines and ciders. Outside seating. Children welcome *until 21.00. Mon* is cyclists and bikers evening; *Wed* quiz.

🍺 **Colliers Arms** 66 Park Road, Elland (01422 372704). Between Elland and Park Nook locks. Traditional canalside pub offering real ale. Home-made food (V) – cooked to order – is available *L and E (until 19.30), daily.* Children welcome; dogs must be kept away from eating areas. Award winning canalside garden with quayside seating. Conservatory. Open fires in winter. Quiz, darts and dominoes *Tue and Thur.*

🍺 **Barge & Barrel** Elland Basin (01422 373623). An interesting choice of real ales from their own Barge & Barrel Brewery Co range together with guest beers in a comfortable Victorian style pub. Inexpensive, home-cooked food (V) *L and E (not Sun and winter E).* Children welcome *until 20.30*; dogs in certain areas. Open fires in winter. Pub games and pool. *Wed and Sun* quiz (and *monthly* live music). Moorings.

🍺 ✕ **Millers** Salterhebble (01422 347700). Pub and hotel at the terminus of the Salterhebble Branch. Real ales served in this relaxed, family-orientated establishment. A range of food (V) is available *all day, every day.* Outside seating and play area. Mooring. B & B.

🍺 **Punch Bowl Inn** Salterhebble (01422 366937). By the Salterhebble Branch. Family-run pub serving real ale. Food available *Sun L only.* Children and dogs welcome. Garden and play area. B & B.

Sowerby Bridge

The canal, now relatively narrow, clings to the side of a wooded hill, its clean water alive with small fish. A conspicuous building to the north is Wainhouse Tower, built in 1875 as a 253ft dyeworks chimney (but never used as such) and converted into a viewing tower. A superb example of stonemasonry, it is *open on Bank Holidays* (400 steps to the top). The buildings close in as the navigation approaches the basins at Sowerby Bridge, where the Rochdale Canal once again branches off to cross the Pennines. Now restored throughout its entire length, a third Pennine crossing has been made available offering the opportunity for two dramatic northern cruising rings. The towpath throughout this section is excellent.

Boatyards

Ⓑ **Shire Cruisers** The Wharf, Sowerby Bridge, Halifax (01422 832712; www.shirecruisers. co.uk). Facilities either here or in the basin. 🛉 🪣 🐟 D Gas, pump out, narrowboat hire, overnight mooring, long-term mooring, winter storage, slipway, crane, boat sales and repairs, chandlery, books and maps, boat fitting out, engine sales and repairs, toilets, DIY facilities, gifts.

● **Halifax**
W. Yorks. All services. Well known as the home of the Halifax Building Society, founded in 1853, which now has ultra-modern offices in Portland Place; it is worth the journey north from the canal to visit this industrial town. The splendid Piece Hall (01422 358087 – *open daily 08.00–18.00*), rebuilt in 1779, is the last remaining manufacturers' hall in the country. Here weavers traded their products, the continuation of an industry that dates back to 1275 in Halifax. Now restored, the hall houses arts and craft shops, a museum, art gallery, restaurant and the **Tourist Information Centre** (01422 368725). The parish church of St John the Baptist is Perpendicular in style, battlemented and with a mass of pinnacles, parapets and gargoyles.
Calderdale Industrial Museum Next door to the Piece Hall, Halifax (01422 358087). Steam engines, a Spinning Jenny, a Flying Shuttle loom and toffee wrapping machines, all working. Re-creation of 19th-C Halifax, coal mines and clay mines. *Open to pre-booked groups.* Small charge.
Shibden Hall Folk Museum Shibden Park, Halifax (01422 352246). A 15th-C building with 17th-C furniture and extensive folk exhibits. *Open Mon–Sat 10.00–17.00, Sun 12.00–17.00 (16.00 Dec–Feb).* Charge.
Eureka Museum for Children Discovery Road, Halifax (01426 983191 *24 hour recorded info; www.eureka.org.uk*). Hands-on museum designed for children to touch, listen and smell. Three main exhibition areas: Me and my body, Living and working together, and Invent, create, communicate. *Open 10.00–17.00, daily except Christmas.* Charge.

Bankfield Museum Akroyd Park, Halifax (01422 354823/352334). Magnificent 19th-C mill owner's residence housing a fascinating range of costumes from around the world, displayed in exotic surroundings. *Open Tue–Sat 10.00–17.00, Sun 14.00–17.00. Closed Mon except B Hols (10.00–17.00).* Charge.

● **Sowerby Bridge**
W. Yorks. All services. Although this is an industrial town, the scale and grandeur of the surrounding landscape dominate the mill chimneys and factory roofs that are dotted about. This rare subservience to nature makes the town human and attractive. The 19th-C classical church is in a good position, overlooking the restored deep lock and tunnel.

● **Sowerby Bridge Basin**
PO, tel, stores. This great canal centre is a classic example of the functional tradition in industrial architecture, and has thankfully survived to be given a new life in restoration, while many other such examples have disappeared. The Rochdale Canal was built to accommodate vessels up to 72ft in length, so goods had to be transshipped here into the shorter Calder & Hebble craft before they could continue their journey; hence this important centre grew in stature.

● **Rochdale Canal**
One of three canal routes across the Pennines, its 92 wide locks over a distance of 33 miles virtually guaranteed its ultimate commercial failure. With the new tunnel and deep lock out of the basin open, it is once again possible to cruise across the Pennines to Manchester: hard work but the effort is amply rewarded.

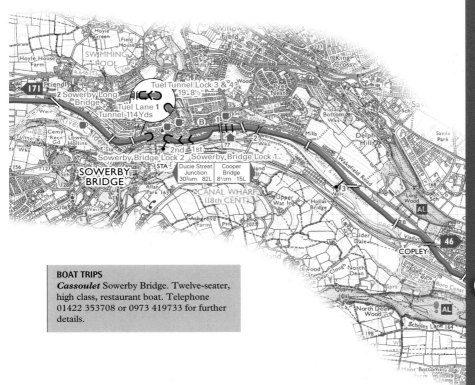

BOAT TRIPS
Cassoulet Sowerby Bridge. Twelve-seater, high class, restaurant boat. Telephone 01422 353708 or 0973 419733 for further details.

Pubs and Restaurants

🍺 **Navigation Inn** By bridge 1. Friendly canalside pub dating back to 15th C complete with inglenook fireplace and Victorian cast iron range. Four rotating guest real ales, including the local Barge & Barrel Brewery Co's range, and an extensive bar menu. *Open all day* with food(V) *available L and E, daily.* Children welcome *until* 21.00; dogs when food is not being served. Regular entertainment. Two gardens.

🍺 ✕ **Moorings** No 1 Warehouse, Sowerby Bridge Basin (01422 833940). A good choice of bar food (V) is served together with real ale in this attractive conversion. Food *available L and E, daily.* Children welcome in dining area. No smoking area *after 21.00.* Patio, family room.

✕ ♀ **Tenujin** No 2 Warehouse, Sowerby Bridge Basin (01422 835500). Specialists in Mongolian barbecues. *Open E, every evening.*

✕ ♀ **Java Restaurant** Wharf Street, Sowerby Bridge (01422 831654). By the basin. A restaurant specialising in Indonesian food (*E only*). *Open 18.30–23.00 daily.*

🍺 **William IV** 80/82 Wharf Street, Sowerby Bridge (01422 833584). A good selection of real ales are served in this friendly pub close to the basin. Children welcome. Beer garden and pub games.

🍺 **Rams Head Inn** 26 Wakefield Road, Sowerby Bridge (01422 835876). *Open evenings and all day Sat and B Hols.* The Ryburn Brewery's sole tied house, close to the plant, dispensing their full range of real ales. The pub is just as traditional as you'd expect: open fires, pub games and *weekend* sing-alongs. Food (V) is also *available Mon–Sat L and E (until 21.00) and Sun 12.00–19.00.* Children welcome *until 20.00.* Garden.

HUDDERSFIELD CANALS

MAXIMUM DIMENSIONS

Length: 70' 0"
Beam: 6' 10"
Headroom: 7' 0"

MANAGER

0161 819 5847;
enquiries.spring@britishwaterways.co.uk

MILEAGE

ASHTON-UNDER-LYNE
Junction with Peak Forest Canal to
Stalybridge: 2 miles
Mossley: 6 miles
Diggle: 8¹/₂ miles
Marsden: 12 miles
Linthaite: 16 miles

HUDDERSFIELD
Junction with Huddersfield Broad Canal:
19¹/₂ miles

British Waterways produces a *Navigational Guide for Boaters* available from the manager's office listed above, regularly updated to cover the provision of new facilities on the South Pennine Ring network of canals.

To book a passage through Standedge Tunnel, telephone Standedge Visitor Centre (01484 844298; info@standedge.co.uk). Advance booking is essential. Charge.

The visitor centre will provide a comprehensive set of Navigational Notes which are essential reading before tackling this canal.

One of three transPennine canals, and by far the shortest route, this waterway was conceived in 1793, at the height of 'Canal Mania' (the bulk of canal construction was concentrated into the 1790s), and encouraged by the success of the Ashton and Huddersfield Broad canals. Benjamin Outram was retained as engineer and he reported in favour of a narrow canal (in the interest of cost saving) following the route of the present navigation. There was the inevitable conflict with local millowners over water supply and a total reservoir capacity of 20,000 locks full of water was provided by way of appeasement.

As always optimism was in far greater supply than the capital raised from the initial share issue following the enabling Act passed on 4 April 1794. The estimated cost was some £183,000, of which nearly one-third was allocated to the construction of a 3-mile tunnel under the Pennines. As work progressed the canal was opened in sections to generate income; the first section opened in March 1797 between Huddersfield and Slaithwaite and two more, linking Slaithwaite to Marsden and Ashton to Greenfield, were completed late in the following year. It was not until 12 years later that the first boat passed through the completed Standedge Tunnel. From the outset the waterway was dogged by shoddy workmanship and flood damage. In its 436ft rise to the eastern tunnel portal at Marsden, the canal follows the Colne Valley, whilst from the west end of the summit pound – 645ft above sea level – it follows the Tame Valley, dropping 334ft in 8¹/₂ miles to Ashton-under-Lyne. Damage extended along 16 miles of canal after flooding during the winter of 1799 and Robert Whitworth, called in to report during Outram's absence through illness, observed that the masonry and earthworks along the navigation 'were the worst executed of any he had seen'. Benjamin Outram resigned in 1801 and he was not replaced, although subsequently, five years later, Thomas Telford was asked to survey the work to date and advise on its completion. Two further Acts were passed to raise more capital before the navigation was officially opened on 4 April 1811 at a final cost of over £300,000. However, this was only after another disastrous flood occasioned after Swellands Reservoir (recommended by Telford as an addition to

Outram's design) burst its banks and inundated large areas of the Colne Valley. Six people were drowned and many factories and mills severely damaged.

High tolls, in conjunction with an additional charge levied on boats using the tunnel, suppressed use of the waterway and although individual communities along the route expanded and thrived, within the climate of industrial prosperity brought by the canal, profits were disappointing. With the reduction of dues in the 1830s, trade was greatly stimulated, only to fall in the face of the inevitable railway competition which came with the completion of the Leeds and Manchester Railway in 1841. Three years later the Huddersfield and Manchester Railway Company was formed with the aim of building a line closely following the route of the navigation, which it acquired in 1845. The existing canal tunnel at Standedge was linked at intervals by cross adits to the infant railway tunnel during construction, thereby greatly reducing time and expense. Subsequent railway tunnels, built as traffic increased, also benefited immensely from the existence of the canal tunnel.

Much trade was surrendered to the railways over the years and by the time of its official abandonment in 1944, regular cargoes were limited to coal and iron ore. The last end-to-end voyage was made by Robert Aickman and fellow IWA members, in *Ailsa Craig*, during 1948.

WALKING & CYCLING

There is an interesting interpretation board beside the Roaches Lock pub (*see* page 55) detailing the industrial history of the area and setting out a short walk that takes in significant local features. The Oldham Way is a 40-mile trail, linking the newly opened Huddersfield Narrow and Rochdale canals, split up into seven more easily manageable sections. Visit the TIC for further details. The Medlock Valley Way leads walkers from the remote uplands of Saddleworth Moor above Oldham into the heart of Manchester linking meadows, rivers, moors, woodlands and canals along a trail of great diversity. Further information from local TICs. The Public Art Sculpture Trail links a number of pieces installed along the section of the canal running through Oldham. These images reflect life on the canal; they have been inspired by the geography of the area, by a local school and, in many cases, make use of recycled and reclaimed materials. Further details from local TICs and Brownhill Visitor Centre – *see* page 54. The Tameside Trail is a 40-mile circular walk that intersects with the canal at Division Bridge and broadly follows the Tameside boundary linking river valleys, country parks and other places of interest. Further details from Tameside Countryside Service (0161 330 9613). A section of the 268-mile-long Pennine Way runs through wild country along the eastern edge of Saddleworth Moor. *See* Leeds & Liverpool Canal, page 110 for further details.

To negotiate Standedge Tunnel, walkers and cyclists can make use of one of the several way-marked routes over the Pennines, commencing beside the Diggle Hotel. Walkers can also take a bus from Uppermill or a boat trip through the tunnel.

The Colne Valley Circular Walk is 12 miles long and takes in the contrasts of impressive industrial buildings set against a backdrop of a striking river valley. Details from Huddersfield TIC (*see* page 59). The Kirklees Way beats the bounds of this eponymous district, totalling a demanding 72 miles. Again contrasts abound: landscape versus history, scenery versus industry. Details from Huddersfield TIC. The Marsden and Tunnel End Trail is a 'hands on' version of much that is depicted in The Old Goods Yard (*see* page 57 under Marsden Moor Estate) and as such is a fascinating insight into the area. There is a regular series of walks and events based on Marsden Moor estate's 5,685 acres of unenclosed moorland. For a programme and copies of the trail detailed above, visit The Old Goods Yard or www.nationaltrust.org.uk/marsdenmoor, or telephone 01484 847016.

Apart from the range of walks detailed above, the presence of the transPennine railway line close to the waterway throughout makes planning expeditions along the canal straightforward. Trains run at frequent intervals, some stopping at all stations and some only at major stations. All trains carry bicycles free of charge although space is limited on Arriva Transpennine Express services and it is advisable to book in advance during busy periods. Telephone 08457 48 49 50 for details.

Huddersfield Canals Introduction

Stalybridge

The canal follows the River Tame east out of Portland Basin, crossing it just over 1 mile later to arrive at the first newly constructed lock in Stalybridge. In 1947 the section from here through the town was culverted and the enthusiasm for the recently exhumed navigation, ascending a series of locks amidst busy streets, is universal. Replacing a forgotten drain, there is now a vibrant waterway, a bustle of activity made colourful with boats: a scene reminiscent of a Dutch town, the canal its central focus, roads subservient. Good moorings are plentiful, well distributed between locks 4W and 8W. The Pennines beckon over the rooftops of Stalybridge, as the waterway continues on its steady climb towards Scout Tunnel, ducking directly between the legs of an unfortunately sited electricity pylon, more recently placed in its path. The climb is unremitting, though largely through leafy glades with just the occasional glimpses of open hill views, punctuated with the dereliction of past industry – largely coal mining. Throughout its ascent, the waterway remains discrete, almost shunning the outside world, winding through woods and passing several attractively sited, waterside picnic areas. Whilst road crossings do briefly intrude, it is the transPennine railway that keeps constant company with the waterway: a not altogether unwelcome diversion bringing a source of well-ordered activity and flashes of colour on a dull day.

BOAT TRIPS
The **Stalybridge Canal Carrying Company** operates *nb Staly Rose* on regular trips along the Huddersfield Narrow Canal, based in Stalybridge. Telephone 01457 878815 for further details.

Pubs and Restaurants

Station Buffet Bar Platform 1, Stalybridge Station, Rassbottom Street, Stalybridge (0161 303 0007). The original station buffet, decorated with old railway photographs and memorabilia, and now dispensing an excellent range of real ales, cider and food (V) *10.00– 20.00, daily.* Children and dogs welcome (dogs' water bowl provided). Outside platform seating and open fires *in winter.* No electronic machines – just the rattle of passing trains. *Open all day.*

Q Inn Market Street, Stalybridge (0161 303 9157). In the *Guinness Book of Records* as the pub with the shortest name in the UK. Real ale and food (V) *L and E.* Pub games. *Open all day.*

Sharkey's Bar Market Street, Stalybridge (0161 303 7098). Heavily mirrored establishment serving real ales and bar snacks *L.* Large-screen TV, pool and darts. Regular live entertainment. *Open all day.*

Old Fleece Hotel Market Street, Stalybridge (0161 338 2827). Real ale and bar meals (V) *available L and E.* Children welcome. B & B.

White House Stalybridge (0161 303 2288). Exposed brickwork, tiled floors and old cast iron radiators create the atmosphere in a pub serving food (V) *L and E (and breakfast)* together with real ale. Children welcome. Pub games and beer garden. *Open all day.*

Bridge Inn Caroline Street, Stalybridge (0161 303 7056). An traditional old pub with extensive wood panelling and a fine selection of wines and real ales. A reasonable standard of dress is required and only over 25s are admitted. *Open Mon–Fri 16.00–23.00, Sat and Sun all day from 12.00.*

Mill Pond Armentières Square, Stalybridge (0161 338 4499). Beside lock 6W. A profusion of glass, a chandelier hanging through an opening in the balconied first floor and wooden floors set the tone in an establishment that maintains a strict dress code and only admits over 25s. Real ale and food (V) *served daily 11.00-21.00 (18.00 Fri and Sat).* *Open all day.* Pub and club activity in Armentières Square can make this a noisy area in which to moor.

Bull's Head Stalybridge (0161 338 4182). Beside lock 7W. Traditional pub, beautifully furnished inside and dispensing real ale. Pub Games. *Takeaways and laundrette* nearby.

Saddleworth

The Pennines rear up ahead, although their full impact is softened by the fringe of woodland accompanying the navigation up the valley. To the west the imposingly situated building of Quickwood church, with its needle-like spire, oversees the bustle of road, rail and waterway activity below. Impressive mills, now sadly decaying, line the canal as it winds its tortuous path towards Uppermill, where it is greeted by what appears to be a castle keep, complete with portcullis. Closer inspection reveals a somewhat elaborate stone facing, topped with iron railings and employed to disguise a concrete box culvert, with further embellishment to hide a vertical gas main! By now the scale of the textile industry is subdued by the imposing bulk of Saddleworth Moor, while the sprawling conurbation of Manchester gives way to a straggle of attractive villages, constructed in the local gritstone and strewn randomly over the surrounding hillsides. Looking back towards the smoking chimneys below, there are wide open views now appearing over the high ground that had seemed to pose such a formidable obstacle when viewed from Stalybridge. Beyond the striking Wool Road Transhipment Warehouse the waterway, still climbing relentlessly, breaks out alongside the railway and together they both pick their way across heathered moorland towards their interlaced passage, deep beneath the Pennines.

● **Mossley**
Gt Manchester. Tel, stores, takeaway, station. A small agricultural hamlet of 1,200 souls in 1821, Mossley had grown into a prosperous cotton town by 1885 with a population of 15,000. There is a useful stores, *open 07.30–22.00*, near Roaches Lock; also an off-licence, takeaway and newsagent.
Mossley Industrial Heritage Centre Longlands Mill, Queen Street, Mossley (01457 838608/835105). Memories abound and are brought to life in an old cotton spinning mill now owned by Emmaus, a charitable organisation which provides work and a home for people who would otherwise be homeless. The Centre now seeks to answer questions about past times in a boom era of cotton and woollen manufacture. Shop and coffee bar. Heritage Centre *open Tue–Sat 14.00–16.00*; Emmaus shop *open Tue–Sat 09.00–17.00*.

● **Greenfield**
Gt Manchester. Tel, stores, station. Another cotton community attempting to adjust to the demise of a past prosperity. The nearest station to Uppermill is here.

● **Uppermill**
Gt Manchester. PO, tel, stores, bank, chemist, butcher, garage. A traditional Pennine village and once the centre of the local cotton and cottage weaving industry, it has become a focus for the tourist trade that has long supplanted all such activity. Now the largest settlement in Saddleworth, it only gained its supremacy in the late 18th C with the coming of the canal and turnpike road, ousting nearby Dobcross.
Saddleworth Museum & Art Gallery High Street, Uppermill (01457 874093; www.museum. saddleworth.net). A family-friendly museum full of intriguing objects from the past telling the story of the people who have created Saddleworth's landscape and character. Gallery with changing exhibitions, many of local interest. Shop. *Open Apr–Oct, Mon–Sat 10.00–17.00, Sun 12.00– 17.00; Nov–Mar, daily 13.00–16.00.* Charge. Disabled access.
Tourist Information Centre High Street, Uppermill (01457 870336/874093; ecs.saddleworthtic@oldham.gov.uk). *Open Mon–Sat 10.00–17.00, Sun 12.00–17.00.*

● **Dobcross**
Gt Manchester. PO, tel, stores. A delightful village, quintessentially Pennine, every building and winding narrow street a gem, the whole presided over by the charming Saddleworth Bank – now fulfilling a more homely role.
Brownhill Countryside Centre Wool Road, Dobcross (01457 872598; oper.rangers@ oldham.gov.uk). Wildlife and historical interpretation centre for the area with changing exhibitions and displays, a woodland 'crawly tunnel' for children, shop, refreshments, toilets and a picnic area. *Open Wed–Sun*, telephone for times. *Outdoor facilities open at all times.*

● **Diggle**
Gt Manchester. PO, tel, bakery, takeaway. Together with its neighbours Dobcross and Delph, Diggle lay at the heart of local handweaving until, in the late 18th C, the Industrial Revolution spawned mills as the centres of production, sited further down the valley for easier access.

Pubs and Restaurants

🍺 **Roaches Lock** Mossley (01457 834288). Canal-oriented pub serving real ales and food *L and E*. Children welcome. Bar games, canalside patio and an interesting selection of reading matter.

🍺 **Tollemache Arms** Mossley (01457 832354). This pub serves real ale and inexpensive bar meals (V) *12.00–18.00* and takeaway food *until 22.00*. Children welcome. Outside seating. Regular *summer* barbecues. *Open all day.*

🍺 **King William IV** 134 Chew Valley Road, Greenfield (01457 873933). East of the canal in the village centre. A cosy village local that welcomes families and serves a good selection of real ales. Traditional bar meals (V) *available all day, every day until 19.30.* Pub games and outside seating.

🍺 **Railway** 11 Shaw Hall Bank Road, Greenfield (01457 872307). West of the canal, opposite the station. Photographs of old Saddleworth adorn the bar in a local that serves a variety of real ales.

Children welcome. Pub games and open fires *in winter.* Live music *Thur and Fri and Sun afternoon.* B & B and camping.

🍺 **Granby Arms** 28 High Street, Uppermill (01457 872348). Real ale and traditional pub food (V) *served daily 12.00– 18.00* in this traditional village local. Children welcome.

🍺 **Waggon** High Street, Uppermill (01457 872376). Cosy village local dispensing real ale and food (V) *L daily.* Also fish & chip special *Fri E 17.00– 19.30.* Children welcome. B & B.

🍺 **Navigation Inn** Wool Road, Dobcross (01457 872418). West of Wool Road Bridge. Serves real ale and food (V) *L and E.* Children welcome. Outside seating and pub games. Brass bands play on *summer Sun afternoons.* Camping.

🍺 **Swan Inn** The Square, Dobcross (01457 873451). Also known locally as The Top House, this 18th-C hostelry serves real ale and home-cooked food (V) *L and E (not Sun E).* Children welcome. No machines. Open fires in *winter.* Non-smoking dining area. Outside seating.

🍷 ✕ **Diggle Nook Bistro** Diggle (01457 810044). Just west of the tunnel mouth. Family-friendly establishment serving home-cooked food (V).

🍺 **Diggle Hotel** Station Houses, Diggle (01457 872741; dawn@digglehotel.freeserve.co.uk). Close to the western tunnel portals (both canal and railway) this one time merchant's house became went on to become a store, and then a pub, and now dispenses real ale and home-made food (V) *L and E Sun–Fri and all day Sat.* Children welcome. Garden with superb Pennine views. B & B.

Map labels

Standedge Tunnel
5686yds 64
Green
56
MP
245
Harropdale Farm
Sch
Diglea
DIGGLE
Kiln Green
Summit Lock 32W
Shaw Lee
31W Geoffrey Dickens Lock
66 Ward Lane Bridge
Weak MS
67 Subway
Fair Banks
Lark Hill
224
Wool Road Lock 24W
30W Dobcross Lock
29W Cast Iron Lock
Pumpout
69 Alice Footbridge
70
28W Embankment Lock
Wool Road Bridge 61yds
27W Coffin Lock
DOBCROSS
26W 12 Mile Lock
25W Navigation Lock
Visitor Centre and Slipway
Ryefields
Tame Water
Brownhill Bridge 73
73 Brownhill Bridge
Saddleworth
74 Railway Aqueduct
Lime Kiln Lock 23W
75 Mytholm Bridge
209
Saddleworth Viaduct 76
Dungebooth Lock 22W
76 Saddleworth Viaduct
13m 53L Aspley Basin
Dukinfield Junction 7m 21L
UPPERMILL
SADDLEWORTH FOLD
Clogger Knoll Bridge
77
78 Upper Mill High Street Bridge
Wade Lock 21W
Clogger 77 Knoll Bridge
MUS
Wade Lock 21W
Upper Mill 78
High Street Bridge 50yds
20W Hall Lock
79 Halls Footbridge
SHAW HALL
STA
Lower Arthurs
80 Frenches Bridge
Shaw Hall Bridge 81
Grasscroft
Royal George Lock 19W
82 Manns Wharf Bridge
Keith Jackson Lock 18W
83 Royal George Bridge
16W Gas Works Lock
Royal George Aqueduct 84
86 Mossley Footbridge
87 Roaches Lock Bridge
A635
Division Bridge 85
15W Roaches Lock
Division Lock 17W
Gas Works Lock 16W
87 Roaches Lock Bridge
ROACHES
15W Roaches Lock
WOOD
15W Roaches Lock
Woodend Lock 14W
53
88
MOSSLEY
Winterford Bridge
13W Wharf Cottage Lock
89 Micklehurst Bridge
MICKLEHURST
91 Bottoms Bridge

Marsden

It comes as almost something of a relief to leave the activity centred around the tunnel mouth and start the long steady descent into Huddersfield. Lock operation is no less arduous going downhill and there is a feeling akin to anti-climax as the waterway drops rapidly through a profusion of trees and almost into Sparth Reservoir. In places the hills lining the Colne Valley step back a little, leaving level grazing and fields for hay and silage making. The infant river is never far away and in places is separated only by a narrow band of trees. From time to time the landscape is punctuated by the gaunt remains of a splendid old mill as views open out briefly before the often tree-lined hills close in once again. The railway shadows the canal into Slaithwaite where once again the harmony wrought by its focal position amidst shops and streets is most satisfactory.

Pubs and Restaurants

♀ ✗ **Water's Edge** Tunnel End, Marsden (01484 846782). Licensed tearooms occupying a unique position at the tunnel mouth. Meals, snacks (V), tea and coffee. Children welcome. Canalside seating. *Open as per the Visitor Centre.*

⬤ **Tunnel End Inn** Reddisher Road, Marsden (01484 844636). Just a 200yd walk up from the Visitor Centre, this little pub provides a warm and friendly atmosphere together with real ale served *Mon–Thur 19.00–23.00, Fri 17.00–23.00, Sat and Sun 12.00–22.30.* Home-made, value for money food (V) is *available E Fri and Sat 18.00–20.00 and L Sat–Sun.* Children and dogs welcome. Outside seating and pub games. Open fires in *winter.* Meals (including breakfast) are *available at other times* but must be booked. It would be worth telephoning to see if opening hours have been extended.

⬤ **Riverhead Brewery Tap** 2 Peel Street, Marsden (01484 841270). Once a grocer's shop, this lively single-roomed brew-pub now dispenses real ciders and an excellent range of its own real ales, which mostly carry the names of local reservoirs. *Open Mon– Fri 17.00–23.00 (Thur 16.00) and all day Sat and Sun.* No children.

✗ **Moonraker Floating Tearooms** Slaithwaite (01484 846370). A boat-based tearoom, moored above Dartmouth Lock 23E, serving home-made meals (V), snacks, cakes, scones, sandwiches, salads, hot and cold drinks of all kinds and ices. *Open Apr–Sep, Tue–Sun 09.00–18.00 (Sun 10.00); Oct–Mar, Wed–Sun 09.00–16.00 (Sun 10.00). Also all B Hols except 25–26 Dec.*

BOAT TRIPS
See opposite for details of trips into Standedge Tunnel.

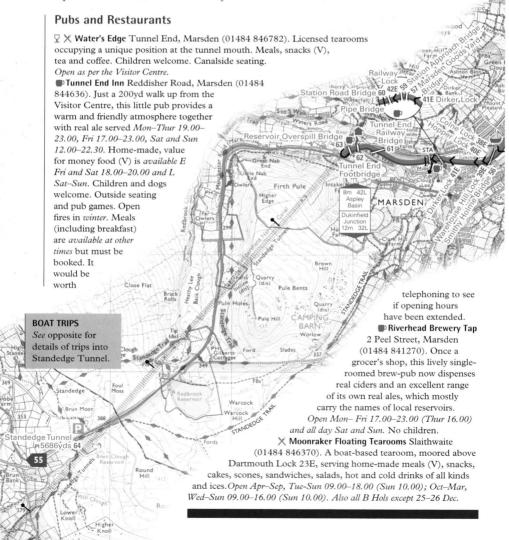

● **Marsden**
W. Yorks. PO, tel, stores, bank, chemist, garage, takeaway, station. Situated at an important transPennine crossing point, Marsden has always been a focus for the weaving industry and is associated with the Luddite riots. Enoch Taylor, pivotal figure in this industrial unrest, is buried beside the fine church and there is a set of stocks nearby. Its popularity as a location for TV soaps now make a different set of dramatic demands upon its environs. To the north of Colne Lock 38 there is a useful stores and off-licence *open Mon–Fri 09.00–22.00 (closed 13.00–15.00), Sat and Sun 10.00–22.00.*

Marsden Information Point 20-26 Peel Street, Marsden (01484 845595; marsden-information-point@kirklees.gov.uk). More than just a TIC – a fund of information and a community lifeline. *Open Tue 14.00–17.00, Wed–Fri 09.30–16.00, Sat 10.00–16.00, Sun 12.00–16.00.*

Marsden Mechanics Institute Peel Street, Marsden (01484 844587). A striking stone building with a colourful wooden tower (the foundations of the main structure were considered inadequate to bear the weight of anything heavier) erected in 1861 to provide education for the betterment of the working man. Now the library and community hall. Also home to the evergreen Mikron Theatre Company (when not touring the waterways on their boat *Tysley*) who can be contacted on 01484 843701; www.mikron.org.uk.

Marsden Moor Estate The Old Goods Yard, Station Road, Marsden (01484 847016; www.nationaltrust.org.uk/marsdenmoor). Over 5,000 acres of moorland in the hands of the NT and accessible through a series of walks and trails. The exhibition in the Old Goods Yard, beside the towpath at Marsden Railway Station, uses a series of excellent displays to provide a wealth of information about every aspect of the area, from natural phenomena through to the relatively recent industrial impact of weaving, water, canal and railway. Free.

Standedge Tunnels At first sight there appears to be an indecently large number of tunnels connecting Diggle with Marsden. The canal tunnel came first, completed in 1811, followed by the single bore of the Huddersfield and Manchester Railway dating from 1845. Two years later this railway company was taken over by the LNWR who built a second single – and parallel – track to cope with increasing demand. In 1894 the present double track tunnel was constructed to cope with the burgeoning traffic. In all instances the canal tunnel, now owned by the railway company and connected to its tunnels by cross-adits, proved invaluable for spoil removal during construction.

Standedge Visitor Centre Waters Road, Marsden (01484 844298; www.standedge.co.uk). All the superlatives marshalled within the confines of one extremely long tunnel: highest, longest and deepest in Britain and largely hewn out of solid rock. The centre offers two floors of interactive activities. *Open Nov–Mar, Wed–Sun 11.00–16.00; Apr–Jun and Sep–Oct, daily 11.00–17.00; Jul–Aug, daily 10.00–18.00. Closed 23 Dec–1 Jan.* Last admission 30 minutes before closing. Charge. Park at Marsden Railway Station and walk west along the towpath. A water taxi service operates during peak periods. Disabled access and disabled parking at the centre itself.

● **Slaithwaite**
W. Yorks. PO, tel, stores, butcher, bank, chemist, garage, takeaway, station. Another settlement founded on the woollen and cotton industries with a fine Georgian church and the 16th-C Slaithwaite Hall.

● **Linthwaite**
W. Yorks. Tel. Although strung out and somewhat detached from the waterway, this village is not without charm and is home to several very striking (and very derelict) mills which tell of its former glory as a textile producer.

Map labels:
44 Brittania Road Bridge
Lees Mill Bridge 41
Old Bank 45 Bridge
Spot Lock 20E
Waterside Lock 21E
42 Waterside Bridge
22E Pickle Lock
Shuttle Lock 24E
23E Dartmouth Lock
SLAITHWAITE
47 Upper Mill Bridge
Shaker Wood Lock 25E
Skew Bridge Lock 26E
Mill Pond Lock 27E
48 Shaw Carr Bridge
Waring Bottom Lock 28E
White Hill Lock 29E
Bank Nook Lock 30E
50 Waring Bottom Bridge
51 Booth Banks Bridge
BOOTH
Booth Lock 31E
52 Booths Bridge
Fisher's Footbridge
53
54
32E Pig Tail Lock
33E Sparth Lock
34E Cellars Lock
35E Moorale Lock
36E White Skye Lock
37E Smudges Lock

Huddersfield

East of Slaithwaite the waterway settles into a broader valley bottom and the hills become a little more submissive. Attractive tree-lined glades alternate with views of a still bold landscape and everywhere there are the gaunt remains of mills: reminders of this area's supremacy as a textile producer and the canal's real purpose. The descent into Huddersfield is steady and not without contrast – pretty stone bridges vie with an imposing railway viaduct and many of the locks (although still in need of more use) appear in attractive settings. The two factory tunnels are an ingenious solution to recent building on the old canal line and, in conjunction with the re-siting of the locks, represent the very best in Northern pragmatism! However, it is with some relief that you leave the stygian gloom of the second tunnel – the towpath employs an above-ground and altogether less elegant solution to the blockage – and, winding between university buildings, arrive at Apsley Basin. Beyond is the remarkable Turnbridge Loco Liftbridge dating from 1865; you will need a Watermate key to unlock it. The outskirts of Huddersfield present a mix of industry, a new waste incineration plant and by way of relief, a vast expanse of green sports fields. The nine locks appear with a steady regularity and, passing through Cooper Bridge Lock, the canal finally enters a river section of the Calder & Hebble Navigation (*see page 44*). Before leaving this lock, boaters should be quite clear of the layout of the junction and of their intended passage.

NAVIGATIONAL NOTES

When joining the Huddersfield Broad Canal at Cooper Bridge, take care to avoid the weir on the river just beyond the entrance to lock 1.

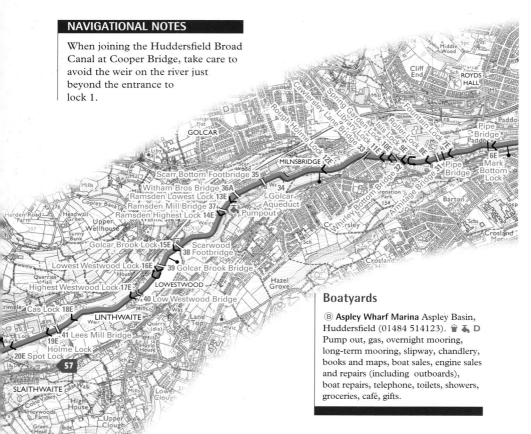

Boatyards

Ⓑ **Aspley Wharf Marina** Aspley Basin, Huddersfield (01484 514123). 🚽 🛢 D Pump out, gas, overnight mooring, long-term mooring, slipway, chandlery, books and maps, boat sales, engine sales and repairs (including outboards), boat repairs, telephone, toilets, showers, groceries, café, gifts.

● **Huddersfield**
W. Yorks. All services. Huddersfield is in the best tradition of Victorian industrial towns: all built to a grand scale of dark local stone, in a happy mixture of 19th-C styles. The most striking part of the town is around the railway station, built in 1847 with its powerful classical façade of Corinthian columns, considered one of the finest examples of railway architecture. The renowned Huddersfield Choral Society operates from the 19th-C town hall.

Alfred McAlpine Football Stadium & UCI Multi-Screen Cinema: Telephone 08700 102030 for full programme details.

Art Gallery Princess Alexandra Walk, Huddersfield (01484 221964). Above the library. Presents an international programme embracing all media together with changing displays from the permanent collection. *Open Mon– Fri 10.00–17.00, Sat 10.00–16.00.* Free.

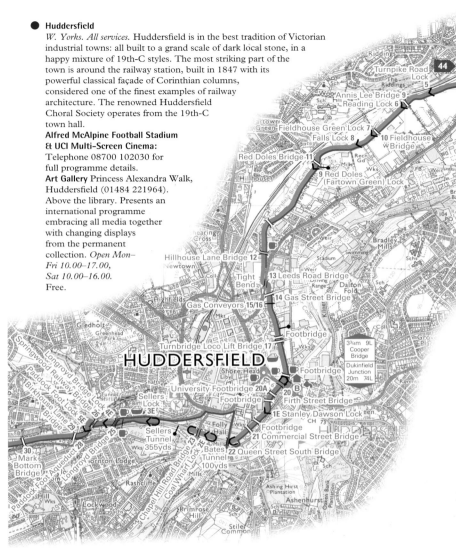

Castle Hill and Jubilee Tower Castle Hill, Almondbury, Huddersfield (01484 223830). A striking local landmark occupied since the Stone Age and now topped by a Victorian tower. Splendid views and an exhibition tracing the hill's 4000 years of history. Charge. Bus no 304 from Huddersfield. Telephone for opening times.

Colne Valley Museum Cliffe Ash, Golcar, nr Huddersfield (01484 659762). The hand weaver's working life c.1850 depicted in a working exhibit in period settings. Also clog making by gas light and a range of changing craft exhibitions. Books, gifts and light refreshments available. *Open weekends and B*

Hols 14.00–17.00. Small charge. Regular buses – nos 301, 302 and 303 – from Huddersfield bus station; or walk up from Holme Mill Bridge on the Narrow Canal.

Holmfirth Nr Huddersfield. An essential visit for all *Last of the Summer Wine* devotees, easily accessible by bus from Huddersfield. Exhibition gallery contains photographs and memorabilia dating from the series beginning in 1972. *Sat* craft market and galleries.

Holmfirth Tourist Information Centre 49–51 Huddersfield Road (01484 222444; holm-firth.tic@kirkleesmc.gov.uk). *Open Mon–Fri 09.00–17.00, Sat 10.00–17.00, Sun 11.00–17.00.*

Kirklees Light Railway Park Mill Way, Clayton West, Nr Huddersfield (01484 865727). Scenic ride on a narrow-gauge railway along a disused branch line. Children's playground and miniature fairground rides. Café. *Open daily Spring B Hol–Aug; weekends and most school holidays in winter.* Charge. Bus no 484 from Huddersfield.
Tolson Museum Ravensknowle Park, Huddersfield (01484 223830). Fine Italianate mansion housing natural history, archaeology and local history exhibits. Workshops, events and children's activities. *Open Mon–Fri 11.00–17.00, Sat and Sun 12.00–17.00.* Free. There are buses from Huddersfield.
Tourist Information Centre 3–5 Albion Road, Huddersfield (01484 223200; huddersfield.tic @kirkleesmc.gov.uk). *Open Mon–Sat 09.15–17.00.*

Pubs and Restaurants

🍺 ✕ **Royal and Ancient Country Inn** 19 Dalton Bank Road, Colnebridge, Huddersfield (01484 425461). East of bridge 2. A fine pub, tastefully furnished, achieving a balance between genuine olde worlde and traditional comfort. An intimate, cosy atmosphere in the separate restaurant area – screens, scatter cushions and an inviting window settle – together with interesting wall decorations and an intriguing array of curios to captivate the eye. An elaborate, varied and exciting range of food (V) – there are 15 fish dishes alone – is available in both the bar and restaurant *L and E (not Mon E)* and a good selection of real ales is dispensed from a bar dominated by a dark burr-oak post, uncarved, but appearing to depict the head of a Hereford bull. Children welcome as are well-behaved dogs in the bar only. Patio seating. Open fires *in winter.*
🍺 **DB's** Huddersfield (01484 423899). South of bridge 8. A handy pub by the cricket pitches. Bar meals *L.* Children welcome *until 19.00.* Outside seating overlooking playing fields.
🍺 **Spinners Arms** Huddersfield (01484 421062). East of the canal, approaching Turnbridge. Inexpensive bar snacks *available all day, every-day.* Large pub geared up around entertainment which includes a stripper *Wed,* karaoke *Fri* and a live act *Sat.*

There are plenty of pubs and restaurants in Huddersfield. These are just a selection close to Aspley Basin:
✕ **Canalside Café** Cooper Bridge, Huddersfield (01484 469429). Immediately to the west of Cooper Bridge, in the middle of an industrial estate, above a dyeworks. Real down-to-earth café (in spite of its first floor location) serving an impressive selection of extremely inexpensive food from breakfasts (they come in all sizes) through sandwiches, hot drinks, soups and snacks, to a variety of full-blown meals. *Open Mon–Fri 07.00–14.00, Sat 07.00–12.00.*
🍺 **County Hotel** 4 Princess Street, Huddersfield (01484 300494). As if to spite its narrow façade this pub is amazingly spacious inside and dispenses excellent real ale. Tucked away behind the Town Hall it serves traditional bar food (V) *L, daily.* Outside seating. Non-smoking area. Pool.
🍺 **Ship Inn** Queensgate, Huddersfield (01484 424123). Large, one-roomed student pub with a poster-covered ceiling. Seven real ales always on tap. Live music *Thur* and quiz *Sun.*
✕ 🍷 **Memsahib Eastern Eatery** 37/39 Queensgate, Huddersfield (01484 422002). Indian cuisine from a restaurant whose proprietor takes a real interest in serving authentic, regional dishes (V) using fresh ingredients. Excellent value and *open E.* Children welcome. Takeaway service – within jogging distance of the basin.
🍺 **Blob Shop** Queensgate, Huddersfield (01484 510974). Next to College Arms. Originally cottages, now with most of the first floor removed to give soaring ceilings; decorated with chintzy wall coverings and bright paintwork. Real ales together with inexpensive bar snacks (V) *L.* Children welcome if eating.
🍺 **College Arms** 33 Queensgate, Huddersfield. Close to the basin. Real ales in this unusual, student pub – formerly the Dog & Gun. Inexpensive bar snacks available *Mon–Sat L.* Children welcome *L only.* Pool.
🍺 **Dr. Brown's** Huddersfield (01484 423009). South of Wakefield Road Bridge. Striking combination of dingy woodwork, exposed brickwork and flagstone floors making these earthy surroundings ideal for the consumption of excellent real ales. A warm and friendly establishment serving an interesting selection of inexpensive bar food *until 21.00.* Beer garden. Children welcome.
🍺 ✕ **Aspley** Aspley Basin, Huddersfield (01484 544250). Whitbread Brewers Fayre Chain. Real ales and food (V) available *all day, every day.* Children welcome. Canalside seating and moorings.

LANCASTER CANAL

MAXIMUM DIMENSIONS	MILEAGE
Preston to Tewitfield Length: 75' Beam: 14' Headroom: 7' 6"	*PRESTON* to Garstang: 16$^1/4$ miles Junction with Glasson Branch: 24 miles Lancaster: 29$^1/4$ miles
Glasson Branch Length: 67' 6" Beam: 16' Headroom: 7' 9"	Carnforth: 37$^1/4$ miles *CANAL TERMINUS:* 41$^1/4$ No locks
MANAGER 01524 751888; enquiries.LANC@britishwaterways.co.uk	Glasson Branch: 2$^3/4$ miles, 6 locks Millennium Ribble Link: 4 miles, 9 locks

Construction on the Lancaster Canal began in 1792. The chosen route included several aqueducts, but only eight locks, at Tewitfield. By 1799 the canal between Tewitfield and Preston, including the aqueduct over the Lune, and the separate section between Clayton and Chorley, was opened. The north end remained separated from the national canal network until 2002. The route north was extended to Kendal in 1819, and the short arm to Glasson Dock, falling through six locks, was opened in 1826, finally providing a direct link with the sea. In 1968 the canal north of Tewitfield was abandoned with the building of the M6 motorway (although restoration is now mooted), and the route in Preston was shortened by about a mile. What remains is remarkably rural, surprisingly quiet and worthy of exploration. The Ribble Link, opened in 2002, at last links this canal to the national network.

NAVIGATIONAL NOTES

1 You will need a special key to use the locks on the Glasson Branch. These keys can be purchased from British Waterways, Lancaster Waterways Office, Main Road, Galgate, Lancaster LA2 0LQ (01524 751888).

2 Those who wish to use the Ribble Link (www.millenniumribblelink.co.uk) MUST obtain the Skipper's Guide and booking form from the address above, as this gives all ESSENTIAL navigational information. A booking form can also be obtained by email from enquiries.LANC@britishwaterways.co.uk. *Five days' notice is required.* As we go to press the charges are £35 for a single journey, £60 for a return. *Opening times are dictated by tides in the Ribble estuary, but a journey can be made Easter–Oct during daylight hours, Nov–Easter on request.* The staircase and sea lock are manned, and the link will operate one way each day. There is no mooring on the Link. As the River Ribble is tidal, boats should carry, *as a minimum*: anchor, chain and warp, VHF radio or mobile phone, lifejackets for all on board, fire-fighting equipment, coastal flares. Your engine must be sufficiently powerful to cope with tidal conditions. Be sure to check that your boat insurance covers tidal waters.

3 If you need help or advice while on the River Ribble, contact Preston Riversway Control on VHF channel 16, or telephone 01772 726871.

4 If you wish to visit Preston Docks, contact Preston Riversway Control on 01772 726871.

5 A pilot service for the Ribble Link (charge) can be obtained from: 01772 632439/ 812462/812250.

6 Navigators entering the Rufford Branch of the Leeds & Liverpool from the sea should remember that they will need a padlock key and a windlass to open the locks.

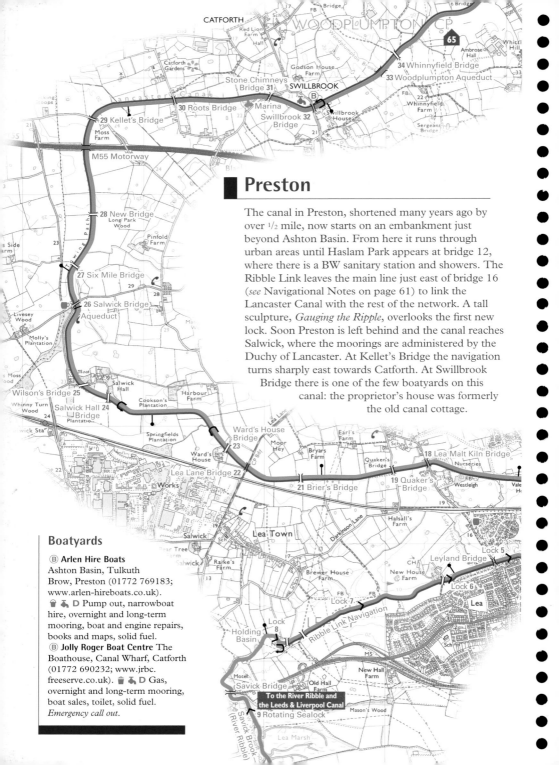

Preston

The canal in Preston, shortened many years ago by over ½ mile, now starts on an embankment just beyond Ashton Basin. From here it runs through urban areas until Haslam Park appears at bridge 12, where there is a BW sanitary station and showers. The Ribble Link leaves the main line just east of bridge 16 (*see* Navigational Notes on page 61) to link the Lancaster Canal with the rest of the network. A tall sculpture, *Gauging the Ripple*, overlooks the first new lock. Soon Preston is left behind and the canal reaches Salwick, where the moorings are administered by the Duchy of Lancaster. At Kellet's Bridge the navigation turns sharply east towards Catforth. At Swillbrook Bridge there is one of the few boatyards on this canal: the proprietor's house was formerly the old canal cottage.

Boatyards

Ⓑ **Arlen Hire Boats** Ashton Basin, Tulkuth Brow, Preston (01772 769183; www.arlen-hireboats.co.uk). 🚿 🛠 D Pump out, narrowboat hire, overnight and long-term mooring, boat and engine repairs, books and maps, solid fuel.
Ⓑ **Jolly Roger Boat Centre** The Boathouse, Canal Wharf, Catforth (01772 690232; www.jrbc. freeserve.co.uk). 🚿 🛠 D Gas, overnight and long-term mooring, boat sales, toilet, solid fuel. *Emergency call out.*

● **Preston**

Lancs. All services. A large industrial town granted a Royal Charter by Henry II in 1179, with the right to hold a Guild Merchant. An outdoor market was also established and still thrives today. The teetotal movement was founded in Preston in 1834, and Joseph Livesey's Temperance Hotel (the world's first) used to stand at the corner of Church Street and North Road. There are many churches, such as St Walburge's (south east of the terminus), whose tall spires are a distinctive feature of the town. There is a good shopping precinct and a large modern bus station. Preston was awarded city status by the Queen in April 2002, in celebration of her Golden Jubilee.

Harris Museum & Art Gallery Market Square, Preston (01772 258248; harris.museum@ preston.gov.uk). The largest gallery space in Lancashire, containing a specialised collection of the Devis family of painters and exhibits illustrating 18th-C and 19th-C art, including ceramics and costume. *Open Mon–Sat, 10.00–17.00; closed B Hols.* Free.

Tourist Information Centre Guildhall Arcade, Lancaster Road, Preston (01772 253731; tourism@preston.gov.uk).

Pubs and Restaurants

🛳 **Last Orders Inn** Water Lane, Aston, Preston (01772 721567). A 1/4-mile south of Ashton Basin. A good basic pub serving bar meals (V) *12.00–19.00 daily.* Singers on *Sun.*

🛳 **Lime Kiln** 228 Aqueduct Street, Preston (01772 493247). Just east of Ashton Basin. This is a very friendly and extremely handy corner pub serving real ale and bar meals (V) *L.* Children welcome.

🛳 **Dr Syntax** 241 Fylde Road, Preston (01772 726413). South east of the terminus, this pub has a garden, and children are welcome. Quiz *Sun.*

🛳 **Fylde Tavern** 300 Fylde Road, Preston (01772 722514). South west of the terminus. Real ale is served, and children

are welcome *until 19.00.* There is a garden, and a 60s. 70s and 80s disco *Fri,* live singer or groups *Sat* and a contemporary disco *Sun.*

🛳 **Grand Junction** Watery Lane, Preston (01772 726698). South west of the terminus. Changing ownership as we go to press.

🛳 **Lane Ends** Weston Road, Preston (01772 671216). East of Blackpool Road Bridge. Real ale is served and children are welcome.

🛳 **Cotty Brook** Lea Road, Lea (01772 723484). A friendly pub serving real ale, and food (V) *L and E Mon–Fri, and 12.00–17.00 Sat–Sun.* Children are welcome. Garden.

🛳 **Hand & Dagger** Treales Road, Salwick (01772 690306). Canalside at bridge 26. Once the Clifton Arms. A welcoming country pub serving real ale and freshly prepared food (V) *L and E and all day Sat–Sun.* Children welcome, and there is a play and barbecue area. Mooring. Karaoke *monthly.*

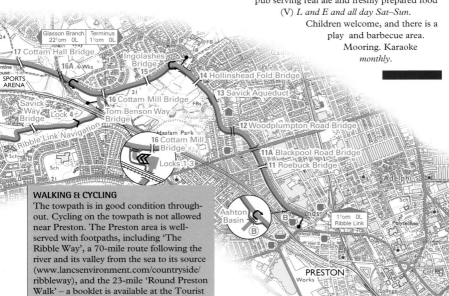

Glasson Branch 22¹/₂m 0L Terminus 1¹/₂m 0L

17 Cottam Hall Bridge

16A Wks

Ingolashes Bridge

15

14 Hollinshead Fold Bridge

SPORTS ARENA

16 Cottam Mill Bridge
21
Tom Benson Way Bridge

13 Savick Aqueduct

Cottam Way Bridge Lock 4

Ribble Link Navigation

Haslam Park

16 Cottam Mill Bridge

Locks 1-3

12 Woodplumpton Road Bridge

11A Blackpool Road Bridge

11 Roebuck Bridge

Ashton Basin

1¹/₂m 0L Ribble Link

PRESTON
Works

WALKING & CYCLING
The towpath is in good condition throughout. Cycling on the towpath is not allowed near Preston. The Preston area is well-served with footpaths, including 'The Ribble Way', a 70-mile route following the river and its valley from the sea to its source (www.lancsenvironment.com/countryside/ribbleway), and the 23-mile 'Round Preston Walk' – a booklet is available at the Tourist Information Centre.

Bilsborrow

Passing the marina at Moons Bridge, the canal gently meanders along its remote route towards White Horse Bridge where, just a 1/4 mile walk to the east, there is a *pub, garage, post office and telephone kiosk*. The canal then sweeps round to enter the village of Bilsborrow on a minor embankment: the A6 joins the canal here, as does the main railway line to Scotland, and the M6. Generally these rival transport routes keep their distance and the canal is for the most part delightfully quiet, still passing through peaceful green farmland, while the foothills of the Pennines begin to converge from the east. The River Brock is crossed on an aqueduct, with a good view to the west. There is a handy *garage and shop* at bridge 49, with limited temporary moorings giving direct access.

Boatyards

Ⓑ **Moons Bridge Marina** Hollowforth Lane, Woodplumpton (01772 690627; www. moonsbridgemarina.co.uk). 🛥 D Gas, long-term mooring, winter storage, slipway, lifting trailer, boat and engine sales and repairs, chandlery, gifts, DIY facilities.

Pubs and Restaurants

🍺 **White Horse Hotel** Barton (01995 640236). 1/4 mile east of bridge 42. Small, comfortable pub serving home-made food (V) *L and E*. Children are made very welcome.

🍺 ✕ **Owd Nell's** Canalside, St Michael's Road, Bilsborrow (01995 640010; www.guysthatched-hamlet.co.uk). At bridge 44. A farmhouse-style thatched pub and restaurant complex, with all sorts of attractions. There are craft shops, a thatched terrace, a timber castle and games areas with cricket pavilion. Generous bar meals, with a children's menu (V) *all day, every day*. Real ales, with a choice of well furnished bars in which to drink them (some with no smoking areas). Morris dancing (to bagpipes) on *summer weekends*. Children welcome. Hotel accommodation.

🍺 ✕ **Roebuck** Garstang Road, Bilsborrow (01995 640234). A pub/restaurant/lodge serving real ale and meals (V) *11.00–22.00 daily*. Children welcome, and there is a large garden.

🍺 **White Bull** Garstang Road, Bilsborrow (01995 640324). Canalside at bridge 44. Friendly village local with an open fire, dispensing real ales and food (V) *Sun–Thur 12.00–18.00, Fri and Sat 12.00–20.00*. Children welcome, and there is a garden. *Weekend* entertainment includes karaoke, singers or perhaps a quiz.

🍺 ✕ **Brock Tavern** Brock (01995 640220). South of bridge 47 on the A6 Garstang Road. A friendly family pub which offers food (V) *L and E Mon–Thur and 11.30–22.00 Fri and Sat*. Children welcome if eating.

FROM PRESTON TO KENDAL, BY WATERBUS

In an age when there is great personal freedom of movement, it is not always easy to imagine that canals, in their time, provided much the same opportunities as buses and trains today. As well as regular water bus services, special excursions were organised. Indeed as early as 1776 boats carried pleasure seekers from Beeston to the Chester Races, on what is now the Shropshire Union Canal.

Such services were scheduled on the Lancaster Canal until 1849. Initially a regular daily service operated between Kendal and Preston, the journey taking 14 hours, with refreshments being provided. In 1833, in order to compete with the stage coaches, an express service was introduced, cutting the journey time to 7 hours 15 minutes, and carrying an incredible 14,000 passengers in the first six months.

'For safety, economy and comfort no other mode of transport could be so eligible.'

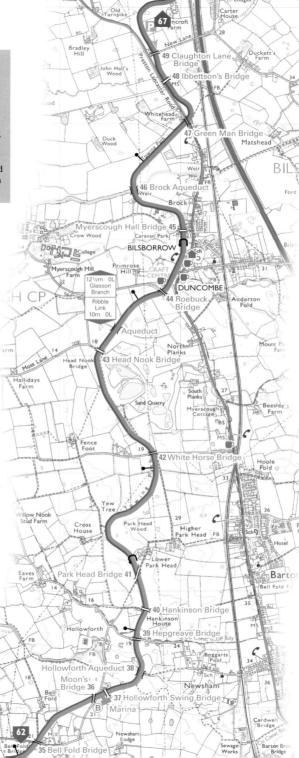

BOAT TRIPS
The Bilsborrow Lady
Old Duncombe House,
Bilsborrow Wharf,
Garstang Road (01995
640336; www.
hotpots.com/Wyre/
billsborrowlady). A com-
fortable 12-seater boat
offering a wide range of
trips and cruises. Bar and
buffet available. Between
bridges 44 and 45.

● **Bilsborrow**
*Lancs. PO, tel, stores,
garage, fish & chips.* A
village which straggles
along the A6. The
church of St Hilda, built
1926–7, is set apart, up
on a hill; there are three
pubs very close to the
canal.

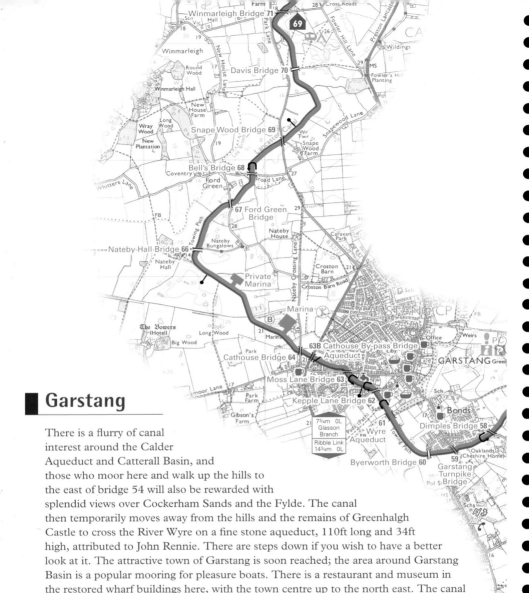

Garstang

There is a flurry of canal
interest around the Calder
Aqueduct and Catterall Basin, and
those who moor here and walk up the hills to
the east of bridge 54 will also be rewarded with
splendid views over Cockerham Sands and the Fylde. The canal
then temporarily moves away from the hills and the remains of Greenhalgh
Castle to cross the River Wyre on a fine stone aqueduct, 110ft long and 34ft
high, attributed to John Rennie. There are steps down if you wish to have a better
look at it. The attractive town of Garstang is soon reached; the area around Garstang
Basin is a popular mooring for pleasure boats. There is a restaurant and museum in
the restored wharf buildings here, with the town centre up to the north east. The canal
then passes a new marina and continues to wind through countryside that is as green
and pleasant as ever, but which is now overlooked by the steep slopes of the Pennines.

Boatyards

Ⓑ **Bridge House Marina** Crossing Lane, Nateby
(01995 603207 or 0870 050 6541). Between
bridges 64 and 66. 🚽 🚻 🔧 D Gas, long-term

mooring, winter storage, slipway, crane,
chandlery, boat sales, boat and engine repairs,
toilets, showers, telephone.

Pubs and Restaurants

🍺 **Kenlis Arms Hotel** Ray Lane, Barnacre (01995 603307) East of bridge 54. A country local serving home-cooked food (V) *L Fri–Sun and E Mon–Sat.* Children are welcome, and there is a family garden with a play area.

🍺 **Th'Owd Tithebarn** The Wharf, Church Street (01995 604486). Canalside at bridge 62. A uniquely old-fashioned establishment where it is hard to discern where the bar ends and the museum, which the building contains, begins. They serve real ale and country fruit wines, and substantial bar and restaurant meals (V) *L and E, daily.* Children welcome. Morris dancing *in the summer.* Canalside terrace.

🍺 **Church Inn** 33 Bonds Lane, Garstang (01995 602387). North of bridge 59. A traditional and cosy pub by the church, serving real ale, and food (V) *L and E.* Children welcome.

🍺 ✕ **Royal Oak Hotel** Market Place, Garstang (01995 603318). A coaching inn, dating from the 1670s but with parts surviving from 1480. Real ale. Bar meals (V) *L and E, daily.* Children, and dogs, welcome. B & B.

🍺 **Eagle & Child** High Street, Garstang (01995 602139). Serves real ale and bar meals (V) *L Mon–Sat.* Children welcome, and there is a small garden. Disco *Sun.*

🍺 ✕ **Flag** Parkside Lane, Nateby (01995 602126). 200yds south of bridge 64. Real ale and bar meals (V) *12.00–21.00 (20.00 Sun).* Indoor play area for children. Live music *Fri,* disco *Sat.*

🍺 **Crown** High Street, Garstang (01995 602152). Serving real ale and meals *L and E (not Sun or Mon E).* Children welcome, and there is a play area and bowling green.

🍺 **Kings Arms** High Street, Garstang (01995 602101). A sport-orientated pub serving real ale and home-made bar meals (V) *L.* Children welcome, outside seating. DJ and large-screen football *Sun.*

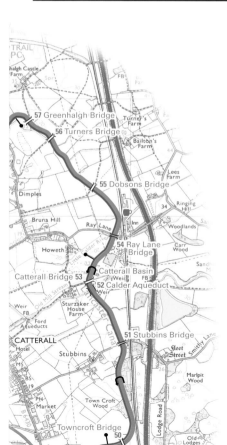

● **Claughton Hall** 1/4 mile east of the canal. This hall was originally an Elizabethan mansion built next to the village church for the Croft family, but in 1932–5 the whole house, except for one wing, was dismantled and reassembled on top of the moor north of the village. It was quite a remarkable undertaking and still stands in defiant isolation.

● **Greenhalgh Castle** Just north of the canal on a grassy knoll are the modest ruins of Greenhalgh Castle. It was built in 1490 by the Earl of Derby, who placed Richard III's crown on Henry Tudor's head after the victory at Bosworth Field. In the 17th C it was destroyed by the Roundheads during the Civil War, when the Royalists made a final stand there. Ask at the adjacent farm to visit the ruins.

● **Garstang**
Lancs. PO, tel, stores, bank, garage. A friendly place, referred to as 'Cherstanc' in the Domesday Book, lying north east of the canal, which retains the atmosphere of a small market town. In the 18th C Garstang was a popular stopping point for coaches en route from London to Edinburgh and the traditional market which still takes place every Thurday dates back to 1310, in the time of Edward II. Near the canal is the 18th-C church of St Thomas, surrounded by a tidy churchyard. Opposite the cobbled market place is an interesting town hall with diminutive bell-tower. Built 1755–64 to acknowledge the town's promotion by the king to borough status, it was rebuilt in 1939. The market cross, erected in 1754, is an elegant column topped by a ball. There was at one time a dozen ale houses in the town; the present six seem quite adequate.

Tourist Information Centre Discovery Centre, Council Offices, High Street, Garstang (01995 602125; www.wyrebc.gov.uk/tourismgarstang).

Potters Brook

Continuing northwards through quiet, modest and unspoilt pasture land, the canal passes countryside which is empty of villages but full of farms and houses which are dotted about the landscape. The absence of any locks certainly makes this an ideal waterway for restful cruising, while the wildlife and the generously proportioned stone-arched bridges always supply interest along the way. From Potters Brook Bridge (81) a lane across the A6 leads to a *telephone* and hotel beside what used to be Bay Horse Station. Just north of Potters Brook is the Ellel Grange estate with its remarkable spired church, ornamental canal bridge and the Grange itself, shrouded by tall trees; unfortunately the estate is private.

Ellel Grange Ellel (01524 751651; www. ellelministries.org). On the banks of the canal. A very fine Italianate villa built for William Preston, a merchant, in 1857–9. It is a large mansion with two broad towers that compete in vain with the graceful spire of the charming little church of St Mary, built in 1873 at a cost of £7000, which stands in the grounds of the house.

It was also built by William Preston. Purchased in 1986 by the Ellel Ministries, it was the first of their centres to be established and it still remains the international headquarters of the work. As well as holding Healing Retreats and Training Courses, Ellel Grange accommodates the Special Ministries Unit which provides longer-term help for those in need.

Pubs and Restaurants

Bay Horse Bay Horse, Forton (01524 791204). North east of bridge 81, across the A6. Real ale is served in this friendly and cosy country pub, which has an open fire *during the* *winter*. Restaurant and bar meals (V) are available L and E *(not Sun E or Mon)*. Children are welcome if you are eating, and there is a garden.

Lune Aqueduct (see page 70)

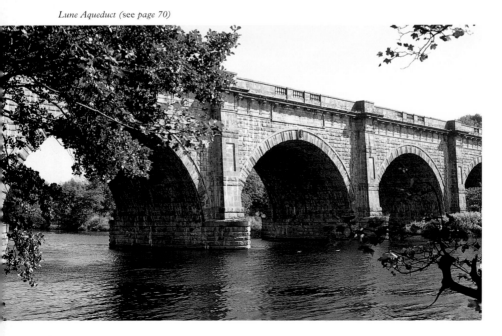

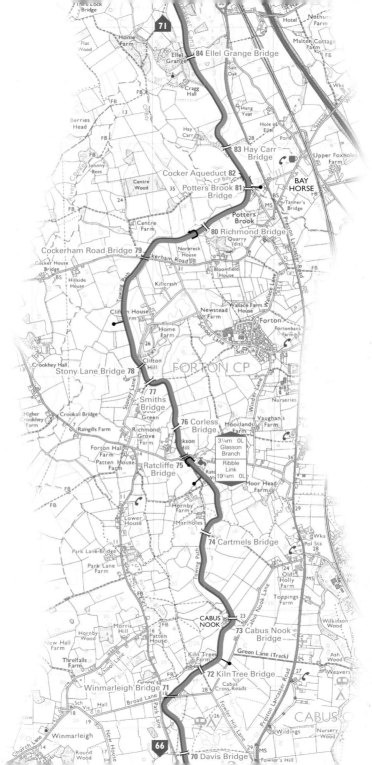

71

84 Ellel Grange Bridge

83 Hay Carr Bridge

Cocker Aqueduct 82

Potters Brook 81 Bridge

BAY HORSE

80 Richmond Bridge

Cockerham Road Bridge 79

Stony Lane Bridge 78

77 Smiths Bridge

76 Corless Bridge

3¼m 0L Glasson Branch

Ribble Link 19¼m 0L

Ratcliffe 75 Bridge

74 Cartmels Bridge

CABUS NOOK

73 Cabus Nook Bridge

72 Kiln Tree Bridge

Winmarleigh Bridge 71

CABUS

66

70 Davis Bridge

The Glasson Branch

Double Bridge marks the end of a rocky cutting and the junction with the Glasson Branch. Just around the corner on the main line is Galgate and a large boatyard and mooring site. The Glasson Branch leads off down to the west to connect the Lancaster Canal with the Lune estuary via Glasson Dock. The branch was finished in 1826, long after the main line of the canal was completed, and provided the canal with its only direct link with the sea. There are six wide locks whose bottom gates feature the same excellent type of sliding paddles seen on the Leeds & Liverpool Canal (*see* Navigational Note 2). Gates must be locked after use, and the locks left *empty*, even when going up. The arm falls through the Conder Valley, a pleasant, quiet stretch of countryside whose proximity to the sea is betrayed by the many seagulls cruising around. After the bottom lock, the canal runs in a straight line through saltings and marshland to Glasson Basin, where there is a large boatyard, mainly for seagoing yachts, and British Waterways moorings.

The main line of the canal continues northwards through beautiful undulating green countryside, then passes through an unusually long wooded cutting, marked by Deep Cutting Bridge, and ends in the outskirts of Lancaster.

NAVIGATIONAL NOTES

1 The entrance lock from Glasson Dock up into Glasson Basin will take boats up to 87' 10" x 26' 3" with 11' 9" draught, and operates *2hrs* before high water. Anyone wishing to use the lock (for which *24hrs* notice is required) should telephone British Waterways, Lancaster Office, Main Road, Galgate, Lancaster LA2 0LQ *during office hours Mon–Fri* on 01524 751888.

2 The locks on the Glasson Branch will take boats up to 67' 6" x 16' with 3' 10" draught. You will need a key to operate them, available from British Waterways Lancaster Office *during office hours Mon–Fri*. Gates must be locked after use, and the locks left *empty*, even when going up.

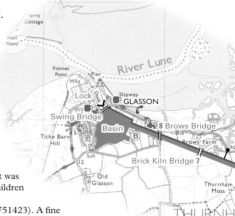

Pubs and Restaurants

🍺 **Thurnham Mill Tavern** Thurnham Mill Hotel, Conder Green (01524 752852). On the Glasson Branch. Real ale and award winning food (V) *L and E, daily,* in a sympathetically restored 17th-C grain mill, which was rebuilt in 1829. For over 100 years it was powered by canal water – an unusual innovation. Children welcome, garden and moorings close by.

🍺 **Victoria** Victoria Terrace, Glasson Dock (01524 751423). A fine family pub with an open fire and a nautical theme, taking its name from the *SS Victoria*. Real ale is served along with home-made bar meals (V) *L and E (all day Sun)*. Children welcome, and there is a waterside garden with a play area. Quiz *Sun*.

🍺 **Green Dragon** Main Road, Galgate (01524 751062). Real ale in a village pub which has its own children's football team. Food (V) *L and E (not Wed L)*. Children welcome. Outside seating. Live entertainment *Fri and Sat*, quiz *Sun*.

✕ **Lantern O'er the Lune Café** Tithebarn Hill, Glasson (01524 752323). Overlooking the basin, this friendly café does main meals along with cakes, teas and coffee. *Open 09.30–18.00 (16.00 in winter, weekends only Jan)*.

✕ **Lock Keepers Rest** Glasson Basin. This converted caravan has provided tea, coffee, cakes and burgers to visitors for many years.

Boatyards

Ⓑ **Marina Park**
Canal Wharf,
Galgate, Lancaster
(01524 751888). 🚽 🚿
⚓ Long-term moor-
ing, slipway, toilets,
showers.

Ⓑ **Glasson Basin Yacht
Co.** Glasson Dock,
Lancaster (01524
751491; info@glasson.
marina.com). ⚓ D
Gas, overnight and
long-term mooring,
winter storage, travel
hoist, boat sales and
repairs, chandlery,
books and maps.

WALKING & CYCLING
The Lune Millennium
Cycleway, which also
forms part of the
Lancashire Cycleway,
follows a former railway
line and connects
Glasson to Lancaster
and Bull Beck picnic
site to the north. The
route of this
footpath/cycleway runs
through Lancaster
before heading up-
stream on the River
Lune towards Caton.

● **Galgate**
Lancs. PO, tel, stores, garage.
An unassuming village on the
A6, dominated by the main
railway to Scotland. The back
of the village up the hill is
quiet; by the church of St
John, built 1906–7, are the
buildings of what is apparently
the oldest surviving silk
spinning mill in England, built
in 1792. There is another,
apparently older, built
originally as a corn mill, close
by. Some of the nearby
cottages were built for the
mill-workers.
Canalside Craft Centre Pear
Tree Barn, Main Road,
Galgate (01524 752223). A
craft shop next to the marina.
Tea, coffee, snacks and full
meals. *Open 10.00–17.00,
closed Mon except B Hols.*

● **Glasson**
Lancs. PO, tel, stores, garage.
A fascinating tiny port built in
1787 to serve Lancaster.
The huge basin is now only
occupied by an assortment
of pleasure boats using its
excellent sheltered moorings.
In the tidal dock, however,
there are often coasters
which discharge into
lorries.

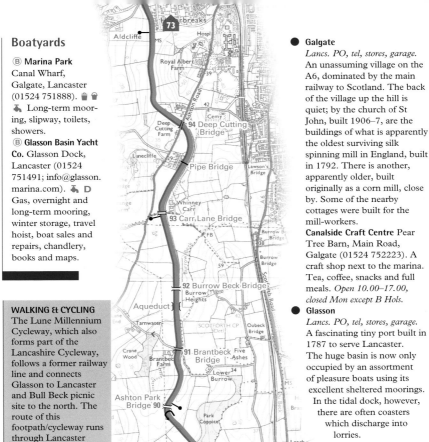

Lancaster

The canal now enters Lancaster, losing its rural identity as buildings close in. There are useful *stores* just west of bridge 98. At bridge 100 the towpath returns to the west side of the canal, where it stays for the rest of the journey northwards. The canal passes through the heart of Lancaster and continues north to cross an aqueduct, built in 1961, over the A683. The imposing aqueduct which carries the canal over the River Lune quickly follows, affording fine views along the Lune valley. The canal then rejoins the side of the valley, turning west, then north again to head towards the sea at Hest Bank.

● **Lancaster**
Lancs. All services. Today Lancaster's quay, once a great shipping port handling more cargo than Liverpool, is a quiet backwater, with pleasant walks. There are some fine canalside buildings.
Lancaster Castle (01524 64998, www.lancaster-castle.com). On the site of Roman fortifications, this is a mainly 13th-C and 14th-C construction, except for the Norman keep, which is surmounted by a beacon tower. *Open daily 10.00–17.00. Guided tours (Court sittings permitting) from 10.30–16.00.* Charge. Gift shop.
Cottage Museum 15 Castle Hill (01524 388716). Opposite the castle, this is part of a 1739 house containing the artifacts of an artisan, c. 1820. *Open Easter–Sep 14.00–17.00.* Charge.
Lancaster Priory & Parish Church Castle Hill, Lancaster, (01524 65338; lancasterpriory@yahoo.co.uk). There has been a church on this site since AD 630. The present building is an attractive 15th-C church in late Perpendicular style, with an original Saxon western doorway. Church *open all year round 09.30–17.00.* Free. Guided tours *Jul–Sep.* Refectory *open Easter–Oct, 10.00–16.00.* Interesting book stall. Nearby are the excavated remains of a Roman bath house.
Lancaster City Museum Old Town Hall, Market Square, Lancaster (01524 64637; museum@lancaster.gov.uk). The history and archaeology of Lancaster. *Open Mon–Sat 10.00–17.00.* Free.
Ashton Memorial Williamson Park, Quernmore Road (01524 33318, www.williamsonpark.

u-net.com). The Taj Mahal of the north. A Butterfly House and Mini Beast Enclosure are among its other delights. *Open Easter–Oct, daily 10.00–17.00; winter, daily 11.00–16.00.* Charge.
Maritime Museum Old Customs House, St George's Quay, Lancaster (01524 64637). Walk towards the river from bridge 99, turning left into Damside. Lifeboats, fine models and artefacts from Glasson Dock. *Open Easter–Oct, daily 11.00–17.00; winter 12.30–16.00.* Charge. Café. The riverside path to the west connects with Glasson Dock about 5 miles away, making an excellent walk or bike ride.
Tourist Information Centre 29 Castle Hill, Lancaster (01524 32878, tourism@lancaster. gov.uk). *Open Mon–Sat 10.00–17.00.*

● **Lune Aqueduct**
This splendid edifice carries the navigation for some 600ft across the River Lune, which is 60ft below. Designed by John Rennie, it was built between 1794–7 by Alexander Stevens, a Scotsman who died before it was completed. The bottom of the channel is apparently 7 or 8ft deep, containing a layer of puddled clay about 3ft thick. There is said to be a plug which can be pulled to drain the structure into the River Lune below. Its total cost was £48,320 18s 6d.

● **Hest Bank**
Lancs. PO, tel, stores, bank, Chinese takeaway. The seashore is only a couple of hundred yards from the navigation, and at low water miles of sandy beach are uncovered.

Pubs and Restaurants

● ✗ **Water Witch** Aldcliffe Road (01524 63828). Canalside between bridges 98 and 99. Warm and friendly, with a stone floor and a good variety of fresh food (V), including an excellent cheeseboard, in the bar or restaurant *L and E (Sun 12.00–18.00).* A wide selection of local real ales is available. Outside seating, mooring.
● ✗ **Farmers Arms Hotel** Penny Street (01524 36368; www.farmersarmslancaster.co.uk). A friendly family-run pub close to the canal, serving real ale and a wide range of bar and restaurant meals (V) *L and E, daily.* Children welcome.
● ✗ **White Cross** Quarry Road (01524 384981). Canalside at bridge 100. Real ales, bar and restaurant meals (V) *L and E, and all day Sat and Sun.* Children welcome. canalside seating.

✗ **Whale Tail Vegetarian Café** 78a Penny Street (01524 845133). Imaginative vegetarian and vegan meals, plus an organic snack menu. Organic main meal on *Fri,* cooked breakfasts, cakes, coffees and herb teas. *Open Mon–Fri 09.30–16.00, Sat 09.30–17.00, Sun 10.30–15.00.* On the first floor, and there is no lift. Chinese restaurant below.
● **Waggon & Horses** St George's Quay, Lancaster (01524 846094). Worth a look in if you are visiting the Maritime Museum, this pub serves real ale, and food *L.* Waterside seats outside.
● ✗ **Hest Bank** 2 Hest Bank Lane (01524 824339). Canalside at Bridge 118. *See* Pubs and Restaurants page 75.

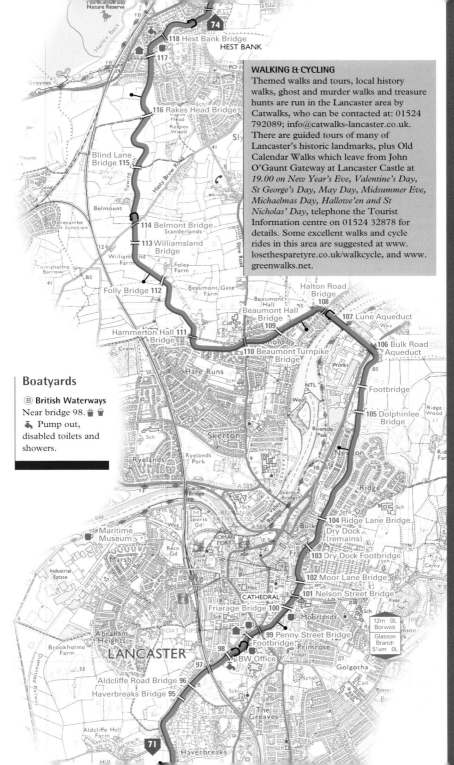

74

118 Hest Bank Bridge
HEST BANK
117

116 Rakes Head Bridge

Blind Lane
Bridge 115

Belmount

114 Belmont Bridge
Standerlands
113 Williamsland
Bridge

Folly Bridge 112

Hammerton Hall 111
Bridge

WALKING & CYCLING
Themed walks and tours, local history
walks, ghost and murder walks and treasure
hunts are run in the Lancaster area by
Catwalks, who can be contacted at: 01524
792089; info@catwalks-lancaster.co.uk.
There are guided tours of many of
Lancaster's historic landmarks, plus Old
Calendar Walks which leave from John
O'Gaunt Gateway at Lancaster Castle at
19.00 on New Year's Eve, Valentine's Day,
St George's Day, May Day, Midsummer Eve,
Michaelmas Day, Hallowe'en and St
Nicholas' Day, telephone the Tourist
Information centre on 01524 32878 for
details. Some excellent walks and cycle
rides in this area are suggested at www.
losethesparetyre.co.uk/walkcycle, and www.
greenwalks.net.

Halton Road
Bridge
108
Beaumont
Hall
Beaumont Hall
Bridge
109
107 Lune Aqueduct
106 Bulk Road
Aqueduct

110 Beaumont Turnpike
Bridge

Footbridge

105 Dolphinlee
Bridge

Boatyards

B **British Waterways**
Near bridge 98.
Pump out,
disabled toilets and
showers.

104 Ridge Lane Bridge
Dry Dock
(remains)

103 Dry Dock Footbridge

102 Moor Lane Bridge

101 Nelson Street Bridge

CATHEDRAL
Friarage Bridge 100

99 Penny Street Bridge
98 Footbridge
Primrose

12m 0L
Borwick

Glasson
Branch
5¼m 0L

LANCASTER
97 BW Office

Aldcliffe Road Bridge 96
Haverbreaks Bridge 95

Aldcliffe Hall
Farm

71

Haverbreaks

Carnforth

The canal now passes Hest Bank and Bolton-le-Sands, with the sea never far away to the west and the A6 beside and below. As the waterway comes into Carnforth, it often affords grand views over Morecambe Bay before sneaking quite inconspicuously through the town, mostly in a cutting, passing a *sanitary station*, *pump out* and *showers*. It then dives under the motorway spur road and finds itself diverted along a new channel for several hundred yards before going under the main line of the M6: this diversion was presumably cheaper to build than a long, finely-angled skew motorway bridge over the navigation. Beyond the motorway lies peaceful green countryside backed, unmistakably, by the foothills of the Lake District. At Capernwray the canal crosses the River Keer on a minor aqueduct built by John Rennie in 1797; the nearby railway, which goes to Leeds, also crosses the Keer, on a very impressive viaduct.

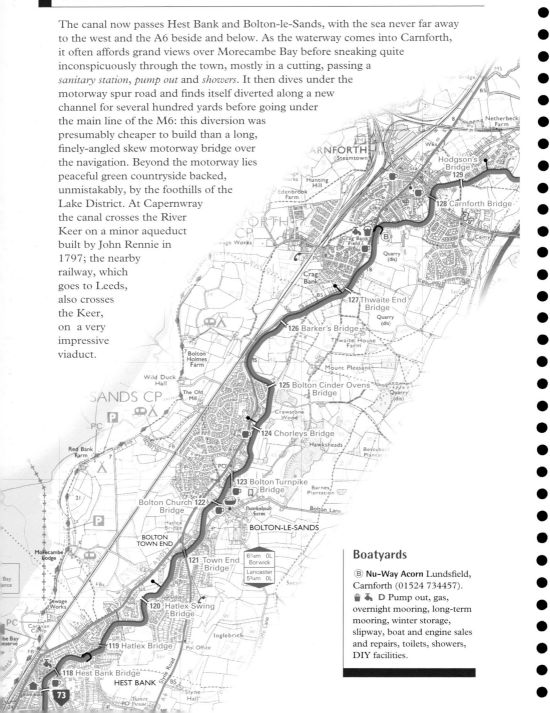

Boatyards

Ⓑ **Nu-Way Acorn** Lundsfield, Carnforth (01524 734457). 🛢 🔧 D Pump out, gas, overnight mooring, long-term mooring, winter storage, slipway, boat and engine sales and repairs, toilets, showers, DIY facilities.

● **Bolton-le-Sands**
*Lancs. PO, tel, stores, fish &
chips.* A pleasant village of narrow streets, with a pub at each end.

● **Carnforth**
Lancs. PO, tel, stores, garage, bank, station. Not
particularly attractive but useful for supplies and of interest as
an important railway junction. It is possible to catch trains not only
north–south but east over the beautiful green hills to Skipton and Leeds, west to
Barrow and right round the coast to Carlisle. Carnforth was the last town in the country to lose its
regular British Rail steam locomotive service in 1968: it is now a centre for steam-hauled railtours over
the national railway system. There is a useful *PO and stores* north west of bridge 127 at Crag Bank.

Pubs and Restaurants

◗ ✕ **Hest Bank** 2 Hest Bank Lane (01524
824339). Canalside at bridge 118. You can
still see the window for the guiding light, which
once showed the way across the sands. Now
this old coaching inn, which dates from 1554,
is justly popular and you can share the shelter
it once offered to abbots and monks, soldiers
and highwaymen, the Duke of Devonshire and
Prince Frederick of Prussia. Real ale and fresh
local food (V), and seafood *L and E, daily*.
Children welcome (not in the public bar), and
there is a fine canalside garden. Quiz *Wed*.
Mooring.

◗ ✕ **Blue Anchor** Main Road, Bolton-le-
Sands (01524 823241). An 18th-C coach
house serving real ale and bar and restaurant
food (V) *L and E (all day Sun)*. Children
welcome. Garden. Quiz *Wed*. B & B.

◗ **Packet Boat Hotel** Main Road, Bolton-le-
Sands (01524 822289). A friendly pub with
'something for everyone', serving real ale and
food (V) *L and E (all day Fri–Sun)*. Children
welcome *until 20.30*, and a free dog chew
for your dog. Outside seating. *Weekend
entertainment and quiz Sun*. Live TV
premiership football.

◗ **Royal Hotel** Bolton-le-Sands (01524 732057).
A choice of real ale, plus a good range of food,
featuring 'Pauline's Pies' (V) *L and E (all day

Sun)*. A large and very comfortable pub where
the original layout remains, although the total
space has been made one area. You can still
find yourself a cosy corner, with books and a
fire *in winter*. Children welcome, and there is a
new play area. Garden.

◗ ✕ **Canal Turn** Lancaster Road, Carnforth
(01524 734750). A very attractive canalside
pub in cottages once known as 'Pig & Piano
Row', and which housed workers from nearby
iron and gas works. Meals (V) are served *L
and E, daily*, along with real ale. Children are
welcome, and there is a waterside garden.

◗ **Shovel** North Road, Carnforth (01524
733402). West of bridge 128. A friendly pub
serving real ale. Children welcome, and there
is a garden. Quiz nights.

◗ ✕ **Royal Station Hotel** Market Street,
Carnforth (01524 732033; royalstation@
mitchellshotels.co.uk). Bang in the centre of
town, this handsome establishment played
host to Trevor Howard, Celia Johnson and
Stanley Holloway in the Noel Coward film
'Brief Encounter', which was filmed around
Carnforth Station. Queen Victoria is also
reputed to have stayed here. They offer real
ale, plus bar and restaurant meals (V) *L and E
(all day Sun)*. Children welcome. The Sports
Bar has a large-screen TV. B & B.

Borwick

Beyond Keer Aqueduct and the railway viaduct is the Capernwray Arm, a short branch to a worked-out quarry, and now offering some attractive sheltered moorings. The canal then winds around the hillside to end abruptly just beyond Borwick and right beside the M6, but fortunately with a decent pub just a stone's throw away. The abandoned Tewitfield locks begin across the road from the present terminus, and it is well worth taking the fenced path by the motorway and under the bridge to go and have a look, and to imagine how they will look when hopefully restored! It is possible to walk the 15 miles or so from Tewitfield to the original terminus at Kendal (and get a bus back). Boats can be left at the moorings here.

● **Borwick**
Lancs. Tel. A small, old and attractive village, spread around a green. Overlooking the canal is Borwick Hall, a large and sombre Elizabethan manor house, built around a high 15th-C tower and with extensive gardens.

● **Warton**
Lancs. PO, tel, stores. About 2 miles west of Borwick. Ancestors of George Washington lived in this village and their family crest, containing the famed Stars and Stripes, is to be seen on the 15th-C tower of the church of St Oswald.

Pubs and Restaurants

● ✕ **Longlands Hotel** Tewitfield Locks, Tewitfield (01524 781256; info@ thelonglandshotel.co.uk). Just north east of the canal terminus. This popular country pub serves real ale and home-made bar and restaurant meals (V) *L and E,* in a friendly atmosphere. Children are welcome, and there is outside seating by copious baskets of flowers. Live bands play *Mon,* disco *Thur and Sat.* B & B.

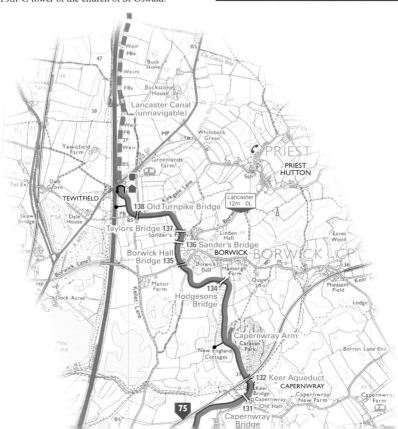

■ LEEDS & LIVERPOOL CANAL

Leeds & Liverpool Canal

Introduction

MAXIMUM DIMENSIONS

Liverpool to Wigan, and Leigh Branch
Length: 72'
Beam: 14' 3"
Headroom: 8' 6"

Wigan to Leeds	*Rufford Branch*
Length: 60'	Length: 62'
Beam: 14' 3"	Beam: 14'
Headroom: 8'	Headroom: 8'

MANAGER

Central Waterway Office covering the entire canal: 01282 456978; enquiries. leedsliverpool@ britishwaterways.co.uk

Liverpool to Greenberfield Bridge 156: 01942 242239; enquiries.whitebear@ britishwaterways.co.uk

Greenberfield Bridge 156 to Leeds: 01274 611303

MILEAGE

LIVERPOOL. Canal terminus to Burscough, junction with Rufford Branch: 24½ miles
Wigan, junction with Leigh Branch: 35 miles
Johnson's Hill Locks: 47¼ miles
Blackburn, Top Lock: 56 miles
Burnley: 72½ miles
Skipton: 98 miles
Bingley Five Rise: 110¾ miles
Apperley Bridge: 118 miles
LEEDS, River Lock: 127 miles
Locks: 91
Leigh Branch: 7¼ miles, 2 locks
Rufford Branch: 7¼ miles, 8 locks

BW produce an excellent navigation guide for this canal (obtainable, free, from lock keepers and the managers offices listed above) to assist boaters in the safe operation of the many swing bridges and staircase locks.

With a length of 127 miles excluding branches, the Leeds & Liverpool Canal is the longest single canal in Britain built by a single company. The canal has its beginnings in the River Douglas, a little river made navigable by 1740 from Wigan to Parbold, Tarleton and the Ribble estuary. Several ambitious trans-Pennine canal schemes had been mooted; one for a canal from Liverpool to Leeds, to connect with the head of the Aire & Calder Navigation. The Leeds & Liverpool Canal was authorised in 1770, and construction began at once, with John Longbotham as engineer. The first (lock-free) section from Bingley to Skipton was opened within three years; by 1777 two long sections were open from the Aire & Calder at Leeds to Gargrave (incorporating many new staircase locks) and from Wigan to Liverpool. The L & L bought out the River Douglas navigation at an early stage to gain control of its valuable water supply. It was replaced by a proper canal branch to Rufford and Tarleton, where it joined the (tidal) River Douglas. In 1790 work began again, with Robert Whitworth as the company's engineer; but after 1792 and the outbreak of war with France, investment in canals declined steadily. The whole of the main line from Leeds to Liverpool was finished by 1816 actually *sharing* the channel of the Lancaster Canal for 10 miles from Wigan Top Lock to Johnson's Hill Bottom Lock. The Lancaster used to branch off up what became the Walton Summit Branch. In 1820 a branch was opened to join the Bridgewater Canal at Leigh. A short branch (the Springs Branch) was also made to rock quarries at Skipton and an important 3-mile-long canal from Shipley to Bradford. The cut down into the Liverpool Docks was made in 1846. The prosperity of the company after 1820 was not, at first, greatly affected by the advent of railways. The scale of the navigation (the locks were built as broad locks 62ft by 14ft, allowing big payloads to be carried along the canal) contributed to the high dividends paid to shareholders for several years. Water supply was, however, a problem and in spite of the building of copious reservoirs, the canal had to be closed for months on end during dry summers, driving carriers' custom away to the railways. Use of the navigation for freight has declined throughout this century; the hard winter of 1962/63 finished off many traders. Today this canal offers boaters, walkers and cyclists an exhilarating link between two superb cities.

Liverpool

The first ³/4 mile of this canal has been filled in, so the navigation now begins just north of bridge 'B'. It runs north from the city centre for about 6 miles, parallel and close to Liverpool Docks, before turning east to Aintree, Wigan and the Pennines. Liverpool, while at one time not an attractive place from the canal, is slowly changing and although some factories still have their backs to the waterway, considerable effort has been made to improve the access to the towpath which is alive with walkers, fishermen and cyclists. The water, however, is surprisingly clear. Eldonian Village forms an attractive backdrop to the moorings in the terminus basin. There is a *PO* beside bridge 2A together with a very comprehensive range of *shops*.

NAVIGATIONAL NOTES

1 Just north of the terminus is the Stanley Dock Branch. This useful connection from the canal down into Liverpool Docks and the River Mersey is nowadays the main *raison d'être* of the west end of the Leeds & Liverpool Canal. There are four locks on the branch: they can be opened only by the resident lock keeper *during working hours Mon–Fri*. Boaters wishing to use these locks should give *24hrs notice* to the BW Whitebear office (01942 242239; enquiries.whitebear@britishwaterways.co.uk). Immediately below the locks is Stanley Dock: this belongs to the Mersey Docks & Harbour Company, whose permission should be sought before one enters the dock – telephone 0151 949 6000. The MD & HC is unlikely to refuse such a request, but does not like pleasure boats to tie up in the dock. Navigators are encouraged to move straight on to the big lock down into the tidal River Mersey. The lock is operated *24hrs a day*.

2 Those navigating the Leeds & Liverpool will need, as well as a windlass, a British Waterways handcuff key and a Watermate key.

3 Mooring at unrecognised sites in the city centre is not recommended.

4 If you wish to navigate the remainder length (Liverpool to Aintree) and require assistance or details of safe mooring locations, please contact BW on 01942 242239; enquiries.whitebear@britishwaterways.co.uk.

Liverpool
Merseyside. All services. In the first century AD it was 'lifrugpool', a settlement next to a muddy creek; now it is one of Britain's largest ports with a population of over half a million. Famous worldwide as the place where the Beatles began their march to fame, and equally well known for the exploits of Liverpool Football Club. There is much to be seen in this ancient port. The Anglican Cathedral, begun in 1904 and finished in 1978, is the largest in the world; the Roman Catholic Cathedral has stained glass by John Piper and Patrick Reyntiens. The superb Albert Dock development and Liverpool Tate Art Gallery are attracting increasing numbers of tourists. On the pierhead is a memorial to the engineers lost on the *Titanic*, which sank in 1912.
Tourist Information Centres Queen Square Centre (0906 680 6886; www.visitliverpool.com). *Open Mon–Sat 09.00–17.30 (Tue from 10.00), Sun and B Hols 10.30–16.30.* Atlantic Pavilion, Atlantic Dock (0906 680 6886; www.visitliverpool.com). *Open daily 10.00–17.30.* There is a great diversity of Liverpool Tours – from walking to travelling in a converted (and updated) wartime DUKW. Ask at the TIC for further details.

Beatles Story Britannia Vaults, Albert Dock, Liverpool (0151 709 1963; www.cavern-liverpool.co.uk). *Open daily, Mar–Oct 10.00–18.00; Nov–Feb 10.00–17.00. Last admission 1 hr before closing. Closed 25 and 26 Dec.* Charge.
Liverpool Museum William Brown Street, Liverpool (0151 478 4399; www.liverpoolmuseum. org.uk). *Open Mon–Sat 10.00–17.00, Sun 12.00–17.00. Closed 23–26 and 1 Jan.* Free.
Conservation Centre Queen Square, Liverpool (0151 478 4999; www.conservationcentre.org.uk). Housed in an impressively restored, listed Victorian warehouse (the former Midland Railway Goods Offices) this interactive exhibition provides a rare insight into work that normally goes on behind the scenes. Surrounded by classical sculpture, the Café Eros makes a good place to meet and eat. *Open daily 10.00–17.00. Closed as per Liverpool Museum. Free. Full disabled access.*
HM Customs & Excise National Museum Albert Dock, Liverpool (0151 478 4499; www. customsmuseum.org.uk). *Open daily 10.00–17.00, last admission 16.00. Closed as per Liverpool Museum.* Free.
Lady Lever Art Gallery Port Sunlight Village, Bebington, Wirral (0151 478 4136;

www.ladyleverartgallery.org.uk).
Close to Bebington railway station.
Gallery shop and restaurant. *Open
as per Liverpool Museum.* Free.
Museum of Liverpool Life Albert
Dock, Liverpool (0151 478 4080;
www. museumofliverpoollife.org.uk).
*Open daily 10.00–17.00. Closed 23–26
Dec and 1 Jan.* Free.
Mersey Ferries Pier Head, Liverpool
(0151 630 1030). A 50 min heritage
cruise with commentary and
spectacular views. *Daily cruises
weekdays 10.00–15.00 and weekends
10.00–18.00.*
Merseyside Maritime Museum Albert
Dock, Liverpool (0151 478 4499;
www.merseysidemaritimemuseum.
org.uk). *Open as per HM Customs &
Excise National Museum.* Free. **Note:**
Visitors can purchase a Waterfront
Pass that includes entrance to the
Maritime Museum, Museum of
Liverpool Life, Beatles Story and
Mersey Ferry Heritage Cruise.
Available from Albert Dock Tourist
Information Centre.
Port Sunlight Heritage Centre
Greendale Road, Port Sunlight
(0151 644 6466). Near Port
Sunlight railway station. Discover
the architectural delights of this
garden village built by William Lever
for his workers. *Open daily 10.00–
16.00, Sat and Sun from 11.00 in winter.
Closed Xmas and New Year.* Charge.
Sudley Mossley Hill Road, Liverpool
(0151 724 3245; www.sudleyhouse.
org.uk). Take the train to either
Airburth or Mossley Hill stations.
Victorian interior decoration and
craftsmanship. *Open as per Liverpool
Museum.* Free. Victorian tearooms *open
Sat and B Hols 10.00–16.30, Sun
12.00–16.30.*
Tate Liverpool Albert Dock, Liverpool
(0151 702 7400; www.tate.org.uk/
liverpool). *Open Tue–Sun and B Hol Mons
10.00–17.50. Closed 24–26 Dec.* Free to see
collection; charge for touring exhibitions.
Walker Art Gallery William Brown
Street, Liverpool (0151 478 4199;
www.walkerartgallery. org.uk). *Open as
per Liverpool Museum.* Free.
Western Approaches Museum 1 Rumford
Street, Liverpool (0151 227 2008). Recreation of the underground centre that
orchestrated the Battle of the Atlantic during
World War II. *Open Mar–Oct, Mon–Thur and
Sat 10.30–16.30. Last admission 15.30.* Charge.

Pubs and Restaurants

There are many to be found here.

Leeds & Liverpool Canal Liverpool

Maghull

North of Litherland the canal turns east to Aintree. Soon the first of many swing bridges is encountered; for the first few miles these bridges have to be padlocked to combat vandalism. All navigators should ensure that they have the requisite key before reaching these bridges (obtainable from the British Waterways offices at Wigan and Apperley Bridge). Aintree marks the limit of Liverpool's outskirts and here is of course the Aintree Race Course. At the east end of the racecourse is another swing bridge; this carries a main road and traffic lights are installed, but boat crews operate the bridge themselves. The canal turns north again and emerges into open countryside, although Maghull soon interrupts this with a series of swing bridges.

Pubs and Restaurants

Cooksons Bridge Litherland, Liverpool (0151 476 7327). Beside bridge 4A. Newly refurbished pub offering pool; bingo *Tue*; karaoke *Wed and Sun* and live music *Sat*. Children welcome. There are a useful selection of *shops and a PO*, beyond the pub to the north of the canal.

Old Roan Netherton (0151 526 8422). Near Old Roan Bridge 7D. Real ales are served amidst multiple TV screens. Sensibly priced bar food (V) served *L and E Mon–Fri and 12.00–19.00 Sat–Sun*. Children welcome. Outside seating. Disco *Fri and Sun*.

Horse & Jockey Aintree (0151 546 9406). Near bridge 9C. Bar food (V) *available L daily*. Children's play area. *Mon* Karaoke, *Wed* Quiz and live music *Fri–Sun*.

✕ Bootle Arms Rock Lane, Melling (0151 526 2886). Continental, Asian and traditional food (V) is served *L and E daily* together with real ale in this family restaurant and pub. Children are welcome; dogs in the bar area only. Garden with children's play area.

Hare & Hounds Maghull (0151 526 1447). Near bridge 14. Real ales and traditional bar meals (V) are available

12.00–20.00 daily in this roadside pub. Patio seating area. Quiz *Mon and Wed*.

Red House 31 Foxhouse Lane, Maghull (0151 526 1376). Genuine, traditional, suburban local dispensing real ales. Food (V) is available *12.00–20.00 Mon–Sat and 12.00–17.00 Sun*. Children welcome; patio seating area. *Monthly* live music and/or karaoke *Fri or Sat*.

Coach & Horses Maghull (0151 526 1093). On A567 east of the canal between bridges 15 and 16. Snacks and bar meals (V) are available *L and E (until 20.00) daily* together with real ales. Children outside only. Garden and children's play area. Quiz *Thur*, live music *Sat*.

Running Horses Maghull (0151 526 3989). Canalside, at bridge 16. Real ales together with home-made bar snacks

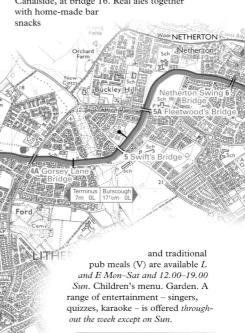

and traditional pub meals (V) are available *L and E Mon–Sat and 12.00–19.00 Sun*. Children's menu. Garden. A range of entertainment – singers, quizzes, karaoke – is offered *throughout the week except on Sun*.

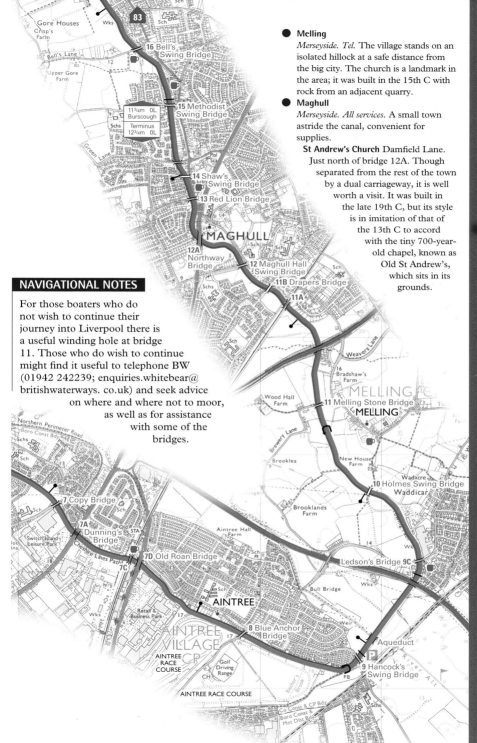

● **Melling**

Merseyside. Tel. The village stands on an isolated hillock at a safe distance from the big city. The church is a landmark in the area; it was built in the 15th C with rock from an adjacent quarry.

● **Maghull**

Merseyside. All services. A small town astride the canal, convenient for supplies.

St Andrew's Church Damfield Lane. Just north of bridge 12A. Though separated from the rest of the town by a dual carriageway, it is well worth a visit. It was built in the late 19th C, but its style is in imitation of that of the 13th C to accord with the tiny 700-year-old chapel, known as Old St Andrew's, which sits in its grounds.

NAVIGATIONAL NOTES

For those boaters who do not wish to continue their journey into Liverpool there is a useful winding hole at bridge 11. Those who do wish to continue might find it useful to telephone BW (01942 242239; enquiries.whitebear@ britishwaterways. co.uk) and seek advice on where and where not to moor, as well as for assistance with some of the bridges.

Haskayne

The canal now enters continuous open countryside, which soon establishes itself as extremely flat and intensively cultivated lowlands: indeed it is more akin to Cambridgeshire or Lincolnshire than to the rest of Lancashire. However, it is pleasant enough and the canal forms one of its more important features – a view which is borne out by the large number of people usually to be seen walking and boating upon it, as well as the hundreds of anglers enjoying their sport in this well-stocked length of canal. As if in compensation for the unexciting landscape, the traveller is offered a truly astonishing number (and variety) of pubs on or near the canal, all the way from Lydiate to Wigan. The digging of the canal is reputed to have commenced in the low cutting between bridges 24 and 25, and this clearly provided an excellent source of stone for local bridges.

● **Haskayne**
Lancs. PO, tel. There are just two pretty houses here: the old post office and a thatched cottage opposite. No sign of a church.

FERTILE RELIEF

This was once an area of low lying marshland, much of it below sea level and, consequently, thinly populated. The original course of the River Douglas ran close by, joining the sea near Southport. At some point its course was blocked – possibly by giant sand dunes thrown up by a great storm – and it found a new, northern mouth in the Ribble estuary, leaving behind the area known today as Martin Mere. This once extended to 15 square miles but in 1787 Thomas Eccleston of Scarisbrick Hall, with the help of John Gilbert, set about draining it for agricultural use (it was Gilbert who, as agent to the Duke of Bridgewater, enlisted James Brindley's help in constructing Britain's first major canal). Once drained the mere required vast quantities of manure to raise its fertility for crop production. 'Night soil' was shipped in along the canal from the large conurbations of Liverpool and Wigan and off-loaded at a series of small wharfs, some still visible today. Part of the mere remains undrained, a haven for migrating geese.

Pubs and Restaurants

Scotch Piper Lydiate (0151 526 0503). 500yds west of canal, access from bridge 19, left at A567 junction. An attractive old world, thatched pub dispensing real ales and good conversation in generous measure. No large (or small) screen TV, fruit machines or juke boxes. Dogs are most welcome but strictly no children. Garden.

Scarisbrick Arms Downholland (0151 526 1120). Canalside, at Downholland Bridge. An original estate-owned pub dating from 1899, now smartly adorned by a host of floral tubs and hanging baskets. Real ales. Wide range of food from bar snacks to full à la carte restaurant menu (V) served *L and E Mon–Sat and all day Sun.* Beer garden running down to canal and patio. Quiz *Fri.* Children welcome. Patio.

King's Arms Haskayne (01704 840245). 100yds north of bridge 21A. A selection of real ales served in this traditional, old-fashioned village local. Snacks available *L.* Outside courtyard seating. *Monthly Sat* live music.

Ship Haskayne (01704 840572; www. shipinnhaskayne.co.uk). Canalside, at Ship Bridge. A well-known canal pub with a garden and waterside terrace serving real ale. Excellent fresh food (V) served in a homely, dark-beamed bar tastefully decorated with horse brasses available – including seafood, steaks and pasta – *L and E Mon–Thur and all day Fri–Sun.* Children welcome. Reputed to be the first pub on the canal, which was started in the adjacent cutting. Quiz *Tue*, pianist *Fri.*

Saracen's Head Halsall (01704 840204). Canalside, at Halsall Warehouse Bridge. Real ales together with a wide range of food (V) served *L and E Mon–Sat and all day Sun.* Children welcome *until 20.00*; garden with children's play area. Quiz *Thur* and live music *Sat.* Full disabled facilities.

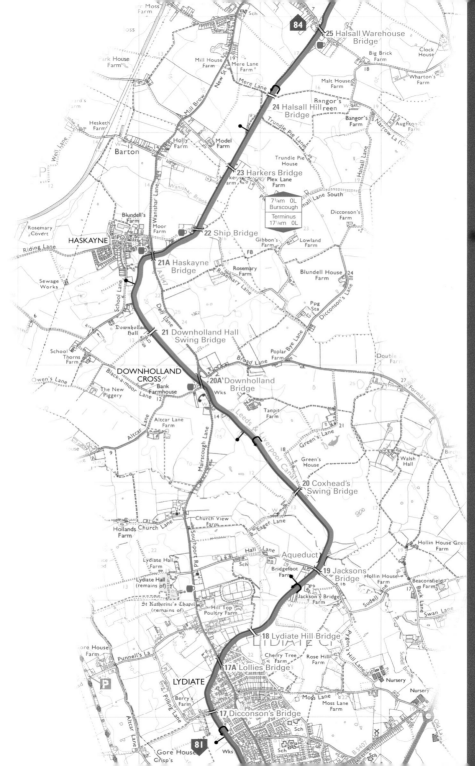

84

25 Halsall Warehouse Bridge

Big Brick Farm

Clock House

Wharton's Farm

Mill House Farm

Mere Lane

24 Halsall Hill Bridge

Malt House Farm

Bangor's Green

Bangor's Farm

Narrow La (Cle

Aughton

Park House Farm

Hesketh Farm

New St

Mill Brow

Trundle Pie Lane

Trundle Pie House

Halsall Lane

Dicconson's Farm

Holly Farm

Model Farm

Barton

23 Harkers Bridge

Plex Lane Farm

Lane South

Rosemary Covert

Blundell's Farm

Wanshar Brook

Moor Farm

7¼m 0L
Burscough
Terminus
17¼m 0L

Blundell House Farm

22 Ship Bridge

Gibbon's Farm

Lowland Farm

HASKAYNE

Riding Lane

21A Haskayne Bridge

Rosemary Farm

Rosemary Lane

Sewage Works

Ppg Sta

Dicconson's Lane

School Lane

Dell Lane

Downholland Hall

21 Downholland Hall Swing Bridge

Poplar Bye Lane

Poplar Farm

School Thorns Farm

Double Farm

DOWNHOLLAND CROSS

Black-a-moor Lane

Bank Farmhouse

20A Downholland Bridge

Broad Lane

Owen's Lane

The New Piggery

Altcar Lane

Altcar Lane Farm

Tanpit Farm

Leeds & Liverpool Canal

Mairscough Lane

Green's Lane

Green's House

Walsh Hall

Formby Lane

20 Coxhead's Swing Bridge

Church View Farm

Eager Lane

Hollands Farm

Church Lane

Southport Rd

Hall Lane

Aqueduct

Hollin House Gree Farm

Lydiate Hall Farm

Bridgefoot Farm

19 Jacksons Bridge

Hollin House Farm

Beaconsfield Farm

Lydiate Hall (remains of)

St Katherine's Chapel (remains of)

Hill Top Poultry Farm

Jackson's Bridge

Sudell

Back Lane

Swan Lane

Sudell Brook

18 Lydiate Hill Bridge

Pregon's Hill Lane

LYDIATE C

Cherry Tree Farm

Rose Hill Farm

17A Lollies Bridge

Nursery

Gore House Farm

Punnell's La

LYDIATE

Berry's Farm

Pilling Lane

Moss Lane

Moss Lane Farm

Nursery

Altcar Lane

17 Dicconson's Bridge

Sch

81

Gore House Crisp's

Wks

B 5407

Burscough

On now past a massive caravan site on one side and attractive woods containing the private Scarisbrick Hall on the other; then out again into the open flatlands. An attractively produced information board, at the north end of bridge 27A, offers a fascinating insight into the history of the parish and the past habitation of the hall. The Southport–Manchester line converges from the north west; it runs near the canal all the way into Wigan, and has some wonderfully remote stations. A flurry of swing bridges brings the canal into Burscough; just beyond is the junction with the Rufford Branch. There is a *pump out* available by bridge 32A.

Halsall

Lancs. PO, tel, garage. 1/2 mile west of canal. There is a handsome tall 14th–15th-C church here (St Cuthbert's), with a fine spire. The choir vestry, erected in 1592, was formerly a grammar school. There is an interesting pair of pulpits/lecterns. One of them is generously illuminated by a solitary overhead window; the other, more sheltered, gives the occupant the unfortunate air of being behind bars . . .

Burscough

Lancs. PO, tel, stores, takeaways, garage, bank, station. Formerly a canal village and a staging post on the one-time Wigan–Liverpool 'packet boat' run, this place attaches more significance nowadays to the benefits of road and rail transport. It still boasts two stations (one is on the Preston–Liverpool line) and suffers from heavy through traffic. A very convenient place for taking on provisions.

Boatyards

(B) **Red Lion Caravan Centre** Scarisbrick Bridge, Southport Road, Ormskirk (01704 840032). ♿ **D E** Gas, solid fuel, large selection of spares and parts for caravans, many of which are 'boat compatible'.

(B) **Lathom Marina** The Workshop, Crabtree Lane, Burscough (01704 894782). **D** Winter storage, slipway, chandlery, boat and engine sales and repairs, salvage, canopy manufacture and repairs.

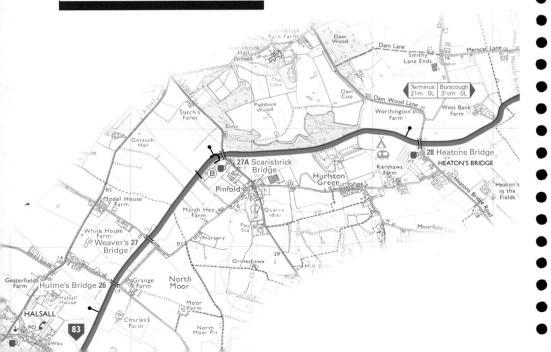

Pubs and Restaurants

🍺 ✕ **Red Lion** Scarisbrick (01704 840317). Near Scarisbrick Bridge 27A. Furnished in brewery chintz, this pub serves real ales and offers an extensive menu (V), including carvery *L and E (available from 17.00).* Children welcome. Outdoor patio and play area.

🍺 **Heatons Bridge** Heatons Bridge (01704 840549). Friendly unspoilt canalside pub, at bridge 28. Real ales together with inexpensive, traditional pub food (V) served *all day, every day.* Children welcome (not in bar area); dogs welcome outside restaurant space. Garden and moorings.

🍺 ✕ **Martin Inn** Mescar Lane, Burscough (01704 892302; www.martininn.co.uk). 200yds north of bridge 29. Extensively refurbished restaurant and inn attracting a wide ranging clientele and serving real ale and an à la carte menu (V) *L and E.* Children and dogs welcome. Patio seating. Live music *Fri and Sat.* B & B.

🍺 ✕ **Farmers Arms** near Burscough (01704 896021). Canalside, by bridge 31. A bright, friendly pub of great character with an open fire, serving real ale. Full à la carte menu together with a wide and interesting range of bar food (V) *L and E daily,* served in nicely furnished surroundings. Children welcome. Large patio area; open fires in winter. Singer *Sat.* Good moorings.

🍺 **Slipway** 48 Crab Tree Lane, Burscough (01704 897767). Attractive canalside setting (beside bridge 32) for this refurbished pub serving real ales and food (V) *L and E Mon–Fri and all day Sat–Sun (no food Mon Jan–Feb).* Children welcome; dogs welcome but not inside while food is being served. Large garden with children's play area and patio. *Monthly* singer. Good moorings.

🍺 **Royal Coaching House** Liverpool Road, Burscough (01704 893231). Real ales in a pub two minutes' walk from the canal. Wide range of interesting snacks and bar food (V) *L daily.* Children welcome as are dogs *until 19.00.* Cobbled courtyard with pond. Quiz *Mon,* karaoke *Wed* and live music *Sat.*

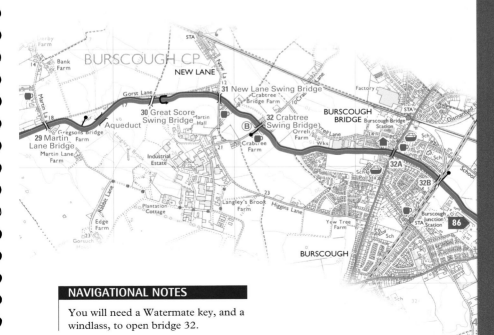

NAVIGATIONAL NOTES

You will need a Watermate key, and a windlass, to open bridge 32.

Parbold and Rufford

The Rufford Branch leaves the Leeds & Liverpool main line just east of Burscough, through an imposing arched bridge dated 1816. A canal settlement, now a conservation area, surrounds the top lock and the roomy dry dock here (also *showers* and the usual *facilities*). The locks come thick and fast to begin with, as the canal falls through the fertile and gently sloping farmland towards the distant Ribble estuary and a connection with the Lancaster Canal. The country is generally quiet, flat and unspectacular. At times the busy A59 intrudes noisily. East of the junction with the Rufford Branch, the canal meanders through the flat countryside to the village of Parbold with its ancient sail-less windmill. Here the canal crosses the River Douglas and then joins the Douglas Valley, a pretty, narrow wooded valley which the canal shares with the railway. Appley Lock is reached: there are two locks alongside, now restored, and you can choose to use either these or the very deep main lock. The shallower locks were once used as a navigable sidepond for boats passing in opposite directions. **As with all subsequent locks, the gates should be closed and the paddles lowered and padlocked after use to combat vandalism and wastage of water.**

NAVIGATIONAL NOTES

You will need a Watermate key to open bridges 33 and 36.

● **Parbold**
Lancs. PO, tel, stores, butcher, takeaway, garage, station. Parbold is prettiest near the canal bridge, where the brick tower of the old windmill is complemented by an equally attractive pub. Unfortunately the rest of the village is being engulfed by acres of new housing. Local landmarks are the tall spires of Parbold's two churches, and Ashurst's Beacon high on a hill to the south. The latter was built in 1798 by Sir William Ashurst in anticipation of an invasion by the French. The beacon was intended as a local warning sign.

● **Douglas Navigation**
The little River Douglas, or Asland, was made navigable in the first half of the 17th C, well before the great spate of canal construction. It provided the Wigan coalfield with a useful outlet to the tidal River Ribble, from which the cargoes could be shipped over to Preston or along the coast. When the Leeds & Liverpool Canal was built, the old river navigation became superfluous. The new company constructed their own branch to the Ribble estuary (the Rufford Branch). Between Parbold and Gathurst it is possible to find many traces of the old navigation, including several locks.

Pubs and Restaurants

🍺 **Ship Inn** Lathom (01704 893117). Near second lock down, on Rufford Branch. An old canal pub formerly known as the 'Blood Tub' – black puddings were once made here, and a bucket of pig's blood could be exchanged for a pint of beer. Rightly described by CAMRA as 'the gem of the area' this establishment serves an ever changing range of real ales. Busy, welcoming, comfortable with excellent bar food (V) *L and E, daily.* Children welcome *until 21.00*; dogs *after 14.30.* Garden. Quiz *Mon.*

🍺 **Ring O'Bells** Lathom (01704 893157). Canalside at bridge 34. Tastefully modernised country pub serving an interesting variety of bar meals (V) *all day, every day* along with real ales. Canalside tables, indoor and outdoor children's play areas. Quiz *Wed.*

🍺 **Railway Tavern** Hoscar Station (01704 892369). North east of bridge 35. Small country pub serving real ale and excellent food (V) *L and E* daily. Children's menu, beer garden, Quiz *Thur.* Pub games.

✕ **Rocking Horse Tearoom** Parbold (01257 462026). Canalside, bridge 37. Traditional chintzy tearoom serving coffee, lunch and tea. Tasty ice creams. All food home-made including soups and cakes. *Open Mon 10.00–16.00, Tue–Sat 10.00–17.00 and Sun 11.00–17.00.*

🍺 **Windmill** Parbold (01257 462935). Beside bridge 37. Old village local dispensing real ale, and an imaginative selection of traditional, home-cooked food (V) *L and E (not Mon E).* Children welcome *until 20.00*; dogs on a lead only. A huge collection of brassware decorates the pub, and there is outside seating.

🍺 ✕ **Stocks Tavern** Alder Lane, Parbold (01257 462220). South of bridge 37. Fine traditional country pub, dating from 1810 and serving excellent meals (V) *L and E Mon–Fri and all day Sat and Sun*, together with a selection of real ale. Children welcome; small outside seating area and quiz *Sun.*

✕ **Wayfarer Restaurant** 1 Alder Lane, Parbold (01257 464600). South of bridge 37. Dating back to before 1668 this cosy pub-cum-restaurant serves real ale and food (V) *L and E Mon–Sat and all day Sun.* The à la carte restaurant is *open Mon–Sat 18.00–21.30* and good fresh local produce is used wherever possible. Children welcome; patio area with pond and Koi carp. Log fires *in winter.*

🍺 **Water's Edge** Mill Lane, Appley Bridge (01257 253755). East of bridge 42. Family pub, *open all day*, serving real ale together with inexpensive home-cooked food (V) *all day, every day.* Children welcome *until 21.00.* Moorings and outside seating.

🍺 ✕ **Railway** Appley Bridge (01257 252112). Canalside beside bridge 42. Real ale served together with food (V) *L and E and all day Sun* from predictable brewery menu. Children welcome. Canalside seating area.

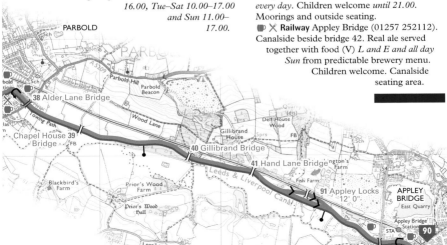

Tarleton

A line of trees and the spire of Rufford church are followed by the beautiful Rufford Old Hall, on the west bank. Then the waterway leads back out into open, flat and fairly featureless countryside, with the River Douglas never far away but initially out of sight. Beside bridge 10 there is an attractively landscaped *picnic area*. At Sollom there used to be a lock, but now it is no more. This is where the canal turns into the old course of the River Douglas, and it twists and turns as though to prove it. The towpath has been ploughed up from here onwards. The 'new' course of the Douglas (which was once navigable from the sea right up to Wigan) comes alongside the canal at the busy road bridge near Bank Hall, a house hidden by trees. From here it is only a short distance to the final swing bridge and Tarleton Lock, where the canal connects with the tidal River Douglas – which in turn flows into the River Ribble near Preston forming the newly opened Ribble Link with the Lancaster Canal.

NAVIGATIONAL NOTES

1 Navigators entering the Rufford Branch canal from the sea should remember that they will need a padlock key – as well as a windlass – to open the locks up the branch. Both available from James Mayor's boatyard.
2 Those who wish to use the Ribble Link (www.millenniumribblelink.co.uk) MUST obtain the Skipper's Guide and booking form from the address on page 61, as this gives all ESSENTIAL navigational information. A booking form can also be obtained by email from: enquiries.LANC@britishwaterways.co.uk. *Five days' notice is required.* As we go to press the charges are £35 for a single journey, £60 for a return. *Opening times are dictated by tides in the Ribble estuary, but a journey can be made Easter–Oct during daylight hours, Nov–Easter on request.* The staircase and sea lock are manned, and the link will operate one way each day. There is no mooring on the Link. As the River Ribble is tidal, boats should carry, *as a minimum*: anchor, chain and warp, VHF radio or mobile phone, lifejackets for all on board, fire fighting equipment, coastal flares. Your engine must be sufficiently powerful to cope with tidal conditions, and be sure to check that your boat insurance covers tidal waters.
3 If you need help or advice while on the River Ribble, contact Preston Riversway Control on VHF channel 16, or telephone 01772 726871.
4 If you wish to visit Preston Docks, contact Preston Riversway Control on 01772 726871.
5 A pilot service for the Ribble Link (charge) can be obtained from: 01772 632439, 812462 or 812250.

Rufford
Lancs. PO, tel, stores, garage, station. Main road village noted for its Hall. The church is a small Italianate Victorian building containing many monuments to the Heskeths who owned Rufford Hall for several centuries; obviously a prolific family, judging by one large sculpture depicting a brood of 11 children, dated c.1458. The family now resides in Northamptonshire.
Rufford Old Hall NT (01704 821254; rrufoh@ smpt.ntrust.org.uk). On the west bank of the canal. A medieval timber-framed mansion with Jacobean extensions given to the National Trust in 1936. The interior is magnificently decorated and furnished in period style, especially the great hall with its hammerbeam roof and 15th-C intricately carved movable screen – one of the few still intact in England. The Hall also houses a folk museum and an exhibition. Gardens and tearoom. *House open daily Apr–Oct 13.00– 17.00 (except Thur and Fri). Gardens as per house 12.00–17.30.* Charge.
Note: although the Hall is beside the waterway, it is not possible to enter the grounds directly from the canal. Navigators should therefore tie up near bridge 8, walk up to the village and turn left at the main road. The entrance is a few hundred yards along the wall on the left.

Tarleton
Lancs. PO, tel, stores, garage, bank. A large village luckily avoided by the A59 road. There are some useful shops, and a good takeaway pizzeria opposite the Cock & Bottle.

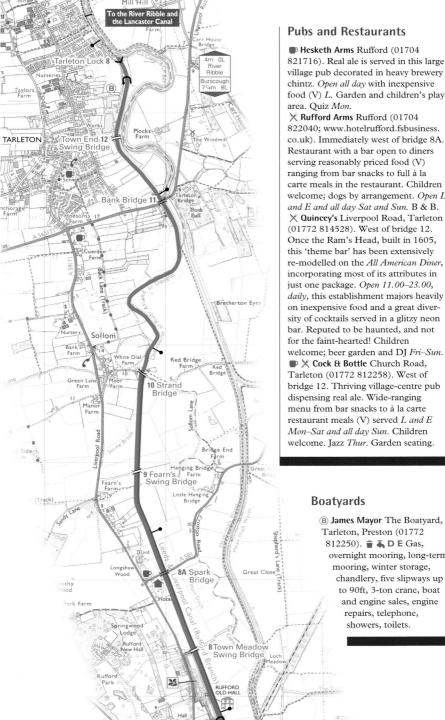

Pubs and Restaurants

Hesketh Arms Rufford (01704 821716). Real ale is served in this large village pub decorated in heavy brewery chintz. *Open all day* with inexpensive food (V) *L.* Garden and children's play area. Quiz *Mon.*

✕ **Rufford Arms** Rufford (01704 822040; www.hotelrufford.fsbusiness. co.uk). Immediately west of bridge 8A. Restaurant with a bar open to diners serving reasonably priced food (V) ranging from bar snacks to full à la carte meals in the restaurant. Children welcome; dogs by arrangement. *Open L and E and all day Sat and Sun.* B & B.

✕ **Quincey's** Liverpool Road, Tarleton (01772 814528). West of bridge 12. Once the Ram's Head, built in 1605, this 'theme bar' has been extensively re-modelled on the *All American Diner*, incorporating most of its attributes in just one package. *Open 11.00–23.00, daily,* this establishment majors heavily on inexpensive food and a great diversity of cocktails served in a glitzy neon bar. Reputed to be haunted, and not for the faint-hearted! Children welcome; beer garden and DJ *Fri–Sun.*

✕ **Cock & Bottle** Church Road, Tarleton (01772 812258). West of bridge 12. Thriving village-centre pub dispensing real ale. Wide-ranging menu from bar snacks to à la carte restaurant meals (V) served *L and E Mon–Sat and all day Sun.* Children welcome. Jazz *Thur.* Garden seating.

Boatyards

ⓑ **James Mayor** The Boatyard, Tarleton, Preston (01772 812250). ⛴ ♿ D E Gas, overnight mooring, long-term mooring, winter storage, chandlery, five slipways up to 90ft, 3-ton crane, boat and engine sales, engine repairs, telephone, showers, toilets.

Wigan and the Douglas Valley

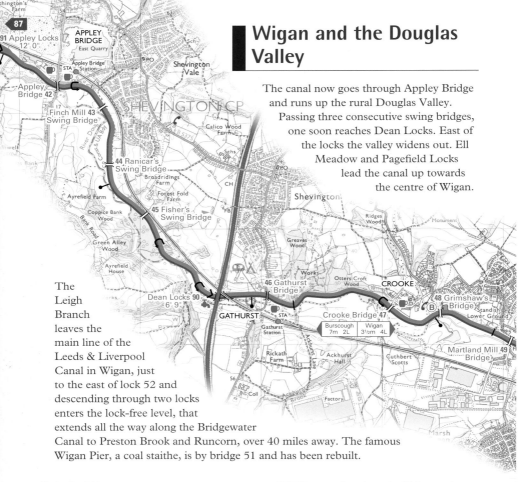

The canal now goes through Appley Bridge and runs up the rural Douglas Valley. Passing three consecutive swing bridges, one soon reaches Dean Locks. East of the locks the valley widens out. Ell Meadow and Pagefield Locks lead the canal up towards the centre of Wigan.

The Leigh Branch leaves the main line of the Leeds & Liverpool Canal in Wigan, just to the east of lock 52 and descending through two locks enters the lock-free level, that extends all the way along the Bridgewater Canal to Preston Brook and Runcorn, over 40 miles away. The famous Wigan Pier, a coal staithe, is by bridge 51 and has been rebuilt.

- **Appley Bridge**
  Lancs. PO, tel, stores, station. Canalside hamlet.
- **Wigan**
  Gt Manchester. All services. A large, heavily industrialised town whose skyline is now a mixture of industrial chimneys and towering concrete blocks of offices and flats. There is a covered market hall in the traditional mould, and an Olympic-size swimming pool.
  All Saints Church A very large and impressive parish church surrounded by beautiful rose gardens. There are several fine stained-glass windows, including a charming William Morris example depicting St Christopher.
  History Shop Rodney Street, Wigan (01942 828128; www.wiganmbc.gov.uk). Heritage Service project offering a display depicting the impact of coal on the area, exhibitions, genealogical research centre, shop and meeting room. *Open Mon 10.00–19.00, Tue–Fri 10.00–17.00 and Sat 10.00–13.00.*
  Wigan Pier Complex Wallgate, Wigan (01942

323666; www.wiganpier.net). *All the attractions below are part of this complex and are open Mon–Thur 10.00–17.00, Sat and Sun 11.00–17.00. Closed Fri except G Fri.* Charge.
  Opie's Museum of Memories A visual journey through time in an interactive experience, where memories from the past 100 years come flooding back.
  The Way We Were A stunning exhibition/museum/theatre illustrating the lives of local people around the turn of the century.
  Trencherfield Mill Probably the largest working mill engine in Europe, installed when the mill was built in 1907. Steamed *daily on the half hour.*
  Waterbus Operates *daily* to transport visitors around the Wigan Pier Complex.
  Pantry at the Pier Café, shops, restaurant, walks.
  Waterways Gardens By Seven Stars Bridge. Boats, stonemason's blocks and a lock-keeper's garden.
  Tourist Information Centre Trencherfield Mill (01942 825677; www.wiganmbc.gov.uk). *Open daily 10.00–17.00.*

Pubs and Restaurants

■ ✗ **Navigation** Gathurst (01257 252856; www.thenavigationinn.com). Canalside, at bridge 46. Rural pub in a picturesque valley, popular with walkers, boaters, fishermen and bird watchers, serving real ales. Food available *L and E (Mon–Fri), all day Sat and Sun.* Children welcome; garden which borders the canal. Boules court. Singer *last Fri in month.* Moorings.

■ ✗ **Crooke Hall Inn** Crooke, Wigan (01942 247524). Near bridge 47. Cosy village pub, with friendly atmosphere, in the pretty Douglas Valley serving a selection of real ales. Inexpensive bar snacks and meals (V) available *L and E (except Tue).* Children welcome in dining room only. Canalside garden, moorings.

■ **Seven Stars Hotel** Wallgate, Wigan (01942 243126). Canalside. Real ale and food (V) *Mon–Fri L.* Children

welcome, outside seating. Live music *Fri and Sat.*

■ **Moon Under Water** 5-7a Market Place, Wigan (01942 323437). Real ale dispensed in a busy, town centre, ex-building society premises. Food (V) *available all day, every day.* Children's room and no smoking area.

■ **Swan & Railway** Wallgate, Wigan (01942 495032). Friendly town pub serving real ales and food *L Mon–Fri.* Beer garden. B & B.

■ **Orwell** Wigan (01942 323034; www. wiganpier.co.uk). Large converted cotton warehouse on Wigan Pier; recently an CAMRA pub of the year so there are always an excellent range of real ales available. Food (V) served *12.00–14.30 Mon–Sat* and there is a *Sun carvery 13.00–15.00.* Children welcome. Canalside seating in summer. No smoking eating area and full disabled access.

NAVIGATIONAL NOTES

1 You will need a Watermate key to open bridge 43.
2 The locks (nos 85–1) between Wigan and Leeds are 60ft long and cannot accommodate a full-length narrowboat.
3 You will require a British Waterways handcuff key.

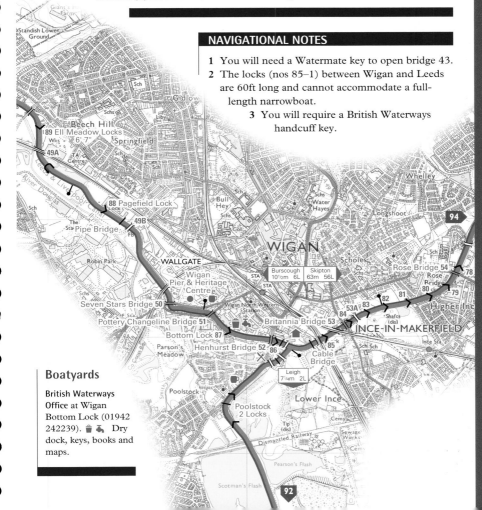

Boatyards

British Waterways Office at Wigan Bottom Lock (01942 242239). 🛠 Dry dock, keys, books and maps.

Plank Lane

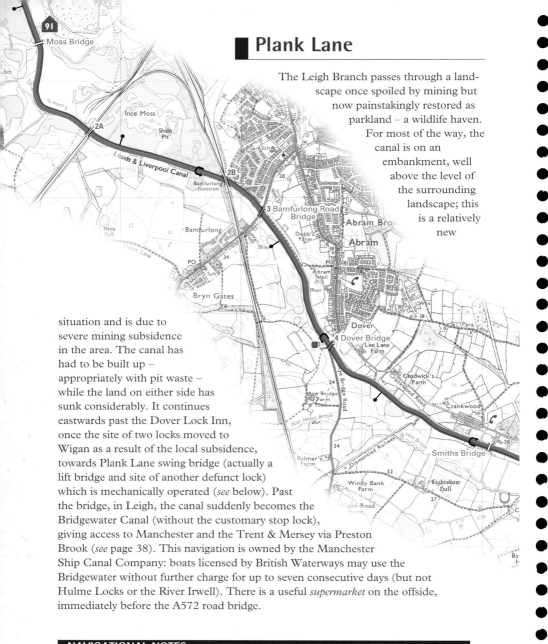

The Leigh Branch passes through a landscape once spoiled by mining but now painstakingly restored as parkland – a wildlife haven. For most of the way, the canal is on an embankment, well above the level of the surrounding landscape; this is a relatively new situation and is due to severe mining subsidence in the area. The canal has had to be built up – appropriately with pit waste – while the land on either side has sunk considerably. It continues eastwards past the Dover Lock Inn, once the site of two locks moved to Wigan as a result of the local subsidence, towards Plank Lane swing bridge (actually a lift bridge and site of another defunct lock) which is mechanically operated (*see* below). Past the bridge, in Leigh, the canal suddenly becomes the Bridgewater Canal (without the customary stop lock), giving access to Manchester and the Trent & Mersey via Preston Brook (*see* page 38). This navigation is owned by the Manchester Ship Canal Company: boats licensed by British Waterways may use the Bridgewater without further charge for up to seven consecutive days (but not Hulme Locks or the River Irwell). There is a useful *supermarket* on the offside, immediately before the A572 road bridge.

NAVIGATIONAL NOTES

Plank Lane swing bridge is *open summer: 08.00–18.00; Jun, Jul, Aug 08.00–20.00; winter: weekdays 08.00–16.30, weekends 10.00–14.00. Closed for lunch daily 12.00–12.45.* The bridge is operated by a bridge keeper. Contact British Waterways by telephoning 01942 242239 to confirm times.

Pubs and Restaurants

🍺 **Dover Lock Inn** Warrington Road, Abram (01942 866300). Canalside at Dover Bridge on the Leigh Branch. Real ales are served together with bar meals (V) and snacks *L and E daily during boating season (no food Mon–Thur L out of season)*. Children welcome *until 21.00*; no dogs. Large south-facing beer garden. Karaoke *Fri*, singer *Sat*.

🍺 **Nevison** Plank Lane, Leigh (01942 671394). 400yds from the swing bridge. An original old-fashioned pub with lots of brass and a piano serving a good selection of real ales and home-cooked food (V) with real chips *daily 12.00–19.30. No food Mon except by prior arrangement*. Children welcome outside bar areas; no dogs. Large enclosed garden with children's play area. Gas lighting in bar area and real fires in winter. Quiz *Wed*.

Note: Winter afternoon drinkers take note of bridge operating times and moor appropriately!

🍺 **Eagle & Hawk** Chapel Street, Leigh (01924 606600). Lively establishment dispensing real ales, good company and bar food (V) *all day, every day*. Children welcome. Quiz *Thur* – also other regular entertainment. Outside seating area.

🍺 **Musketeer** Lord Street, Leigh (01942 701143). *Open all day* and serving real ale and food (V) *L Mon–Sat*. Children welcome.

🍺 **Red Brick Inn** Twist Lane, Leigh (01942 671698). A warm, comfortable boater-friendly pub offering real ales. Food available (V) available *Tue–Sun L and E until 20.00*. Children welcome away from the bar. Outside seating. Disco *Fri*, karaoke *Sat*. B & B.

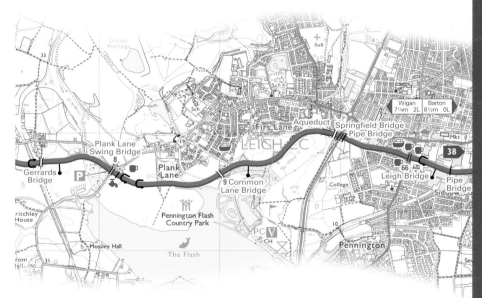

● **Leigh**
Gt Manchester. All services. Once the archetypal mill town, most of the tall buildings and chimneys have now been demolished. In the market place you can see the fine Edwardian baroque town hall, built 1904–7, facing the battlemented church of St Mary. This church was originally built in 1516 but was extensively rebuilt in the late 19th C and is the burial place of Thomas Tyldesley, killed at the battle of Wigan Lane.
Pennington Flash Country Park St Helen's Road, Leigh (01942 605253; www.wiganmbc.gov.uk). 1100-acre park centred on the flash or lake.

Walks, birdwatching, sailing, fishing, golf, picnic areas and information centre. *Open daily.*
Three Sisters Recreation Area Bryn Road, Ashton-in-Makerfield (01942 720453; www.wiganmbc.gov.uk). Site of the Wigan Alps: three colliery spoil tips now landscaped to provide an international karting circuit (01942 270230), racing circuit, boating lake, picnic area and visitor centre. Telephone for details or visit their website.
Turnpike Gallery Turnpike Centre, Leigh (01942 679407; www.wiganmbc.gov.uk). Home to major touring arts exhibitions.

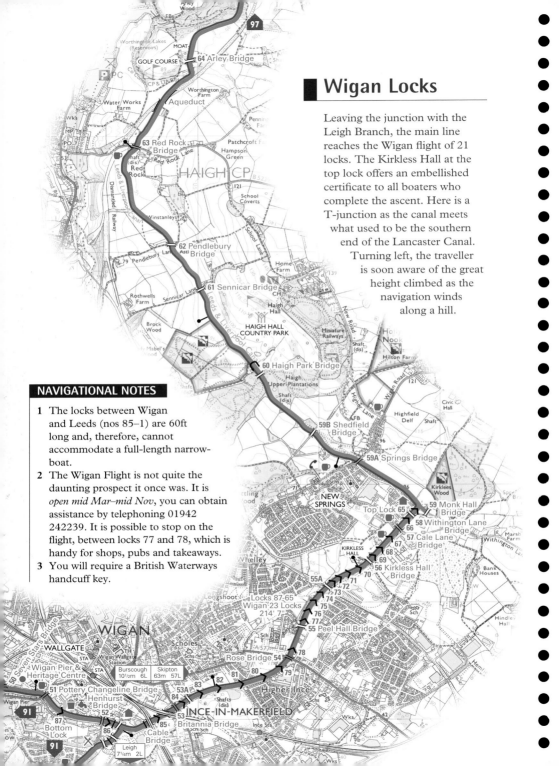

Wigan Locks

Leaving the junction with the Leigh Branch, the main line reaches the Wigan flight of 21 locks. The Kirkless Hall at the top lock offers an embellished certificate to all boaters who complete the ascent. Here is a T-junction as the canal meets what used to be the southern end of the Lancaster Canal. Turning left, the traveller is soon aware of the great height climbed as the navigation winds along a hill.

NAVIGATIONAL NOTES

1 The locks between Wigan and Leeds (nos 85–1) are 60ft long and, therefore, cannot accommodate a full-length narrow-boat.
2 The Wigan Flight is not quite the daunting prospect it once was. It is *open mid Mar–mid Nov*, you can obtain assistance by telephoning 01942 242239. It is possible to stop on the flight, between locks 77 and 78, which is handy for shops, pubs and takeaways.
3 You will require a British Waterways handcuff key.

● **New Springs**

Gt Manchester. A suburb of Wigan. Once an industrial hub with collieries and ironworks lining the canal as it struggled up the 21 locks to the summit. The acres of partially land-scaped waste ground today belie the past activity of Rose Bridge Colliery (near bridge 54) and Ince Hall Coal and Cannel Company higher up (cannel is a dull coal that burns with a smoky, luminous flame). Hardest of all to imagine is the massive operation of Wigan Coal and Iron Co. who, at the turn of the century, employed 10,000 people at their works beside the top nine locks of the flight. Then one of the largest ironworks in the country, it mined 2 million tons of coal to produce 125,000 tons of iron annually. The skyline here was dominated by 10 blast furnaces, 675 coking ovens and a 339ft high chimney. It must have been an impressive sight on the night skyline, viewed from the streets of Wigan.

Haigh Hall Wigan (01942 832895; www. haighhall.net). On east bank of the canal. The pre-Tudor mansion was rebuilt by its owner, the 23rd Earl of Crawford, between 1830 and 1849. The reconstruction was designed and directed by the Earl, and all the stone, timber and iron used on the job came from the estate. The Hall is now owned by Wigan Corporation, who allow the citizens to use it for private wedding receptions, etc. There is little to see in the house and it is not normally open to the public. The park and grounds around the hall are *open daily all year, except 25–26 Dec and 1 Jan* and contain much that caters for the family: there are children's amusements, gardens and woodlands, a nature trail and selection of waymarked walks, miniature rail-way, a model village, crazy golf course, shop and cafeteria. Entry to the park is free but there is a charge for the amusements which are *open May–Sep.* Audio trail for the blind and partially sighted using a braille map and tape player.

Stables Centre Haigh Country Park, Wigan (01942 832895). Daily art and craft workshops for groups and individuals. Hands-on creativity – painting, batik, stencilling, clay, canal art – for adults and children. *Available Mon–Fri 10.30–12.00 and 13.30–15.00. Weekends by arrangement.* Charge.

Pubs and Restaurants

🍺 **Commercial Inn** New Springs, Wigan (01942 238856). Canalside, at bridge 57. A small, sturdy working man's pub offering bar snacks on request *Mon–Sat.* Children welcome. Outside seating.

🍺 **Kirkless Hall** New Springs, Wigan (01942 242821). Canalside, near Wigan Top Lock. Distinctive black and white building housing spacious and comfortable bars. A wide range of excellent food (V) is offered *L and E daily* from both table d'hôte and à la carte menus. Children welcome. Canalside patio. Karaoke *Sat.*

🍺 **Crown Hotel** New Spring, Wigan (01942 242539). West of bridge 59A. Extensively refurbished, this pub offers real ales and food (V) *available daily until 20.30.* Children welcome *until 20.30.* Garden. Karaoke *Fri and Sat.*

🍺 **Colliers Arms** New Springs, Wigan (01942 831171). Above bridge 59A. Real ale dispensed in a charming 17th-C listed hostelry overlooking the canal. Children welcome *until 21.00.* Patio seating.

🍺 **Crawford Arms** Red Rock Lane, Haigh (01257 421313). *Open all day from 12.00,* serving inexpensive bar food (V) *daily until 20.00.* Temporary jail to a 17thC murderer, this pub now dispenses real ale rather than justice. Children welcome. Outside seating. Quiz *Thur. 48hr* mooring outside.

Adlington

The canal continues to run as a 9-mile lock-free pound – known as the Lancaster Pool – along the side of the valley from which the industries surrounding Wigan can be viewed in the distance. It enjoys a pleasant and quiet isolation in this lightly wooded area. Already the navigation is well over 300ft above the sea, and the bleak hills up to the east give a hint of the Pennines that are soon to be crossed. The conspicuous tower east of Adlington stands on a hill that is over 1500ft high. Wandering northwards, beyond the village, the waterway remains hemmed in for much of the way by woodland and is undisturbed by the railway and main roads that for a while follow it closely. Soon the greenery gives way to views of Chorley's rows of rooftops across the valley. The canal crosses this valley, but shuns the town. There is a *slipway* just to the north of Cowling Bridge 75A, on the towpath side.

Pubs and Restaurants

Bridge Adlington (01257 480507). East of bridge 69. Traditional local serving real ale and bar snacks *L Mon–Sat*. Pub Games and outside seating.

Waggon & Horses Adlington (01257 480767). East of bridge 68. Good value, home-cooked food available *all day, every day (except 14.00–17.00 Sat), served until 20.00 (19.30 Sat)*. Dating from 1818, this busy pub dispenses real ale and offers live entertainment *Sat* and a Quiz *Tue*. Children welcome. Outside seating.

White Bear Market Street, Adlington (01257 482357). West of bridge 69. An old roadside pub serving real ales and inexpensive bar food (V) available *L and E (not Mon E) and all day Sun*. Tea and coffee *always available*. Garden with children's play area. B & B. *Open all day*.

Cardwell Arms Chorley Road, Adlington (01257 480319). East of bridge 71. Real ales in a boisterous (*at weekends*) pub. Garden and outside play area. Food available *weekends all day until 19.00*. *Sun* disco and jackpot.

Mariners Coffee Shop Adlington (01257 474454). East of bridge 69, beside the marina. Friendly establishment serving breakfasts, lunches (V), snacks (all home-made and predominantly low fat), coffee and tea. *Open 09.30–16.00, closed Mon*.

White Horse Heath Charnock (01257 481766). East of bridge 71, top of Rawlinson Lane. Smart, welcoming pub serving real ale. Reasonably priced food (V) *L daily, Fri E and all day Sat and Sun (no food after 17.00 Sun)*. Children welcome. Patio, pool and pub games. Quiz *Tue*.

Hop Pocket Carr Lane, Chorley (01257 275597). West of bridge 75. Real ale in a modern estate pub offering live artists on *Sat and Sun*. Food (V) available *L daily*. Children welcome. Garden and outside seating area.

Boatyards

ⓑ **White Bear Marina** Park Road, Adlington, Chorley (01257 481054). 🚿 🛏 ⚓ D E Pump out, slipway, gas, overnight mooring, long-term mooring, winter storage, boat fitting out, boat and engine sales and repairs, crane, DIY facilities, wet dock, laundrette, showers, toilets, chandlery (mail order), books, gifts and maps, cafe, telephone. *Emergency call out*.

ⓑ **L & L Cruisers** Rawlinson Lane, Heath Charnock, Chorley (01257 480825). ⚓ D Pump out, gas, narrowboat hire, day-hire craft, overnight mooring, slipway, chandlery, books and maps, boat building, engine sales and repairs, gift shop, ice cream, toilets.

- **Adlington**
  Gt Manchester. PO, tel, stores, garage, station. A small industrialised town very useful for pubs and supplies – the local licensed store east of bridge 69 is *open late most evenings* and there is a park nearby.

- **Chorley**
  Lancs. All services. On the west bank of the canal, a busy town based on the manufacture of textiles and spare parts for commercial and public service vehicles. (Leyland, where the vehicles are built, is just a few miles away to the north west.) Chorley has avoided too much industrial grimness by maintaining its market town traditions and by extensive new housing development. Today there are two major markets: the Flat-Iron Market, dating from 1498, *held on Tue* and the Covered Market *held on Tue, Thur, Fri and Sat.* A collectors' market is also *held on Mon.* Sir Henry Tate, the founder of the Tate Gallery in London, was born in Chorley in 1819 and began his career here as a grocer's assistant.

  St Laurence's Church Church Brow. Surrounded by trees in the centre of the town, parts of the church date back to the 14th C. The bones that are enshrined in a recess in the chancel are believed to have belonged to St Laurence and to have been brought back from Normandy.

  Astley Hall Astley Park, Chorley (01257 262166). At the north west end of the town just over a mile from Botany Bridge (78A). Set in 105 acres of wooded parkland beside an ornamental lake, the appearance of this Elizabethan mansion is very striking, for in the 17th C the existing timber framing was replaced by a new façade that is lacking in symmetry. The interior – more home than museum piece – is very fine with splendid restoration ceilings, furnishings, tapestries and pottery. *Open Apr–Oct, daily 12.00–17.00 (closed Mon except B Hols); Nov–Mar, Fri, Sat and Sun 12.00–16.00.* Charge.

  Tourist Information Centre Council Offices Gillibrand Street, Chorley (01257 241693; www.lancashire.gov.uk). *Open Mon–Sat.*

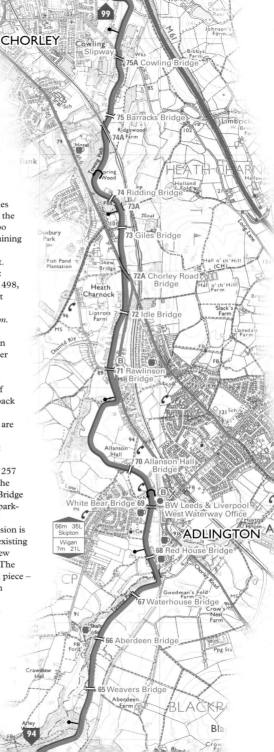

Withnell Fold

The canal sidesteps the town to the east, passing instead some large and resplendent outlying textile mills. There is a *slipway* just to the north of the M61 bridge, on the off-side. Now the boater enters a most delightful stretch of waterway. The junction with the old Walton Summit Branch features a canal cottage and the bottom lock in the Johnson's Hill flight. A short but energetic spell of windlass-wielding is required here, for the seven locks are very close together. It is rewarding work, for the steep countryside yields good views, and the locks are tidily maintained and painted. Near the middle lock is an old toll house and a *telephone*, while at the top lock there is a pub, a boatyard and, together with the usual facilities, showers, toilets and a self-operated pump out. The canal now changes course to north east and flows along a beautifully secluded and often wooded valley at a height of over 350ft above sea level. Even the old paper mills at Withnell Fold, which once brought a glimpse of industry, have been converted into small, discreet, industrial units. There is an excellent nature reserve developed in the old filter beds and sludge lagoons opposite which, derelict for many years, gradually infilled with silt and reedswamp to provide natural plant and animal habitats.

Pubs and Restaurants

Malt 'n' Hops Friday Street, Chorley (01257 260967). Near the railway station. Eight guest real ales that change on a daily basis are dispensed in the congenial surroundings of this displaced antique dealer's! Dogs welcome. *Open all day.*

Tut 'n' Shive Market Street, Chorley (01257 262858). A good selection of real ale and cider served in a pub that's a sports fans' dream: there are 12 TV screens! Lively, young person's establishment serving food (V) *12.00–15.00, Mon–Sat.* Children welcome *until 15.00.* Quiz *Tue;* DJ *Fri–Sun. Open all day.*

Malt House Farm Moss Lane, Whitleywood, Chorley (01257 232889; www.geocities.com/ malthousefarm). A listed farm house recently converted to an upmarket pub and restaurant with exposed timber and masonry; the rustic charm is further enhanced by candlelight and *winter* log fires. Real ales are available together with an extensive range of home-cooked food (V) served *daily 12.00–22.00.* Fresh fish a speciality. Children welcome. Large garden and decking overlooking the canal. Gym and outdoor swimming pool for patrons' use. Jazz *monthly.* B & B.

Red Lion 196 Blackburn Road, Wheelton (01254 830378). A changing selection of real ales served in a popular village pub which is *open all day.* Food available *L Fri–Sun only.* However parties of four or more can pre-book meals *at other times.* Children welcome. Darts and pool.

Railway (01257 279410). Canalside at bridge 78A. Modernised pub and restaurant serving à la carte and bar meals (V) *all day, every day,* with children's menu and outside seating. The railway line has long since disappeared – the viaduct was blown up to make room for the motorway.

Red Cat Blackburn Road, Whittle (01257 263966). Wide ranging, inexpensive Italian menu (V) served *L Fri and Sat, E Mon–Sat and all day Sun* in pleasant surroundings in this listed building. Children's menu and play area. Patio.

Top Lock Copthurst Lane, Heapey (01257 263376). Real ales served in a canalside hostelry at the top of the Johnson's Hill flight of seven locks. Well placed to slake the toiling boaters' thirst, this pub serves a full Asian menu from *11.00–23.00 daily (until 22.00 Mon)* at very reasonable prices. Children welcome; dogs in bar only. Irish and Country music *Wed.* Outside seating and moorings (below the lock please).

Dressers Arms Briers Brow, Wheelton (01254 830041). 3/4 mile east of bridge 82. A superb pub with a fine choice of value for money, home-made food (V) at the bar *L and E Mon–Fri and all day Sat and Sun.* An excellent selection of regular and guest real ales together with their own Dressers Special, are dispensed in the unpretentious, traditional bar: the amalgamation of the original tiny beer house and neighbouring cottages. Children welcome. Quiz *Tue.* Garden seating.

Wam's Cantonese Restaurant Briers Brow, Wheelton (01254 830171). Above the Dressers Arms. A well thought of establishment offering all the Oriental favourites. *Open 18.00–23.00 Mon– Sat and 13.00–20.00 Sun.* Children welcome.

Golden Lion Blackburn Road, Higher Wheelton (01254 830855). A pleasant walk up the footpath south of bridge 86. Real ales in a small, welcoming main road pub. Extensive bar menu (V) *served all day, every day.* Children welcome. Patio seating. Jukebox and free pool *Wed after 19.00.* Quiz *Thur.*

BOAT TRIPS
Royal Sovereign is a charter and trip boat operated from Botany Bay, Chorley (north of bridge 78A) by Boatel Cruises, 7 Botany Bay, nr Chorley. Telephone 01257 273269; shaun@boatelpartycruises.freeserve.co.uk for further details.

● **Wheelton**
Lancs. PO, tel, stores, laundrette, garage. The village is best accessed by walking east from bridge 82. Fish & chip shop *closed Sun, Mon and Thur.*

● **Walton Summit Branch**
The short

branch used to be part of the Lancaster Canal, originally projected to run south from Preston to the Bridgewater Canal. The Lancaster Canal Company, after arranging with the Leeds & Liverpool Company to share a common course between Johnson's Hill Locks and Wigan Top Lock, was daunted by the prospect of constructing an expensive aqueduct over the River Ribble in Preston. A 'temporary' tramroad was built to connect the two lengths of canal between Preston and Walton Summit. The tramway, which opened in 1803, featured a short tunnel and a light trestle bridge over the Ribble. The tramroad was never replaced by a canal; indeed the whole line was closed by 1880. However in 2002, more than 200 years after the truncated Lancaster Canal was completed, the navigation has finally been connected into the rest of the waterways system with the opening of the Ribble Link, using the tidal rivers Douglas and Ribble. Most of the canal branch has been severed by the building of a motorway, although plenty of it still remains in an unnavigable state.

Botany Bay Village Botany Bay, Chorley (01257 273269; www.botanybay.co.uk). Canalside near bridge 78A. Themed shopping centre in a converted mill together with a collection of redundant military hardware. Charge.

● **Withnell Fold**
Lancs. A remarkable, small estate village, built to house workers at the canalside paper mills which are now demolished. Grouped around three sides of a spacious square, the terraced cottages present an intimately united front which is almost unnerving to the casual visitor – especially as on the fourth side of the square is an old set of wooden stocks.

Boatyards

Ⓑ **Wheelton Boatyard and Classic Narrowboats** Wheelton (01257 831333/ 831444). ⚓ **D** Gas, boat servicing and repairs, DIY facilities, boat blacking and painting, boat sales.

Blackburn

Passing under the new M65 extension the canal curls round a steep and thickly wooded valley, crossing it on a high embankment before entering the outskirts of Blackburn. Close to bridge 95 the delightfully named suburb of Cherry Tree provides an excellent range of *shops and takeaways*. There is also a useful *shop* at bridge 94. It seems to take a long time to get through this large town, as there is a flight of six locks here, raising the canal's level to a height of over 400ft above sea level. The lock keeper maintains a tidy flight – indeed most of the passage through the town is now pleasant – there is little rubbish or graffiti, and the views are excellent. A good towpath exists throughout.

Pubs and Restaurants

✕ Boatyard Inn Riley Green (01254 209841). Bridge 91A. Real ale and English and Continental dishes (V) *12.00–21.30 daily*. Children welcome. Terraces, games room, karaoke *Fri and Sun*. Overnight mooring for customers.

Royal Oak Blackburn Old Road, Riley Green (01254 201445). North of bridge 91A. An oak-beamed pub dating from 1620 which serves real ale. Meals and snacks (V) *L and E daily*. Three open fires, no electronic games. Children welcome. Outside seating. *Open all day Sun*. B & B.

Navigation Inn 2 Canal Street, Mill Hill, Blackburn (01254 53230). Canalside, at bridge 96A. Real ale and butties *L* are available in this waterside pub run by Blackburn's longest serving landlady. Children welcome, as are dogs in the Vault. Pub games. Moorings. *Open all day.*

Water's Edge Blackburn (01254 699810). Canalside at bridge 96B. Real ale and bar food (V) *L and until 17.00 on Sun*. Children welcome when eating. Patio. Disco *Fri*, karaoke *Thur and Sat*, quiz *Sun*. Pool.

Moorings Blackburn (01254 664472). By bridge 99. Bar meals (V) available *L and E Mon–Thur and 12.00–18.00 Fri–Sun*. Canalside patio and children's play area.

✕ Blakeys Café Bar King George's Hall, Northgate, Blackburn (01254 503238). Café serving coffee *09.00–16.00* and meals and snacks *09.00–15.30*. Boddingtons and guest real ales available *until 16.00 during the week and evenings Fri and Sat*. Beer Garden.

Malt & Hops 1 Barton Street, Blackburn (01254 699453). Busy, town-centre pub with a late licence dispensing Boddingtons, Flowers, Marston's and guest real ales. Good food (V) available *L and E, daily*. Children permitted if eating. Large-screen TV. Karaoke and live bands *Thur–Sat*. Outside seating.

Postal Order 15-19 Darwen Street, Blackburn (01254 776400). West of bridge 102A. A good selection of real ales and no prizes

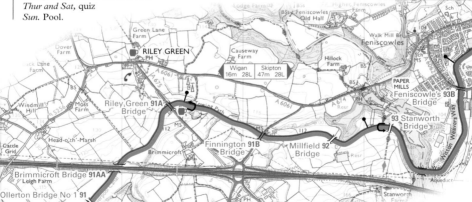

for guessing the original use of this building now under the Wetherspoon banner. Food (V) available *all day, every day*. Children welcome if eating. Non-smoking area. Disabled access. *Open all day.*

Blackburn

Lancs. All services. Few of the Pennine towns which sprang up with the Industrial Revolution can be described as beautiful. In an attempt to rectify this, Blackburn has taken drastic steps in recent years to construct a new town centre. Nevertheless the most impressive features of the town are still the old cotton mills.

Blackburn Cathedral (01254 51491; www.blackburn.anglican.org.uk). Dating from 1820–6, the parish church was raised to cathedral status in 1926. Extensive renovations have been made inside. Very striking 13ft sculpture of 'Christ the Worker' in aluminium and black iron by John Hayward. Large churchyard.

King George's Hall Northgate, Blackburn (01254 582582; www.kinggeorgeshall.co.uk). Entertainment complex promoting a wide-ranging programme of music and theatre. Charge.

Museum & Art Gallery Museum Street, Blackburn (01254 667130; www.blackburn.gov.uk/museum). Exhibits include natural history, pottery, early manuscripts and a large collection of English, Greek and Roman coins. In the art gallery are over 1200 beautiful Japanese prints, as well as English watercolours of the 18thC–20th C. Also incorporated is the Lewis Textile Museum: a series of period rooms demonstrating the development of the textile industry from the 18th C by means of full-size working models, including Hargreaves' Spinning Jenny. *Open Tue–Sat 10.00–16.45; closed B Hols.* Free.

Waves Waterfun Centre Blackburn (01254 51111; www.blackburn.gov.uk). The town's own tropical paradise. Cafeteria. Full disabled access. Technical tours by arrangement. Charge.

Witton Country Park (01254 55423; www.blackburn.gov.uk). Nearly 500 acres of magnificent parkland, including the beautiful landmark, Billinge Hill. Tree and nature trails; wayfaring course; picnic sites and children's play area. Park *always open.* The **Visitor Centre** is *open Apr–Sep, Mon–Sat 12.00–16.45, Sun and B Hols 11.00–16.45; Oct–Mar, Thur, Fri and Sat 12.00– 16.30, Sun 11.00– 16.30.* Free. Restored stables and coach house, displays of carriages. The centre has a natural history room and a live British small mammal collection. Free.

Tourist Information Centre 15-17 Railway Road, Blackburn (01254 53277/681120; www.tourism.blackburnworld.com). *Open Mon–Fri 08.00–17.30 and Sat 09.00–17.00.*

Hoghton Tower Hoghton, Nr Blackburn (01254 852986). Past the Royal Oak at bridge 91A. So enjoyable was a joint of beef that James I knighted the remains 'Sir Loin'. More recently this 16th-C fortified hilltop mansion is visited for its dungeons, dolls houses, picturesque gardens, as well as for the magnificent banqueting hall. *Open Jul, Aug and Sep, Mon–Thur 11.00–16.00; Easter–Oct, B Hols and Sun 13.00–17.00.* Charge.

NAVIGATIONAL NOTES

1 Gates giving access to the towpath in Blackburn are locked at night. For suitable moorings consult the lock keeper.
2 There is the usual range of services, together with showers and toilets, immediately above bridge 99.

Rishton

Of particular interest to those on the canal are the fine canopied wharves of the Depot at Eanam Wharf, now converted for business use with a pub and visitor centre incorporated. The canal leaves Blackburn and embarks upon a course of twists and turns that emphasise the hilliness of the countryside. The scenery varies all the time between heavy industrial development (and its effects) and – just around a corner – green fields, farms and distant views of wild moorlands. The Calder Valley motorway (M65) follows the line of the canal to Burnley. Of interest is the fine wharf building with a large central arch at Simpson's Bridge, now in a serious state of dereliction. Beyond Church, the first of four swing bridges appears (no. 113 requires a handcuff key and a windlass): they are the only ones between Wigan and Gargrave.

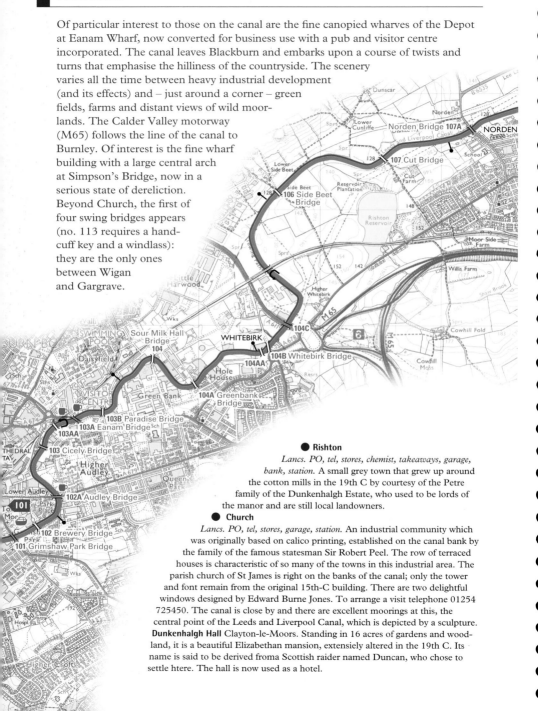

● **Rishton**
Lancs. PO, tel, stores, chemist, takeaways, garage, bank, station. A small grey town that grew up around the cotton mills in the 19th C by courtesy of the Petre family of the Dunkenhalgh Estate, who used to be lords of the manor and are still local landowners.

● **Church**
Lancs. PO, tel, stores, garage, station. An industrial community which was originally based on calico printing, established on the canal bank by the family of the famous statesman Sir Robert Peel. The row of terraced houses is characteristic of so many of the towns in this industrial area. The parish church of St James is right on the banks of the canal; only the tower and font remain from the original 15th-C building. There are two delightful windows designed by Edward Burne Jones. To arrange a visit telephone 01254 725450. The canal is close by and there are excellent moorings at this, the central point of the Leeds and Liverpool Canal, which is depicted by a sculpture.
Dunkenhalgh Hall Clayton-le-Moors. Standing in 16 acres of gardens and woodland, it is a beautiful Elizabethan mansion, extensively altered in the 19th C. Its name is said to be derived from a Scottish raider named Duncan, who chose to settle htere. The hall is now used as a hotel.

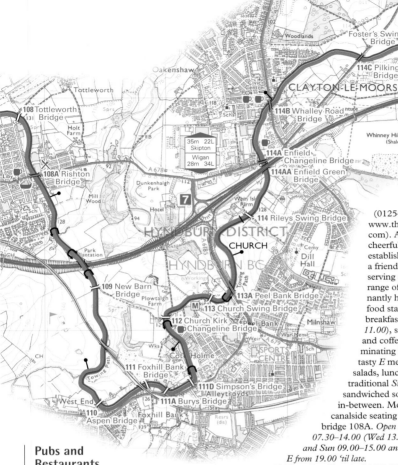

Pubs and Restaurants

🍺 **Wharf** Waterside Bar, Eanam Wharf, Blackburn (01254 678776; www.theeanamwharf.com). A family-run pub glad to welcome all canal users. Good traditional home-cooked food (V) available *L Mon–Sat and E Tue–Fri, Sun 12.00–18.00.* Real ales. Children welcome *until 18.00*; dogs at any time away from food areas. Canalside patio seating. Regular (and varied) entertainment. Close to Thwaites Shire Horse Stables. Moorings.

🍺 **Rishton Arms** Station Road, Rishton (01254886396). Worth the walk for the friendly welcome in this comfortable local beside the railway station. A traditional pub with two rooms serving a range of ales (including a mild) from local brewer Thwaites. Pool and darts. *Open all day Sat and Sun and evenings Mon–Fri.*

✕ ⏲ **Bridge Café** 2-4 Hermitage Street, Rishton (01254 829697; www.thebridgecafe.com). A bright, cheerful and airy establishment with a friendly welcome serving a wide range of predominantly home-made food starting with breakfast (*until 11.00*), snacks, teas and coffee and culminating in enticingly tasty *E* meals; with salads, lunches and traditional *Sun* roasts sandwiched somewhere in-between. Mooring and canalside seating beside bridge 108A. *Open Mon–Fri 07.30–14.00 (Wed 13.00), Sat and Sun 09.00–15.00 and Thur–Sat E from 19.00 'til late.*

🍺 **Thorn Inn** Church (01254 237827). East of bridge 112, behind the church. Cosy, welcoming old pub dispensing real ale. Inexpensive bar meals and snacks *available L (except Sat).* Traditional *Sun* roast and children's menu. Beer garden.

🍺 **Albion** 243 Whalley Road, Clayton-le-Moors (01254 238585). Beside bridge 114A. An excellent selection of real ales from the Rossendale Brewer together with real cider served in a pub astride the halfway point of the canal. To complement the truly stunning array of real ales (and regular *summer* beer festivals), organic bar food is available (V) *Fri–Sun E during the season.* Children and dogs welcome. A unique mix of artwork and entertainment is on offer. Good disabled access and plenty of moorings outside. Garden seating. *Open all day Wed–Sun and evenings Mon and Tue.* Shops and takeaways nearby.

Hapton

The navigation continues to wind eastwards along the side of what turns out to be the Calder Valley with the M65 motorway to the south. High ground rises on each side of the valley, and in the distance the summit of Pendle Hill (1831ft high) can be clearly seen when it is not obscured by cloud. This is an attractive length of canal, unspoilt by industry and greatly enhanced by the ever-changing views from the side of the hill along which the canal is cut, although the motorway is uncomfortably close throughout. Soon the distant mass of dwellings is recognisable as the suburbs of Burnley and the canal ducks through Gannow Tunnel (559yds long) to swing sharply over the M65. BW now have a central Waterway Office at Rose Grove with all the usual facilities including *showers* and *toilets*.

Pubs and Restaurants

🍺 **Bridge House** Hapton (01282 227473). Beside bridge 121. Real ale and bar snacks *available 12.00–20.00.* Children welcome. Beer garden and *Sat* entertainment.

🍺 **Railway** Hapton (01282 779317). Along the road from the Bridge House. Snacks *L.*

🍺 **Gannow Wharf** Gannow Lane, Burnley (01282 421908). Canalside at bridge 127A. Real ale and bar food *L and E.* Quiz *Wed* and live music *Fri and Sat.*

🍺 **Dugdale Arms** Dugdale Road, Burnley (01282 423909). Approach from western end of Gannow Tunnel. Thwaites beers served in a large, modern suburban pub. Children allowed and good disabled access. Bar snacks available *Fri–Sun.* Quiz *Wed*, disco *Fri and Sat*, live music *Sun.* Outside seating and pub games. *Open all day.*

🍺 **Coal Clough** 41 Coal Clough Lane, Burnley (01282 423226; www.coalcloughpub.co.uk). East of motorway slip road, above Gannow Tunnel. An end of terrace traditional northern pub full of friendly folk and good honest real ale. No children or dogs. Folk club *Tue*, entertainment *Thur.* The only Burnley hostelry to dispense Bass Museum beer (Massey's Original). Regular beer festivals. Pub games. *Open all day.*

WALKING & CYCLING

To rejoin the canal beyond Gannow Tunnel leave the towpath and follow the subway under the motorway. Bear round to the right under the A67 and take the path leading uphill to the right of the Derby Hotel. Cross the road and go up the steps and then follow the straight path leading steadily downhill to the eastern tunnel portal. The town of Accrington lies a little to the south of the waterway but is the centre for the Hyndburn District which covers Rishton, Church and Clayton-le-Moors. There is a beautifully produced range of walking and cycling guides to this area which can be obtained (for the most part free) from Accrington Information Centre at the Town Hall (01254 872595; leisure@hyndburnbc.gov.uk).

On the Burnley Embankment
(see *page 106*)

● **Hapton**
Lancs. PO, tel, stores, takeaways, laundrette, station. A small and unmistakably northern town, with regular streets of terraced houses.

Boatyards

Ⓑ **Hapton Boatyard** Hapton (01282 773178; www. haptonboatyard.com). ♿ **D E** Gas, overnight mooring, long-term mooring, winter storage, crane, boat sales, engine repairs, boat building, DIY facilities, hull blacking, paint shop, welding, chandlery.
Ⓑ **Knott's Bridge Moorings** Hapton (01282 774868). **D** Gas, overnight mooring, long-term mooring, DIY facilities.

Burnley

This is an industrial stretch where the canal was once a main artery for the town and its industries. The area around bridge 130, known as the Weavers' Triangle, has been recognised to be of great interest – fine warehouses, tall chimneys and loading bays flank the canal here. At Burnley Wharf there is a museum in the old toll house and wharf master's house. The huge Burnley Embankment carries the navigation across part of the town – called 'the straight mile' it is $^3/_4$ mile long, but no less dramatic for that; 60ft high, it incorporates an aqueduct over a main road. The whole area of the embankment has been tidied up and the towpath opened up offering excellent access to a wealth of pedestrianised shopping, together with good moorings. The town is within easy reach and the attractive Thompson Park (good play area and boating lake) can be found north of the aqueduct after bridge 130H. There is also a useful *supermarket* with footpath access south of bridge 130H. Now the canal negotiates a landscape which alternates between open country, towns and semi-towns, with the massive distant bulk of Pendle Hill in the background. Cobbled streets of terraced houses run down to the canal and old wharves, some disused and overgrown, are under renovation for offices and housing. There is excellent *mooring* immediately south of bridge 140 on the offside, together with an attractive children's playground opposite.

● **Burnley**
Lancs. All services. A large industrial northern town, which has worked hard to improve its appearance. It was once the world centre for cotton weaving. The excellent shopping centre is only 10 minutes' walk from Finsley Gate Bridge, and if you feel like a swim, a sauna or a solarium, the Thompson Centre (01282 664444) is even closer.
Apollo Cinema Hollywood Park, Manchester Road, Burnley (01282 456333). Multi-screen cinema not far from the canal.
Barden Mill Barden Lane, Burnley (01282 420133; www.bardenmillshop.co.uk). Beside bridge 134. A mill shop selling fabrics, clothes, crafts and gifts. Tearoom. Boat trips also available on *nb Barden Broomstick* operating *1 hour 'flights' on Sat and Sun afternoons, May–early Sep.* Telephone 01282 870241 for further details or visit www.boattrips.info.
Queen Street Mill Museum Harle Syke, Burnley (01282 412555; queenstreet@museum.org.uk). North east of Burnley Embankment, along Eastern Avenue and Briercliffe Road from the football ground. This is Britain's only working 19th-C weaving mill: 300 looms powered by the 500hp steam engine 'Peace'. Virtually unchanged until it closed in 1982, the mill has now found a new lease of life, with some of the former employees back again to work the looms. Mill shop and cafe. *Open Apr and Oct, Tue–Fri 12.30–17.00; May–Sep, Tue–Sat 10.30–17.00; Mar and Nov Tue–Thur 13.00–16.00. Also B Hol weekends during season.* Charge.
Rourkes Forge Vulcan Works, Accrington Road, Burnley (01282 458901; www.rourkes.co.uk). Manufacturers of indoor and outdoor decorative ironwork with visitor centre, gift shop and showroom *open Mon–Fri 08.00–17.00 (16.00 Fri) and*

Sun 11.00–17.00. Live demonstrations for groups *Mon–Fri 09.00–15.00 (13.00 Fri).*
Weavers' Triangle The area between bridges 129B and 130B is one of the best-preserved 19th-C industrial districts in the country – there are weaving sheds with 'north light' roofs, engine houses, spinning mills and well-preserved terraces of 19th-C houses. An explanatory leaflet and town trail guide are available from: the Tourist Information Centre or the Toll House Museum of Local History (01282 452403) and the Cotton Industry, which is also the information centre for the Weavers' Triangle. *Open Easter–Sep, Sat–Tue 14.00–16.00; Oct, Sun 14.00–16.00 only.* Free.
Towneley Hall (01282 424213; www.towneleyhall. org.uk). On the southern outskirts of Burnley, 1¼ miles south east of the BW yard. Set in extensive parkland with two golf courses (one 9-hole and the other 18-hole) and play area, the grandiose, battlemented house dating from the 14th C was the home of the Towneley family until 1902. It is now an art gallery and museum with rooms lavishly furnished in period style. The grounds also contain a natural history museum and aquarium. *Open Mon–Fri 10.00–17.00 and Sun 12.00–17.00. Closed B Hols.* Natural history centre *also open Apr–Sep, Sat.*
Tourist Information Centre Burnley Mechanics, Manchester Road, Burnley (01282 664421; tic@burnley.gov.uk). *Open Mon–Fri 10.00–17.15 and Sat 09.30–12.45.*
● **Brierfield**
Lancs. PO, tel, stores, garage, bank, station. A small industrial town merging into Burnley at one end and into Nelson at the other. The parish church of St Luke in Colne Road is a Victorian building with an unusually designed clock tower culminating in a steep pyramid roof.

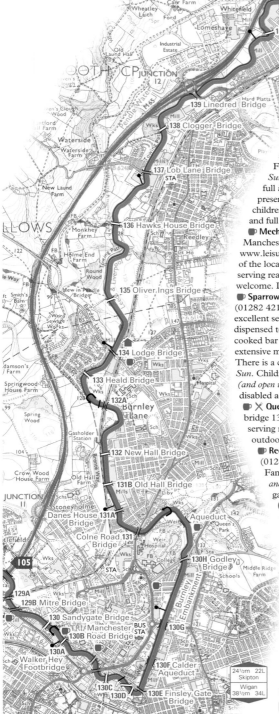

Pubs and Restaurants

There are plenty of pubs in Burnley. This is a selection close to the waterway:

Inn on the Wharf Manchester Road, Burnley (01282 459951). Beside bridge 130B. A weaver's warehouse featuring the original beams, stonework and flagstone floors now dispensing real ale. Food (V) *L and E Mon–Fri and all day Sat, Sun and B Hols*, ranging from bar snacks to full à la carte menu. A family pub, demanding presentable dress, with supervised, upstairs children's play area. Canalside seating, moorings and full disabled access.

Mechanics (Oliver's Bar) Mechanics Institute, Manchester Road, Burnley (01282 664400; www.leisureinburnley.co.uk). Town centre bar, part of the local arts centre, open *Thur–Sat evenings* serving real ales and bar food (V). Children and dogs welcome. Live music *each night*.

Sparrow Hawk Hotel Church Street, Burnley (01282 421551). South west of bridge 130H. An excellent selection of ever changing guest real ales are dispensed together with Belgian bottled beers. Home-cooked bar food (V) *available daily L and E* and a more extensive menu is served in the upstairs restaurant *E*. There is a café/bar open every *E and all day Sat and Sun*. Children welcome *L* only. Pub games. Disco *(and open until 01.00) Fri and Sat*. B & B. Full disabled access.

Queen Victoria (01282 450250). North of bridge 130H. Brewer's Fayre pub and hotel complex serving real ale. Food *available all day*. Indoor and outdoor children's play areas. Canalside seating.

Reedley Hollows 305 Barden Lane, Burnley (01282 425210). 50yds east of bridge 134. Family pub serving real ale and food (V) *L and E (not Mon E)*. Children welcome. Beer garden. Random entertainment

Waggon & Horses Colne Road, Brierfield (01282 613962). Up the road from bridge 139. A beautifully restored pub in Victorian style with an open fire, offering real ale, and food (V) *L and E daily*. Children welcome. Garden. Folk group meets here every *Wed*. B & B. Children welcome. Garden.

Boatyards

(B) **Barden Mill** Barden Lane, Burnley (01282 420333; www.bardenmillshop. co.uk). Pump out, overnight mooring, toilets, café.

Foulridge

The navigation winds as it follows the hillside; but this ceases at Nelson, where it crosses the valley on a minor aqueduct and begins to climb the pretty Barrowford Locks, having finally seen off the motorway. This is a refreshing stretch, in which the canal leaves the succession of industrial towns. It rises through the seven Barrowford Locks, passing Barrowford Reservoir (in which the summit level's surplus water is stored), and at the beautifully kept top lock reaches the summit level of the whole canal. Soon various feeder streams can be seen, continuously pouring vital water supplies into the navigation. Meanwhile, distant mountainous country frames beautiful old stone farms nearer at hand. Soon everything is blotted out by Foulridge Tunnel; at the other end there is an old wharf where it is possible to moor to visit the village.

WALKING & CYCLING

To rejoin the canal beyond Foulridge Tunnel follow the way-marked route along minor roads and footpaths, skirting one of the navigation's extensive water supply reservoirs. Further afield, there is a selection of walks leaflets featuring a variety of treks (from 5 to 45 miles) around Pendle Moors whilst 'Bowland by Bike' is a selection of 10 on- and off-road rides around the area. Available from TICs.

Nelson

Lancs. All services. Nelson is a conglomerate of a number of small villages that combined in the 19th C to form one industrial town. The centre has been redeveloped with a large covered shopping precinct. One of Nelson's more valuable assets is the easy access to the beautiful Moors and Forest of Pendle, behind which looms Pendle Hill.

Barrowford

Lancs. PO, tel, stores. There are still some attractive terraces of stone cottages in this village, which lie a short walk to the west of the locks. The Toll House, the last intact survivor from the old Marsden (Nelson) to Long Preston turnpike road, together with the 17th-C Park Hill (the birthplace of Roger Bannister, the first 'four minute miler') now houses: **Pendle Heritage Centre** (01282 661702; www.pendle.gov.uk/tourism). *Open daily 10.00–17.00 (except Xmas)*. Exhibition on Pendle Witches; 18th-C walled garden and woodland walk; cruck barn with animals; parlour shop and tearoom-cum-restaurant. Also Pendle Arts Gallery. Charge. John Wesley preached from the packhorse bridge in the 1770s; there is a fine park by the river containing traces of a mill dating from 1311.

Tourist Information Centre Pendle Heritage Centre, Park Hill, Colne Road, Barrowford (01282 661701; www.pendle.gov.uk/tourism). *Open daily 11.00–17.00.*

Foulridge

Lancs. PO, tel, stores, takeaway. Attractive around the green, where alleys festooned with washing lines give the place a homely air. In the surrounding countryside are scattered the reservoirs that feed the summit level of the canal. There is a reception centre housing a small museum in the old warehouse on the wharf.

Foulridge Tunnel

1640yds long, with no towpath, this tunnel is, not surprisingly, barred to unapproved boats. The hole in the hill sprang to fame in 1912 when a cow fell into the canal near the tunnel mouth and for some reason decided to struggle through to the other end of the tunnel. The gallant but weary swimmer was revived with alcohol at the Foulridge end. Photographs in the Hole in the Wall pub recall the incident. The tunnel roof drips liberally.

NAVIGATIONAL NOTES

Entrance to Foulridge Tunnel is restricted and controlled by lights. Please obey signs giving instructions.

BOAT TRIPS

M.V. Marton Emperor Canal trips *Easter–Sep, Sun and Tue 14.30*. Also trips through the tunnel to Barrowford run on *last Sun in month end of May–Aug 11.00*. Private charters available throughout year in centrally heated boat. For further details telephone 01282 844033 or visit www.canaltrips.info.

Pubs and Restaurants

Old Bridge Inn Gisburn Road, Barrowford (01282 613983). Cosy village local serving real ales. Children and dogs welcome. Pub games. Garden.

White Bear Gisburn Road, Barrowford (01282 440931). Attractive village local serving real ales and food (V) *L and E, daily*. Children welcome. Outside seating. Quiz Tue and Wed. *Barrowford can be accessed via a footpath near the top of Barrowford Locks.*

Foulridge Restaurant Foulridge Canal Wharf (01282 869159; www.foulridgenet.com). Attractive conversion of the old wharf office and stables to form a tea room and restaurant providing an appetising range of home-cooked snacks and meals (V). Tearoom *open from 10.00 summer, Tue–Sun; winter, Wed–Sun*. Restaurant *open Sat, and for booked groups of six or more, every night.*

Canalside patio seating. Also incorporates a home bakery using organic, stone-ground flour to produce a tasty selection of speciality breads, pies and scones.

Hole in the Wall Foulridge (01282 863568). 250yds east of tunnel, north end. Here is recorded the famous 'cow in the canal' incident. Thirsty boaters, however, are revived with real ale together with an inexpensive range of home-cooked food (V) *L and E (not Mon L)*. Children welcome. Beer garden, pool and darts. B & B.

New Inn Foulridge (01282 864068). Carry on past the Hole in the Wall and cross the main road. A popular village pub serving good food and real ales. Traditional home-cooking with weekly specials available *L and E Wed–Sun*. Children welcome *until 21.30*; dogs in snug area only. Outside seating. Quiz *Mon.*

Barnoldswick

Meanwhile the navigation continues northward through this very fine countryside to Salterforth, crossing over the little 'Country Brook' between bridges 149 and 150. This is one of the more remote sections of the whole canal and probably the most beautiful. There is also much canal interest, for just south of bridge 153 was the junction, now disappeared, of the Rain Hall Rock Branch, essentially a linear quarry where the limestone was loaded directly from the rock face onto the boats. Walk up the road from the bridge (east) and turn right at the top where it will come into view, straddled by a tall three-arched viaduct. A mile further along one rounds a corner and is confronted by Greenberfield Top Lock (*showers, camping*), which introduces the beginning of the long descent towards Leeds – the feeder from the distant Winterburn Reservoir enters the canal at the top lock. The three locks here were built in 1820 to replace the original flight (the old dry bed of the earlier route can be seen on the towpath side) and are set in beautiful uplands – for the next few miles the canal winds through scenery that is composed of countless individual hillocks, some topped by clumps of trees. Beyond are distant mountains.

Boatyards

ⓑ **Lower Park Marina** Kelbrook Road, Barnoldswick (01282 815883). 🕯 D Pump out, gas, overnight mooring, long-term mooring, narrowboat hire, boat sales, winter storage, cranage, DIY facilities, wet dock, solid fuel, boat repairs, chandlery, gifts, books and maps, telephone, groceries, hot drinks and fresh milk.

● **Salterforth**
Lancs. PO (Mon and Thur), tel, stores. A small village of narrow streets and terraced houses in an upland setting. Children will enjoy the playground north of bridge 151.

● **Barnoldswick**
Lancs. PO, tel, stores, garage, bank. Set back from the canal, the mainstay of this town's existence is the Rolls Royce factory, where experimental work is done on aero engines. The centre of the town is compact and dominated by the modern Holy Trinity Church completed in 1960.

Bancroft Mill Engine Trust Gillians Lane, Barnoldswick (01282 865626/842214). A 600 hp steam engine and its two boilers, once powering the looms of Bancroft Mill, saved for preservation. Regular steaming and weaving demonstrations. Refreshments, shop and full disabled access. *Open every Sat* for static viewing. Charge. *Telephone for details of steaming days.*

Tourist Information Centre The Old Library, Fernlea Avenue, Barnoldswick (01282 666704; www.pendle.gov.uk/tourism). *Open Mon and Wed–Fri 09.00–17.00, Tue 10.00–13.00 and Sat 10.00–14.30.*

Pennine Way The Pennine Way is a walking route covering 268 miles of Pennine highland from Edale in the south to Kirk Yetholm in the north. Because of the nature of the route much of the Way is rough, hard walking, but it gives a superb view from the mountains. At East Marton the Pennine Way shares the canal towpath for a short distance – you will notice that the stones here abound with fossils.

Pubs and Restaurants

▶ ✕ **Anchor Inn** Salterforth Lane, Salterforth, Barnoldswick (01282 813186). Canalside, at bridge 151. An historic village canalside pub serving real ales, where a second building was built on top of the first – hence where you now drink was once the bedrooms. Wide range of good, traditional pub food (V) served *L and E* *Mon–Sat and Sun 12.00–20.00.* Built beside the old packhorse road, the downstairs room (and now the cellar) hosts a spectacular display of stalactites. Garden. Good moorings, children's menu and outdoor play area. *Sat* singer. *Open all day.*

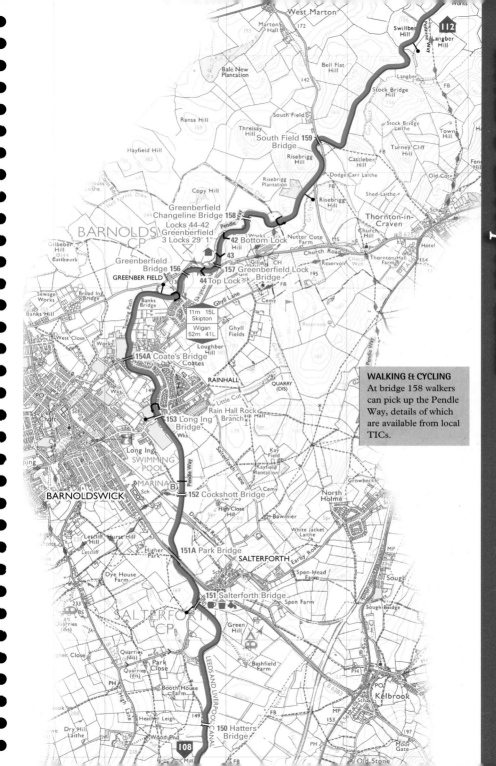

WEST MARTON

Swillber Hill

112

Langber Hill

South Field 159 Bridge

Greenberfield Changeline Bridge 158
Locks 44-42
Greenberfield 3 Locks 29' 1"

BARNOLDS CP

42 Bottom Lock

43

Greenberfield Bridge 156

157 Greenberfield Lock Bridge

GREENBER FIELD

44 Top Lock

11m 15L Skipton
Wigan 52m 41L

154A Coate's Bridge
Coates

RAINHALL

153 Long Ing Bridge

Long Ing SWIMMING POOL

MARINA

BARNOLDSWICK

152 Cockshott Bridge

151A Park Bridge

SALTERFORTH

151 Salterforth Bridge

SALTERFORTH CP

Kelbrook

149

150 Hatters Bridge

108

WALKING & CYCLING
At bridge 158 walkers can pick up the Pendle Way, details of which are available from local TICs.

Gargrave

Around East Marton, after skirting the isolated church, the surroundings change briefly: the navigation enters a cutting, passes under a double-arched main road bridge and enters a sheltered fold housing a farm, a pub and some moorings. A steep wooded cutting leads the canal back into the rugged moorlands. There is a useful *shop* and *restaurant* at Wilkinsons Farm, together with B & B and *camping*, by bridge 162, which can also be reached via a lane to the side of the Cross Keys. This is another outstanding stretch, in which the navigation continues to snake extravagantly around the splendid green and humpy hills that fill the landscape. The six Bank Newton Locks lower the canal into Upper Airedale, yielding excellent views across the valley to the hills and moors beyond.

The River Aire flows in from the north, accompanied by the railway line to Skipton and Leeds from Morecambe, Settle and distant Carlisle. The canal crosses the river by a substantial stone aqueduct. Meanwhile, yet more locks take the canal round Gargrave; the beauty of the area may be judged by the fact that the Yorkshire Dales National Park borders the navigation along here.

● **Gargrave**
N. Yorks. PO, tel, stores, garage, station. A very attractive and much-visited village. Holding an enviable position near the head of Airedale between the canal and the river, this place is the ideal centre for boat crews to explore the surrounding countryside. The River Aire cuts Gargrave in two, and the bridge over it forms the centre of the village. There is a charming station, and some pretty stone cottages along the green. The church is mostly Victorian, except for the tower, which was built in 1521. There is a coal and firewood merchant beside bridge 171.

Pubs and Restaurants

✕ ♀ **Abbot's Harbour Restaurant** Newton Lane, East Marton, Skipton (01282 843207). Charming canalside restaurant set in a 12th-C building constructed by Cistercian monks who worked the land and provided shelter to travellers between abbeys. Traditional English home-cooked food (V) *available 09.00–17.00 daily*. Children welcome, dogs by arrangement. Outside seating.

▣ ✕ **Cross Keys Inn** East Marton, Skipton (01282 844326). Traditional 16th-C inn, overlooking the canal and recently refurbished in a more contemporary style. A range of real ales is available together with an English/Mediterranean menu (V) served *L and E, daily*. Children and dogs welcome. Outside seating. Telephone kiosk nearby.

▣ ✕ **Anchor Inn** Gargrave (01756 749666). By Anchor Lock. Usual Brewers Fayre pub serving real ale and food (V) *all day, every day until 21.00*. Large garden with children's play area. B & B.

▣ **Mason's Arms** Gargrave (01756 749304). An attractive old local pub with a bowling green at the rear dispensing real ales and food (V) *L and E, daily*. Children and dogs welcome. *Sun* quiz; music *Tue*. This pub features a beer-drinking horse. B & B (telephone to confirm).

▣ ✕ **Old Swan** Main Street, Gargrave (01756 749232; www.yourlocal.co.uk/ theswanatgargrave). Imposing village centre pub and restaurant serving real ales and traditional home-cooked food (V) *L and E (all day in spring and summer)*. *Winter* log fires. Children and dogs welcome; children's play area. Garden and pub games. Quiz *Tue*. B & B.

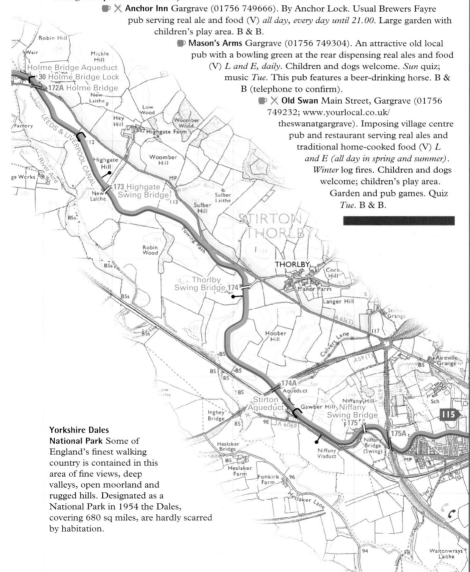

Yorkshire Dales National Park Some of England's finest walking country is contained in this area of fine views, deep valleys, open moorland and rugged hills. Designated as a National Park in 1954 the Dales, covering 680 sq miles, are hardly scarred by habitation.

Skipton

The canal now turns south east and proceeds down Airedale, a valley which contains it from here right through to Leeds. Upper Airedale is a flat, wide valley defined by tall steep hills. The countryside is open, unploughed and very inviting to walkers, especially with the moorlands stretching away over the top of the hills. In this robust landscape the navigation hugs the hillsides just above the valley floor, enjoying a lock-free pound that is 17 miles long – although the navigator's relief at the absence of locks may be tempered by the abundance of swing bridges. Entering Skipton, which is usually bristling with pleasure boats, the navigator will see the Springs Branch, a little arm packed with moored craft, that leads off past the town centre and soon finds itself in what is virtually a ravine, overlooked by the castle more than 100ft above. (Navigation is limited – *see* Navigational Note, opposite.) At the junction is a boatyard: next door is a restored canal warehouse. On leaving Skipton the canal continues along the hillside down the valley of the River Aire, with the main road just beside and below the navigation. Excellent views are offered up and down this splendid valley and the surrounding countryside. The village of Bradley has an attractive waterfront – the *PO stores* are situated beyond the imposing mill building. Visitor moorings are *on the towpath side only*.

Pubs and Restaurants

There is a wide choice of pubs in Skipton. This is just a selection within reach of the canal:

🍺 ✕ **Herriots Hotel** Broughton Road, Skipton (01756 792781; www.mgrleisure.co.uk). Canalside, near bridge 176. 'Modern Victorian' decor and home-made food (V) to suit all tastes are on offer *L and E (not Sun E)* in this bar and à la carte restaurant. Children welcome. B & B.

🍺 **Rose & Crown** Coach Street, Skipton (01756 793884). By the junction with the Springs Branch. Real ale and freshly prepared food (V) *L only* are served in this town centre pub. Children welcome and outside seating. Karaoke and discos *Wed–Fri and Sun.*

🍺 **Royal Shepherd** Canal Street, Skipton (01756 793178). Friendly, welcoming family-run pub (overlooking the Springs Branch) offering home-cooked food (V) *L and E* and a selection of real ales. Dogs and children welcome. Inside there are historic photographs and Royal connections. Garden and play area. Fun quiz with music *Sun.*

✕ 🍷 **Hatters** 17 Otley Street, Skipton (01756 791534). A tasty range of inexpensive, home-cooked traditional English food served in a continental style establishment. *Open Mon–Sat 09.00–17.00 and Sun 10.30–17.00.* There is also a tea garden, and a sandwich bar next door *open Mon–Sat 08.30–14.30.*

🍺 **Cock & Bottle** Swadford Street, Skipton (01756 794734; www.cockandbottle.co.uk). Exposed stone walls and beamed ceilings make this 18th C coaching inn a congenial pub in which to enjoy a good selection of real ales. *Open all day,* serving excellent value, pub grub (V) *L.* Children welcome. Outside seating. *Bi-monthly*

live rock bands and 'view-in' cellar visible from both the bar and street.

🍺 **Narrow Boat** 38 Victoria Street, Skipton (01756 797922). A lively real ale drinkers pub that pays homage to the traditional brewery and to the canal. Furnished with old pews, this hostelry dispenses at least six ever-changing cask ales and a variety of Belgian and German bottled beers. Absolutely no machines and no smoking downstairs. Food (V) *L.* Outside seating and pub games. Jazz *Tue*; folk *Sun.*

🍺 ✕ **Tadpole** Snaygill, Bradley, Nr Skipton (01756 797711). Aiming to provide a 'relaxed, informal experience', this chain pub offers real ale and food (V) *daily 12.00–10.00 (Sun 21.30).* Comprehensive wine selection and log fires in *winter.* Children welcome. Garden and decking overlooking the canal.

🍺 ✕ **Henri's Bistro & Bar** Keighley Road, Snaygill, Nr Skipton (01756 796428). Mediterranean style bar with a large dining area, serving continental lagers and beers together with a mix of Italian and Spanish cooking (V) available *daily 12.00–23.00.* Children welcome *until 18.00.* Outside terrace seating.

🍺 **Slaters Arms** Crag Lane, Bradley (01535 632179). Near bridge 182A. 18th-C quality local complete with inglenook fireplace and log fires in *winter.* Home-made food (V) is available daily *L and E* – lamb Henry and No 4 Slaters grill are two of their specialities. Children welcome *until 21.00;* dogs at any time in the tap room if food is not being served. Large garden, with orchids, overlooking the canal and Aire Valley.

NAVIGATIONAL NOTES

1 Bridges 173, 174, 175, 176 and 177 require handcuff keys.

2 Turning in the Springs Branch is restricted and craft over 35ft should be confident that they can reverse out avoiding moored craft. Craft less than 35ft may still have to reverse to find a turning area.

White Hills
Short Lee Lane
Stirtonber
Aireville Grange
Park Hill
Storems Laithe
Skipton Castle
Spring Gardens
Springs Branch
2 Mill Bridge
Coach Street Bridge 1
Brewery
Swing Bridge 177
113
Gawflat Swing Bridge 176
178 Belmont Bridge
179A Gallows Footbridge
Middle Town
Pinder 179A Bridge
179C Tin Footbridge
New Town Mill

63m 56L Wigan
Leeds 29m 29L

SKIPTON
Greatwood
179B
179D
Great Wood Plantation
Great Wood Laithe
Cemetery
Burnside
Horse Close
Horse Close Hill
Waltonwrays Laithe
Crem
Sewage Works
Carleton Bridge
180 Horse Close Bridge
Cawder Hall Farm
Horse Close Farm
High Laithe
Shaygill Farm
Gill Bottom
181 Snaygill Swing Bridge
LOW SNAYGILL
High Bradley
Butler Hill
182 Snaygill Stone Bridge
Heights Farm
Skipton Road
Keighley Road
LEEDS AND LIVERPOOL CANAL
Langroods Farm
Ghyll Farm
Quarry (dis)
Woods Laithe
Old Hall
LOW BRADLEY
Cononley Ings
Bradley Ings
Cemy
182A Bradley Swing Bridge
Lane End Farm
Mill Br
183 Hamblethorpe Swing Bridge
Low Bradley Moor
Cairn
Lower Sire Bank Farm
Black Hill
Jubilee Tower (Mon)
Farnhill Wood
Farnhill Moor
Works
FARNHILL C.P.
Reservoir
Quarry (dis)
118
183A Farnhill Bridge

BOAT TRIPS

Pennine Boat Trips Waterside Court, Coach Street, Skipton (01756 790829; info@canaltrips.co.uk). *Daily and evening trips (Jul–Aug, Sun and Wed)* and party hire in *Cobbydale* and *Dalesman*.
Nb Leo offers daily trips along the Springs Branch *mid Mar–Oct 10.30–17.00 departing on the hour and on the ½ hour*. For further details telephone Pennine Cruisers on 01756 795478 or visit www.penninecruisers.com.

Stockbridge (see page 119)

Stockbridge (see page 119)

WALKING & CYCLING

British Waterways (01274 611303; enquiries.leedsliverpool@britishwaterways.co.uk) publishes a canal heritage trail for Skipton aimed at introducing the whole family to the history of the canal. The route takes in 10 information posts, nine of which have pictures to take rubbings from – so remember crayons and paper. The walk can be started from any point and takes approximately 1 hour. Details from BW or the Tourist Information Centre.

Boatyards

ⓑ **Pennine Cruisers** The Boat Shop, 19 Coach Street, Skipton (01756 795478; www.penninecruisers.com). At junction with Springs Branch. 🚽 🎁 ⚓ D E Pump out, gas, narrowboat hire, day-hire craft, overnight mooring, long-term mooring, winter storage, dry dock, chandlery, books, maps and gifts, engine repairs.

ⓑ **Snaygill Boats** Skipton Road, Bradley, Nr Skipton (01756 795150; www.snaygillboats.co.uk). At bridge 182. 🚽 🎁 D E Pump out, gas, narrowboat hire, overnight mooring, long-term mooring, chandlery, dry dock, books, maps and gifts, engine repairs, toilet, shower.

● **Skipton**
N. Yorks. All services (including cinema) and excellent shops. Skipton is probably the most handsome town along the whole Leeds & Liverpool Canal. It is an excellent place for visiting from the canal, for one can moor snugly and safely about one minute's walk away from the centre. It still maintains its importance as a market town, which is referred to in its name: Saxon 'Scip-tun' means sheep-town. The wide High Street is very attractive, lined with mostly Georgian houses, and headed at the northern end by the splendid castle and the well-kept grave-yard of the parish church. There is an interesting water mill beside the Springs Branch.
Church of the Holy Trinity Standing opposite the castle, it is a long battlemented church, encircled by large lawns and flourishing gardens. It is in Perpendicular style dating from the 14th C, though it was greatly renovated after suffering serious damage during the Civil War. It has a fine oak roof and a beautifully carved Jacobean font cover.
Craven Museum Town Hall, High Street, Skipton (01756 794079; museum@cravendc.gov.uk). Outstanding local geology and archaeology collection together with a colourful insight into life in the Craven Dales. *Open Apr–Sep, Wed–Sat 10.00–17.00 and Sun 14.00–17.00; Oct–Mar Mon, Wed–Fri 13.30–17.00 and Sat 10.00–16.00. Free.*
Cycle Hire Dave Ferguson Cycles, Skipton (01756 795367) and the Bicycle Shop 3-5 Water Street, Skipton (01756 794386).
● **Springs Branch**
A short (770yds) but very unusual branch that leaves the Leeds & Liverpool Canal, passes the centre of Skipton and soon finds itself in what is virtually a ravine, overlooked by the castle that towers 100ft above. The branch is navigable by small craft, and makes an interesting diversion by boat or foot. (The towpath continues past the arm, into Skipton Woods.) It was built by the Earl of Thanet, the owner of Skipton Castle, to carry limestone away from his nearby quarry. It was

extended by 240yds in 1797 from the water-mill bridge through the deep rock cutting, and 120ft-chutes were constructed at the new terminus to drop the rock into the boats from the horse tramway that was laid from the quarry to the castle. The quarry still flourishes, but the canal and tramway have not been used since 1946. Trains and lorries have replaced them. Now a picturesque backwater the Springs Branch acted for many years as a feeder to the Leeds & Liverpool Canal, taking water from Eller Beck, which runs beside it.
Skipton Castle Skipton (01756 792442; www.skiptoncastle.co.uk). A magnificent Norman castle, with 17th C additions, that dominates Skipton High Street. After a three-year siege during the Civil War, Cromwell's men allowed the restoration of the castle, but ensured that the building could never again be used as a stronghold. The six massive round towers have survived from the 14th C and other notable features are the 50ft-long banqueting hall, a kitchen with roasting and baking hearths, a dungeon and the 'Shell Room', the walls of which are decorated with sea shells. Picnic area, licensed tearooms and shop. *Open daily 10.00–18.00 (16.00 Oct–Feb). Closed Sun until 12.00.* Charge.
Tourist Information Centre Craven Court, High Street, Skipton (01756 792809; www.skiptononline.co.uk). *Open Mon–Sat 10.00–17.00 and Sun 11.00–15.00.*
Skipton Woods Fine woods leading up the little narrow valley from the Springs Branch. For access, just keep on walking up the towpath of the branch.
Embsay and Bolton Abbey Steam Railway (01756 710614; www.embsayboltonabbeyrailway.org.uk). Talking timetable (01756 795189). 1 mile north of Skipton off the A59/65 bypass. Bus service from Skipton. A 4-mile round-trip either steam or diesel hauled. Bookshop, café and picnic site (at all stations). Disabled access at Bolton Abbey Station. *Services throughout year on Sun 11.00–16.15 (every hour); Jul, Tue and Sat; Aug, daily (except Mon and Fri); most B Hols and 26 Dec; plus various 'specials'.*

THE SETTLE–CARLISLE RAILWAY
O.S. Nock, the well-known railway writer, described this line (accessible from Skipton station) as 'the only mountain railway in the world built for express trains'. Completed in 1876, at a cost of almost £3.5 million; 72 miles long – including 20 large viaducts, 14 tunnels and no sharp curves and, in common with so many canal projects, some 50% over budget, it very nearly fell to the neo-Beeching axe. It was both one of the most awesome feats of Victorian railway engineering and one of the most fiercely contested closure battles. It is, therefore, fortunate that in the light of today's burgeoning rail freight, common sense finally prevailed, saving the line for a rapidly growing commercial traffic – and our wonder and enjoyment. Ed Burkhardt's initial success with the English, Welsh and Scottish freight operation, together with ever increasing pressure on the West Coast Mainline, will undoubtedly ensure the future of the line well into the new millennium.

Silsden

There is a fine wooded stretch north of Kildwick; then one curves sharply round the
outcrop on which crouches Farnhill Hall, a mellow stone building. The intriguing
village of Kildwick has some well-restored canalside buildings now used as private
residences. There are good moorings here prior to quieter country: the main road and
the railway cut the valley corner while the canal takes the longer route round to Silsden.
Overlooking Airedale, the green hills are very steep and beautifully wooded in places.
The distant rows of chimneys, factories and terraced houses across the valley comprise
Keighley; most of its industrial and suburban tentacles are quickly passed by the canal,
although the constant succession of little swing bridges regularly impedes a boat's
progress. This type of swing bridge is prone to intermittent stiffness due to the
elements, and all require a handcuff key. There are a *PO* and *stores* south of bridge 197,
and an attractive mooring by woods, to the east of bridge 195.

Pubs and Restaurants

 White Lion Priestbank Road, Kildwick (01535
632265). 17th-C coaching inn near the canal: a
sign on the towpath shows the way! Real ales and
food (V) *daily L and E*. Traditional jazz on *Tue
night* and quiz *Wed*. Children welcome. South-
facing garden offers sun and views.
 Bridge Inn Bradford Road, Silsden (01535
653144). Cosy canalside local which predates the
waterway, serving a good selection of real ales.
Food (V) is available *all day from 12.00 Tue–Sun*.
Children welcome. Disco *Fri and Sat*; karaoke
Sat and Sun (from 16.00). Moorings. Pub games.
B & B.
 King's Arms Bolton Road, Silsden (01535
653216). Friendly, welcoming pub serving real
ales and food (V) *L daily*. Children welcome,
garden. Karaoke *Fri*, disco Sat.
 Brewery Arms 17 Long Croft, Keithley (01535
603102).Serious real ale establishment with a

choice of 10 beers to wash down pie and pease
which are always available. Alternative fare (V) is
also served. Children and dogs welcome. Pub
games and outside seating. *Open all day*.
 Boltmaker's Arms 117 East Parade, Keighley
(01535 661936). Intimate, one-roomed pub dispensing real ale and at least 50 whiskies.
Sandwiches are available *all day, every day*.
Children welcome. Pub games.
 Globe Inn 2 Parkwood Street, Keithley (01535
610802). Well worth the walk and an excuse to
view the K&WV Railway close up. This genuine,
friendly local offers excellent real ale free from the
distractions of any machines together with bar
meals (V) *L (meals E can be booked in advance)*.
Open fires *in winter*; pub games and regular *weekend* entertainment. Disabled access.

There are plenty of other pubs in Keighley.

Boatyards

Ⓑ **Silsden Boats** Canal Wharf, Elliot Street,
Silsden, nr Keighley (01535 653675; www.
silsdenboats.co.uk). **D** Pump out, gas,

narrowboat hire, overnight mooring, slipway,
engine repairs, books, maps and gifts, toilets.

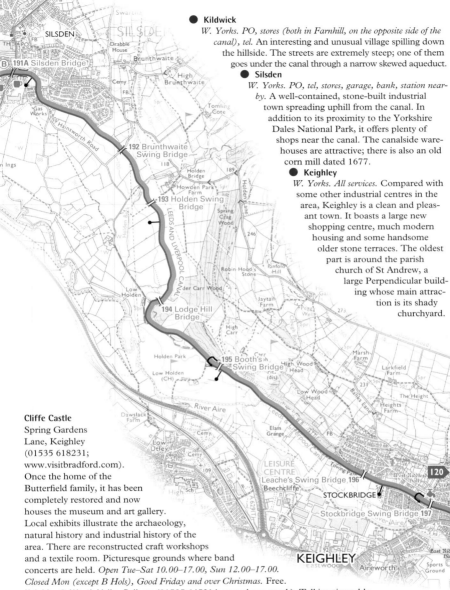

● **Kildwick**
W. Yorks. PO, stores (both in Farnhill, on the opposite side of the canal), tel. An interesting and unusual village spilling down the hillside. The streets are extremely steep; one of them goes under the canal through a narrow skewed aqueduct.

● **Silsden**
W. Yorks. PO, tel, stores, garage, bank, station nearby. A well-contained, stone-built industrial town spreading uphill from the canal. In addition to its proximity to the Yorkshire Dales National Park, it offers plenty of shops near the canal. The canalside warehouses are attractive; there is also an old corn mill dated 1677.

● **Keighley**
W. Yorks. All services. Compared with some other industrial centres in the area, Keighley is a clean and pleasant town. It boasts a large new shopping centre, much modern housing and some handsome older stone terraces. The oldest part is around the parish church of St Andrew, a large Perpendicular building whose main attraction is its shady churchyard.

Cliffe Castle
Spring Gardens Lane, Keighley (01535 618231; www.visitbradford.com). Once the home of the Butterfield family, it has been completely restored and now houses the museum and art gallery. Local exhibits illustrate the archaeology, natural history and industrial history of the area. There are reconstructed craft workshops and a textile room. Picturesque grounds where band concerts are held. *Open Tue–Sat 10.00–17.00, Sun 12.00–17.00. Closed Mon (except B Hols), Good Friday and over Christmas.* Free.

Keighley & Worth Valley Railway (01535 645214; www.kwvr.co.uk). Talking timetable *24hrs* (01535 647777). Privately preserved by volunteers of the Keighley & Worth Valley Railway Preservation Society, the line runs for 5 miles from the British Rail station at Keighley up to Haworth, the home of the Brontë family, and Oxenhope. British Railways closed the line in 1961, but the Society eventually succeeded in reopening it in 1968 with a regular service of steam trains. In the mornings, the service is operated by diesel railbuses, but in the afternoons magnificent steam engines puff their way along the track. In the goods yard at Haworth the Society has a splendid collection of steam engines and carriages, mostly ancient. The line was made famous by the film *The Railway Children*.

Tourist Information Centre 2/4 West Lane, Howarth (01535 642329; www.visithaworth.com). *Open daily Apr–Oct 09.30–17.30; Nov–Mar 09.30–17.00.*

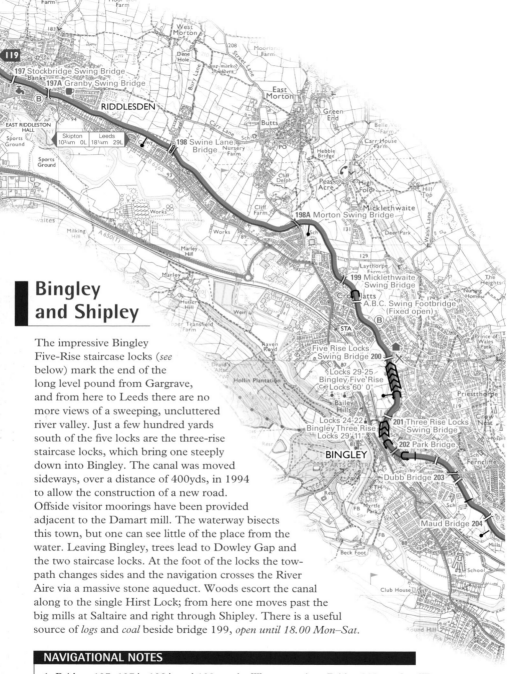

Bingley and Shipley

The impressive Bingley Five-Rise staircase locks (*see below*) mark the end of the long level pound from Gargrave, and from here to Leeds there are no more views of a sweeping, uncluttered river valley. Just a few hundred yards south of the five locks are the three-rise staircase locks, which bring one steeply down into Bingley. The canal was moved sideways, over a distance of 400yds, in 1994 to allow the construction of a new road. Offside visitor moorings have been provided adjacent to the Damart mill. The waterway bisects this town, but one can see little of the place from the water. Leaving Bingley, trees lead to Dowley Gap and the two staircase locks. At the foot of the locks the towpath changes sides and the navigation crosses the River Aire via a massive stone aqueduct. Woods escort the canal along to the single Hirst Lock; from here one moves past the big mills at Saltaire and right through Shipley. There is a useful source of *logs* and *coal* beside bridge 199, *open until 18.00 Mon–Sat*.

NAVIGATIONAL NOTES

1 Bridges 197, 197A, 198A and 199 need a Watermate key. Bridge 209 needs a Watermate key and a windlass.
2 Opening times for Bingley Five-Rise Locks vary (see latest edition of BW Navigation Guide or telephone 01274 611303). They may be used only under the supervision of the lock keeper.

Pubs and Restaurants

Marquis of Granby Riddlesden (01535 607164). At swing bridge 197A. Real ales are served at this long-established canalside pub. Children welcome *until 20.00*. Quiz *Thur.* Beer garden and moorings outside. *PO and stores south of bridge 197.*

Brown Cow Ireland Bridge, Bingley (01274 569482). 1/4 mile west of bridge 202. An excellent selection (seven) of real ales and good quality home-cooked food (V) at pub prices served *L and E Mon–Sat and Sun 12.00–16.00*. Children and dogs welcome. Garden and ghost. Quiz *Tue.* B & B.

Ferrands Arms Queen Street, Bingley (01274 563949). 250yds south of bridge 202. Lively pub with a late night licence (*until midnight Thur–Sat*) dispensing real ales and food (V) *all day until 19.00, every day*. Children welcome *until 20.00. Thur* karaoke, DJ *Fri and Sat.*

✕ Five Rise Locks – Cafe & Store Beck Lane, Bingley (01274 562221). An inexpensive selection of hot and cold, freshly made sandwiches and home-made soup available *until 14.30*. Home-made cakes and gateaux, tea and coffee available *all day. Open Apr–Sep, daily 10.00–17.00; similar opening times during winter school holidays otherwise weekends only Oct–Mar*. Shop sells canal memorabilia, souvenirs, books, etc.

Fishermen's Dowley Gap, Bingley (01274 561697). Canalside, above Dowley Gap locks. A comfortable pub serving real ales and home-made food (V) *L and E (not Sun E)*. Children welcome *until 21.30*. Extensive patio area with views over the Aire Valley. Quiz and games *Wed.*

✕ Boathouse Inn Victoria Road, Saltaire (01274 590408). Between river and canal at bridge 207A. Flying in the face of a century and a quarter of local tradition this is the first licensed premises in Saltaire, and it dispenses real ale. Food (V) *L and E Mon–Sat and 12.00–18.00 Sun*. Children welcome. Quiz and folk music *Wed*. Children welcome in the restaurant. Riverside terrace and beer garden. There are a wide range of pubs in Shipley: several excellent examples being south of the canal between the town and Saltaire.

Noble Comb Quayside, Shipley (01274 585770). Beside 207C. Spacious family pub, newly built, serving real ale and traditional pub food (V) *daily 12.00–10.00 (21.30 Sun)*. Children welcome. Outside seating. *Monthly entertainment.*

Bull 76 Briggate, Shipley (01274 583925). South of bridge 207D. A pub with its own pigeon loft serving real ale and good cheer. Children and dogs welcome. Pool, darts and dominoes. Karaoke *Fri and Sat. Open all day.*

BOAT TRIPS
Apollo Canal Cruises have a water bus operating a scheduled service *up to twice daily in summer*. They also offer *lunchtime and supper* cruises *throughout the year* aboard their restaurant boat *Water Prince* and waterbus *Apollo*. For further details telephone 01274 595914 or visit www.apollocanalcruises.co.uk.

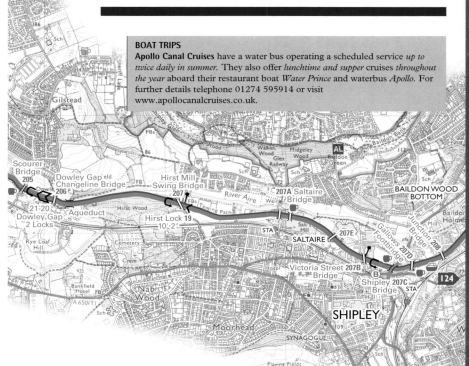

Bingley Five-Rise Locks

Boatyards

ⓑ **Puffer Parts** Excelsior Works, Riddlesden, Keithley (01535 605703/07831 366990; www.pufferparts.co.uk). 150yds south east of bridge 197A. An extensive and varied supply of sensibly priced chandlery (also mail order). Books, maps and gifts. General assistance available to the boater – Dougie himsel' will tell you.

ⓑ **Hainsworth Boatyard** Fairfax Road, Bingley (01274 565925; www.boattransporter.co.uk). 200yds above the five-rise. 🚽 🔧 D Pump out, gas, overnight and long-term mooring, winter storage, slipway, chandlery, boat sales and repairs, engine repairs, toilets. National boat transporters. *24hr emergency call out.*

ⓑ **Apollo Canal Cruises** Wharf Street, Shipley (01274 595914; www.apollocanalcruises.co.uk). 🚽 🚽 🔧 D Pump out, gas, day-hire craft, overnight and long-term mooring, toilets, showers, telephone, gifts.

● **Baildon**

W. Yorks. All services. 1¹/₂ miles north of
Shipley. A very old industrial town huddled
on a hilltop on the edge of Baildon Moor.
Stretching from Baildon to Bingley is the
Glen, a wooded valley that curves below the
heights of the moor. A splendid scenic
tramway carrying two tramcars connects the
coach road to the higher parts of Baildon
Moor – *in summer a frequent service operates,
but in winter it is arranged only to suit the needs
of residents at the upper level.*

Shipley

W. Yorks. All services. A dark stone town built
on a generous scale and based on textile and
engineering industries. There are powerful-
looking mills to be seen, as well as the town
hall and a suitably battlemented Salvation
Army citadel. Shipley is lucky enough to be
on the edge of Baildon Moor and Shipley
Glen. The 3-mile-long Bradford Canal used
to join the Leeds & Liverpool in Shipley, by
bridge 208, but this has all been filled in for
years. Today there are some very real
improvements in the town that directly affect
the boater. There is a new pub and restaurant
beside bridge 207C together with a useful
canalside supermarket between bridges 207D
and 208. There are new public moorings at
Ashley Lane – near bridge 207B – with town
centre shopping a relaxed 5 minutes' walk
away.

● **Saltaire**

W. Yorks. PO, stores, station. An estate village
that owes its existence to the Utopian dream
of Sir Titus Salt, a wealthy Victorian mill
owner. He was so appalled by the working
and living conditions of his workers in
Bradford that he decided to build the ideal
industrial settlement. This he did in 1850 on
the banks of the canal and the River Aire –
hence the name Saltaire. He provided every
amenity including high standard housing, but
no pub – for he was a great opponent of
strong drink. The village has changed little
since those days (save the recent addition of a
pub!); everything is carefully laid out and the
terraced houses are attractive in an orderly
sort of way. There is an Italianate church near
the canal, and a large park beside the river.
Admirers of David Hockney's work should
visit the art gallery.

**Museum of Victorian Reed Organs and
Harmoniums** Victoria Hall, Victoria Road,
Saltaire (07976 535980). Music and musical
nostalgia. *Open Sun–Thur 11.00–16.00; closed
Dec and Jan. Please telephone before visiting lest
the proprietor has been called out on an urgent
musical consultation.* Charge.

Salt's Mill Saltaire (01274 531163;
www.saltsmill.org.uk). The 1853 Gallery
showing David Hockney's work; an inexpensive diner and several furniture and furnishing
retail outlets. *Open daily 10.00–18.00 except
Xmas.*

Tourist Information Centre 2 Victoria Road,
Saltaire (01274 774993;
www.saltaire.yorks.com/touristinfo). *Open
daily 10.00–17.00.*

● **Bingley**

W. Yorks. All services. An industrial town now
known nationally as a centre for thermal
underwear. Standing at the south east end of
the town, amidst several old cottages, is the
large parish church of Holy Trinity, with its
massive spire conspicuous from the canal.

Bingley Five-Rise Locks A very famous and
impressive feature of the canal system built in
1774 in 'staircase' formation. They are all
joined together rather than being separated by
pounds of 'neutral' water. The top gates of
the lowest lock are the bottom gates of the
lock above, and so on. This means it is not
possible to empty a lock unless the one below
is itself empty. The rapid elevation thus
resulting is quite daunting. The BW Sanitary
Station is housed in a handsome old stable,
where towing horses were once rested.

East Riddlesden Hall (01535 607075). NT.
Just south of swing bridge 197A. A 17th-C
stone manor house complete with tithe barn.
Fine collection of Yorkshire oak furniture,
textiles, pewter, paintings and armour. The
house is set in mature grounds with beech
trees, ducks and a pond and the Starkie Wing
provides a striking backdrop to a garden
planted with lavender, flowers and a fragrant
herb border. Also an orchard garden with
wild flowers, bulbs, perennials and, of course,
apple blossom. *Open daily Apr–Oct except
Mon, Thur and Fri 12.00–17.00 (13.00 Sat).
Also open G Fri; B Hol Mon and Mon Jul–Aug.*
Shop, picnic area and tearoom (*open as per
house except 12.00 on Sat*). Events. Charge.

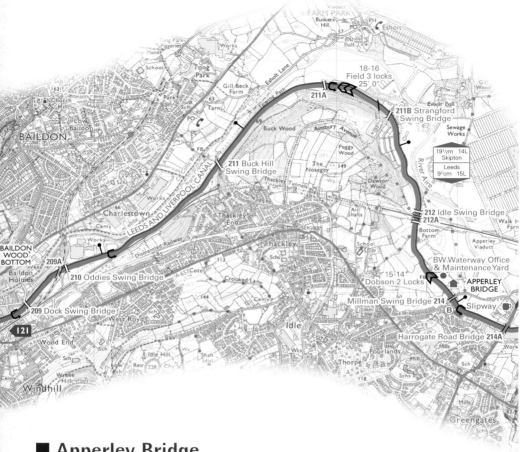

Apperley Bridge

This section sees the end of the wide open moorlands that frame the scenery further upstream: from now on, industry and housing begin to feature more as one approaches the outskirts of Leeds. The navigation, however, is thankfully sequestered from these intrusions into the landscape. Leaving Shipley, the adjacent railway cuts through a 500ft-high hill in two mile-long tunnels. The canal goes all the way round this delightfully wooded hill, tenaciously following the Aire Valley. Halfway round the long curve are Field Locks. Beyond the main railway bridge is a British Waterways maintenance yard at the head of Dobson Locks. This is also the local Waterway Office housed in a former canal warehouse. Temporarily traversing a built-up area, the navigation emerges yet again onto a wooded hillside overlooking the still rural and charming valley that contains the River Aire.

NAVIGATIONAL NOTES

Bridge 214 needs a Watermate key. Bridge 215 is padlocked open to the canal.

● **Rodley**
W. Yorks. PO, tel, stores. A useful village on the canal bank. There are two pubs, several shops and good visitor moorings.

Pubs and Restaurants

🍺 **Shoulder of Mutton** Otley Road, Baildon (01274 584071). ¹/₄ mile east of bridge 210. Real ales and food (V) available daily *L and E Tue–Sat*. Garden with swings. Quiz *Thur and Sun*, live entertainment *Fri*. Disabled access.

🍺 **Woolpack** Esholt, Shipley (01274 582425). As featured in the TV series *Emmerdale*. From bridge 211 follow the footpath to the main road, turn right, then take the turning to the right signposted Esholt. Real ale together with *snacks L (not Sun)* served in this well-known pub. Children's room and garden. Quiz *Thur*.

🍺 **Railway** Calverley Bridge, Rodley (0113 257 6603). Beside bridge 216A. Traditional canal-side pub serving real ale and food (V) *L and E*. Children and dogs welcome. Children's play area, moorings and outside seating.

🍺 **Rodley Barge** Rodley, Leeds (0113 257 4606). Unpretentious canalside pub by bridge 217 serving real ale. Inexpensive home-cooked bar meals (V) available *L Mon–Fri, although weekend L food can be pre-booked*. Children (*until 19.00*) and dogs welcome. Barbecues. Quiz *Mon and Wed*. Canalside garden and moorings. *Open all day Fri–Sun*.

🍺 ✕ **Owl Hotel** Town Street, Rodley (0113 256 5242). A very friendly, family-run pub majoring on live entertainment and serving real ale and a wide variety of food (V) *L and E, daily*. Children and dogs (outside restaurant) welcome. Secure garden. Quiz *Tue and Wed*, live entertainment *Thur*, karaoke *Fri and Sat* and live jazz *Sun*.

Boatyards

Ⓑ **BW Apperley Bridge** Dobson Locks (01274 611303). 🚽 🚿 🔧 .

Ⓑ **Calder Valley Marine** Apperley Bridge, Bradford (01924 467976). 🔧 D Pump out, gas, overnight mooring, long-term mooring, engine sales and repairs, boat sales and repairs, chandlery, coffee shop.

Ⓑ **Swiftcraft** The Boathouse, Parkin Lane, Apperley Bridge, Bradford (01274 611786). By bridge 214B. D Gas, overnight mooring, long-term mooring. DIY facilities.

Ⓑ **Rodley Boat Centre** Canal Wharf, Canal Road, Rodley, Leeds (0113 257 6132). By bridge 216A. 🚽 🚿 🔧 D E Pump out, gas, overnight mooring, long-term mooring, winter storage, slipway, chandlery, books and maps, boat building and repairs, boat sales, engine sales and repairs (including outboards), generators and electrics, gifts. *24hr emergency call out*.

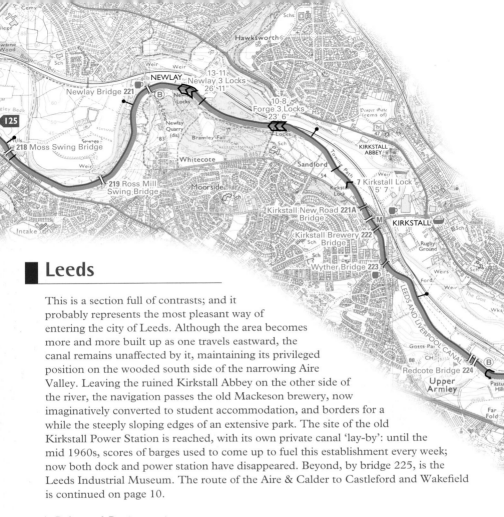

Leeds

This is a section full of contrasts; and it probably represents the most pleasant way of entering the city of Leeds. Although the area becomes more and more built up as one travels eastward, the canal remains unaffected by it, maintaining its privileged position on the wooded south side of the narrowing Aire Valley. Leaving the ruined Kirkstall Abbey on the other side of the river, the navigation passes the old Mackeson brewery, now imaginatively converted to student accommodation, and borders for a while the steeply sloping edges of an extensive park. The site of the old Kirkstall Power Station is reached, with its own private canal 'lay-by': until the mid 1960s, scores of barges used to come up to fuel this establishment every week; now both dock and power station have disappeared. Beyond, by bridge 225, is the Leeds Industrial Museum. The route of the Aire & Calder to Castleford and Wakefield is continued on page 10.

Pubs and Restaurants

Abbey Inn 99 Pollard Lane, Newlay, Leeds (0113 258 1248). 50yds downhill from bridge 221. Small friendly country pub – once used by the nearby Abbey as a morgue – but now serving real ales and excellent food (V) *L and E (15.00–19.00)* to a somewhat less moribund clientele. Children welcome *until 19.00 unless still eating*. Outside seating.

Old Bridge Inn Kirkstall, Leeds (0113 274 9508). 100yds east of bridge 222. Real ales and a tasty selection of food (V) available *L and E Mon–Sat and Sun 12.00–17.00*. The fish and steak pie is a renowned speciality. Excellent *Sun* roast. This welcoming old pub is open all day and in past times is reputed to have served as both mortuary to the monks at nearby Kirkstall Abbey

and, more recently, the police cells. Riverside seating beside a very attractive cast iron bridge over the Aire. Children welcome *until 19.30*; dogs in the garden on a lead. Quiz *Tue*.

Old Vic 17 Whitecote Hill, Bramley, Leeds (0113 256 1207). South of the canal, almost equidistant from bridges 218 or 221, although a steep climb from the latter. A traditional and very friendly local serving an excellent range of real ales that more than justify the walk. Once a vicarage, this comfortable pub offers open fires *in winter* and freedom from machines. Pub games and a quiz *Thur*. Disabled access. *Open all day Sat; from 16.00 Mon–Thur and 14.00 Fri.* Disabled access. There is a *PO*, *stores*, *off-licence* and *takeaway* nearby.

Leeds

W. Yorks. All services. See also page 12.

Leeds Industrial Museum Armley Mills, access from bridge 225A (0113 263 7861). There have been corn and fulling mills on this site since at least 1559, with the present building dating from 1805. When built it was the most advanced in the country and it now houses a superb range of real-life exhibits demonstrating the local textile, heavy engineering, tanning and printing trades. There are working cranes, locomotives and waterwheels, and a cinema of the 1920s. *Jack* the locomotive runs on 'steaming up' days. Shop and picnic area. Disabled access. The little stone bridge over the canal here dates from around 1770. *Open Tue–Sat 10.00–17.00 and Sun 13.00–17.00.* Small charge.

Kirkstall Abbey (0113 230 5492). The large elegant ruins of a Cistercian abbey founded in the 12th C. The remaining walls narrowly escaped demolition in the late 19th C, but are now carefully preserved, surrounded by a small, attractive park. *Open daily during daylight hours.* Free.

Abbey House Museum (0113 230 5492). Just near the abbey is the splendid folk museum illustrating the life and work of the people of Yorkshire during the last 300 years. As well as exhibiting toys, costumes and pottery, it houses three streets of fully furnished 19th C shops, cottages and workshops, including those of a saddler, chemist, tanner and blacksmith. *Open Tue–Fri and Sun 10.00–17.00; Sat 12.00–17.00. Last admission 16.00.* Small charge.

Tourist Information Centre The Arcade, Leeds, City Station, Leeds (0113 242 5242; www.leeds.gov.uk). *Open Mon–Sat 09.30–18.00 and Sun 10.00–16.00.*

NAVIGATIONAL NOTES

During the summer the canal between Newlay Three-Rise locks and Leeds is available during the day for normal passage (for opening times, see the latest edition of BW Navigation Guide or telephone 01274 611303).
Additional staff are also on duty throughout the day. Assisted passage is also available if required but must be booked (*minimum of 72 hours' notice*).

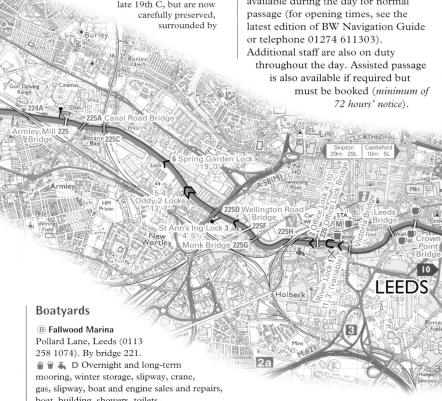

Boatyards

ⓑ **Fallwood Marina** Pollard Lane, Leeds (0113 258 1074). By bridge 221. 🛏 🚿 🏕 D Overnight and long-term mooring, winter storage, slipway, crane, gas, slipway, boat and engine sales and repairs, boat building, showers, toilets.

ⓑ **Aire Valley Marina** Redcote Lane, Kirkstall, Leeds (0113 279 8997). 🛏 🚿 🏕 D Pump out, gas, overnight mooring, long-term mooring, winter storage, slipway, crane, boat sales and repairs, DIY facilities, toilets, showers, laundrette.

Wigan Locks (see page 94)

Newlay Locks (see page 126)

MACCLESFIELD CANAL

MAXIMUM DIMENSIONS
Length: 70'
Beam: 7'
Headroom: 7'

MILEAGE
HARDINGS WOOD JUNCTION
(Trent & Mersey Canal) *to:*
Congleton Wharf: 5³/4 miles
Bosley Top Lock: 11¹/2 miles
Macclesfield: 17 miles
Bollington: 20 miles

MARPLE JUNCTION
(Peak Forest Canal): 27³/4 miles

Locks: 13

MANAGER
01782 785703;
roger.teagle@britishwaterways.co.uk

With the completion of the Trent & Mersey Canal in 1777, demand was created for an alternative canal link between the Midlands and Manchester, and a direct line through the manufacturing town of Macclesfield was an obvious choice. But it was not until 1825 that Thomas Telford was asked by promoters of the canal to survey a line linking the Peak Forest Canal and the Trent & Mersey Canal. The 28-mile line he suggested was the canal that was built, from Marple to just north of Kidsgrove, although Telford did not supervise the construction, leaving to go and build the Birmingham & Liverpool Junction Canal (now the Shropshire Union). William Crosley was the canal's engineer.

The canal, which runs along the side of a tall ridge of hills west of the Pennines, does, however, bear the distinctive hallmarks of Telford's engineering. Like the Shropshire Union, the Macclesfield is a 'cut and fill' canal, following as straight a course as possible, and featuring a many great cuttings and embankments. Apart from the stop lock at Hall Green, where a 1ft rise was insisted upon as a water preservation measure by the Trent & Mersey Canal Company – to whose Hall Green Branch the Macclesfield Canal connected at the stop lock, all the locks are grouped into one flight of 12 at Bosley. The canal is fed from nearby reservoirs, at Bosley and Sutton.

In spite of intense competition from neighbouring railways and the Trent & Mersey Canal, the Macclesfield carried a good trade for many years. Much of this was coal, along with cotton from the big mills established along its northern reaches. Following its purchase in 1846 by the Great Central Railway Company, the canal began a slow, but steady, decline. The Macclesfield Canal today is an extremely interesting cruising waterway, and forms part of the popular 100-mile Cheshire Ring canal circuit. Look out for the original, and very large, stone milestones showing distances from Hall Green stop lock (the original end of the canal) and Marple. These were removed during World War II in fear of helping invading forces. They have been lovingly restored to their former glory by the Macclesfield Canal Society.

Hardings Wood

The junction of the Macclesfield Canal with the Trent & Mersey Canal is exciting and unusual. The Macclesfield leaves the Trent & Mersey on the south side at Hardings Wood Junction, then crosses it on Poole Aqueduct after the T & M has fallen through two locks. The Macclesfield Canal then crosses Red Bull Aqueduct to begin its journey to Marple.

It is thus a busy area, with canalside pubs, British Waterways moorings and plenty of boats contributing to an interesting canal scene. Leaving Hardings Wood, the Macclesfield Canal passes through a stop lock in the cutting at Hall Green, to enter glorious open countryside at Kent Green. To the east, Mow Cop crowns the ridge of tall hills that stretches parallel to the navigation for miles to come. You can take a good walk to the top, on footpaths to the east from bridge 85. Beyond this point, the canal loses itself in splendid countryside for several miles as it approaches Congleton.

Boatyards

Ⓑ **Heritage Narrowboats** Kent Green, Scholar Green, Kidsgrove (01782 785700; www.sherbornewharf.co.uk). ⛽ 🚽 ⚓ D Pump out, gas, narrowboat hire, day hire craft, overnight and long-term mooring, boat sales and repairs, engine repairs, chandlery, toilets, books, maps and gifts, solid fuel.

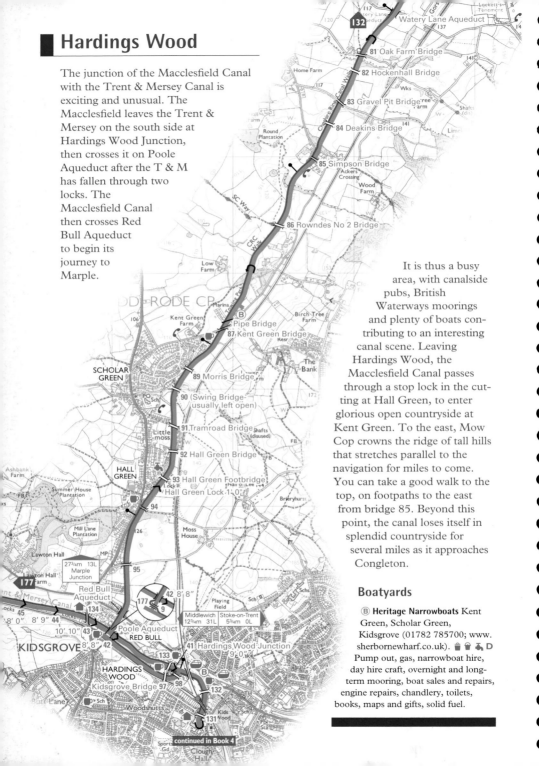

81 Oak Farm Bridge
82 Hockenhall Bridge
83 Gravel Pit Bridge
84 Deakins Bridge
85 Simpson Bridge
86 Rowndes No 2 Bridge
87 Kent Green Bridge
89 Morris Bridge
90 (Swing Bridge – usually left open)
91 Tramroad Bridge
92 Hall Green Bridge
93 Hall Green Footbridge
Hall Green Lock 1.0
94
95
Red Bull Aqueduct
Poole Aqueduct RED BULL
41 Hardings Wood Junction
Kidsgrove Bridge 97

SCHOLAR GREEN
HALL GREEN
KIDSGROVE
HARDINGS WOOD

continued in Book 4

● **Little Moreton Hall**
Congleton (01260 272018; littlemoretonhall
@ntrust.org.uk). NT. Just 3/4 mile west of the
canal, but access is not straightforward –
moor by bridge 85, walk south along the lane,
cross bridge 86 and follow the footpath. This
fabulous moated house is arguably the finest
example of black and white timbered architecture in the UK, and is well worth the walk
from the canal. It was built between 1559 and
1580 with carved gables and ornate windows,
and has scarcely changed since. It contains a
fine collection of oak furniture and pewter.
*Open late Mar–Oct, Wed–Sun and B Hols
11.30–17.00; early Nov–late Dec, weekends only
11.30–17.00 or dusk.* Charge. Restaurant.

● **Mow Cop**
NT. Walk east from bridge 85. A hill nearly
1100ft above sea level, which gives a magnificent view across the Cheshire Plain, beyond
Stoke and into Wales, which looks particularly
good at night. On top of the hill is Mow Cop
Castle, an imitation ruin built in 1754 by
Randle Wilbraham, a local squire. It was on
this spot that Hugh Bourne, a wheelwright,
climbed to the summit to create the Primitive
Methodists in 1807. Their first meeting lasted
14 hours, and was an endeavour to create a
simpler form of religion. The memorial
church was erected in 1862 on the site of
this meeting. A hundred years later 70,000
disciples climbed to the top to worship on
what had become, for them, a Holy
Mountain. Bourne died at the age of 80,
having seen over 5000 Methodist chapels
founded. Coal from collieries to the east of
Mow Cop was carried down to the canal by a
tramway known as 'The Brake'.

● **Kent Green**
Ches. Tel, stores.

NAVIGATIONAL NOTES

The Macclesfield Canal is generally quite shallow, and mooring is usually only
possible at recognised sites.

WALKING & CYCLING
The towpath is in good condition throughout the length of this canal. Ambitious walkers will
want to walk to the top of Mow Cop, which is best accessed from bridge 85. From the top
you can follow a section of The Gritstone Trail north towards the Old Man of Mow, a 65ft-tall
gritstone pillar left as the rock around it was quarried away. Just before a radio mast turn downhill as waymarked to pass through Roe Park Woods, then bear right to reach the lane leading to
Ackers railway crossing and the canal. The Staffordshire Way leaves Mow Cop to head towards
Kinver, on the Staffordshire & Worcestershire Canal.

Pubs and Restaurants

● **Blue Bell** Canalside, at Hardings Wood
Junction (01782 774052). Friendly, quiet,
one-bar local which has no juke box, pool
table or gaming machines, but there are four
separate drinking areas, including a no-smoking section. Winner of many CAMRA
awards, it serves real ale, plus a range of specialist bottled beers, including many from
Belgium, plus real cider and perry. Note the
trapdoor in the lounge ceiling. Snacks are
available *at weekends.* Well-behaved children
welcome *until 21.00. Open Tue–Fri
19.30–23.00, Sat 13.00–16.00 and
19.00–23.00, Sun 12.00–16.00 and
19.00–22.30. Closed Mon.*

● **Canal Tavern** Hardingwood Road (01782
775382). Canalside by bridge 133. Food (V)
is served *L and E,* and there is a large garden.
Children are welcome *until 19.30.* Karaoke at
weekends.

● ✕ **Red Bull Hotel** Congleton Road South,
Church Lawton (01782 782600). By lock 43
on the Trent & Mersey. A popular pub, close
to Hardings Wood Junction, serving real ale
and bar meals, including fish dishes (V) *L and
E,* along with good wine. Children welcome.
Canalside seating area. Quiz nights *each Tue.*

● **Bleeding Wolf Hotel** 121 Congleton Road
North, Scholar Green (01782 782272). Near
bridge 94. A large and lively thatched country
pub with a conservatory, offering real ale and
food (V) (including a carvery) *L and E (not
Mon E).* Children welcome in the lounge.
Large garden and children's play area, with
goats and a potbellied pig. *PO, tel, garage and
stores* nearby.

● **Rising Sun** Station Road, Scholar Green,
(01782 776235). Near the canal. A friendly
and welcoming pub offering real ale, and
excellent home-cooked food, including steak
and ale pie, curry and chilli dishes, (V) *L and E
(not Mon L).* Children welcome. Patio.

Congleton

The canal continues north east, crossing Watery Lane Aqueduct. To the east the ever-present range of hills is a reminder that the Pennine Chain lies just beyond. Passing a golf course, the embanked wharf which over-looks Congleton soon appears, with an aqueduct over the road that runs down into the town. The warehouse at the wharf, once handsome, now looks forlorn, and ripe for devel-opment. There is a useful parade of *shops* a short distance south east (uphill) of bridge 75. Beautifully elegant 'roving' bridges, 76 and 77, follow. These are known locally as 'snake bridges' and, in the days of horse-drawn boats, changed the towpath from one side to the other without having to un-hitch the horse. Past Congleton railway station, the canal is carried on a high embankment – a common feature of the Macclesfield – across a narrow valley, affording a good view westward of the tall and elegant railway viaduct crossing the same valley. Meanwhile the looming fell known as the Cloud, over 1000ft high and topped with remains of ancient earthworks, is given a wide berth as the navigation continues on its lonely lock-free course through this very fine landscape. There is a good walk to the top of the Cloud along footpaths east of bridge 71. The canal then continues its lonely course, turning east to cross the River Dane on an embankment – not very impressive from the boat, but superb when viewed from the river – and arrives at the foot of Bosley Locks, in a really delightful setting which is semi-wooded and semi-pastoral. There are good, quiet moorings here.

WALKING & CYCLING

'Crossroads around Congleton' is a 20-mile cycle ride suitable for family cyclists – details from www.cheshire.gov.uk/countryside/cycling, or telephone 01270 764773 – which will take you past Marton Church, the oldest half-timbered church in Europe still in use, and Cheshire's oldest oak tree, estimated to be 600 years old. You can also walk from Congleton to Astbury Mere Country Park, where there is a network of paths all worthy of exploration. Call in at the visitor centre, telephone 01260 297237 or email astbury@cheshire.gov.uk

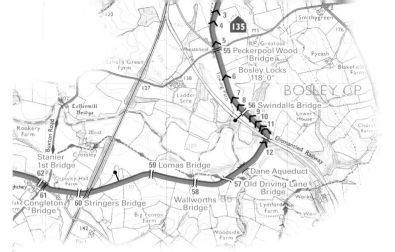

- **Astbury**
  Ches. Tel, stores. About 1 mile north west of
  bridges 79 and 80. A pretty village set just off
  the A34. St Mary's Church is amazing: its
  light interior and wide aisles are complemented
  by generous battlements along the roof and a
  tower standing quite separate from the body
  of the church.
  Astbury Meadow Garden Centre Just along the
  main road from the village (01260 276466).
  Lots of plants, and nice tearooms. *Open
  Apr–Oct and Dec, Mon–Sat 09.00–18.00; Nov,
  Jan–Mar, Mon–Sat 09.00–17.00; also Sun all
  year 10.00–17.00.*
- **Congleton**
  Ches. All services. A compact and busy market
  town.

- **Tourist Information Centre** Town Hall, High
  Street, Congleton (01260 271095; tourism@
  congleton.gov.uk). *Open Apr–Sep Mon–Sat
  09.00–17.00, Oct–Mar Mon–Fri 09.00–17.00,
  Sat 09.00–13.00. Closed Sun.*
- **Bosley Locks**
  Effectively the only locks on all the 27 miles
  of the Macclesfield Canal, these handsome
  constructions are deep, raising the canal level
  by fully 118ft to well over 500ft above sea
  level. Each lock has a pair of mitred top gates
  instead of the more usual single one, and are
  a good example of Telford's practice of
  grouping locks together in flights; here there
  are 12 within just one mile.

Pubs and Restaurants

🍺 ✕ **Egerton Arms** Astbury (01260 273946;
www.egertonarms.com). A handsome and
justly popular village pub built c.1560 opposite
the 11th-C church, serving real ale. Home-
cooked food (V) is available in the restaurant
L and E, daily. Children, with well-behaved
parents, are welcome *untill 21.00*, and there is
a large garden with a play area. B & B.

🍺 **Wharf** 121 Canal Road, Congleton (01260
272809). Near Congleton Wharf. Real ale in a
very pleasant red-brick locals pub, decorated
with flowers in the summer. Food (V) *L and E,
daily.* Children are welcome, and there is a
children's playground in the garden. Large-
screen TV.

🍺 **Moss Inn** 140 Canal Road (01260 273583).
South of Congleton Wharf. A warm and
friendly family-run pub, serving real ale. Food
(V) is served *L and E, daily.* Large safe garden
with a children's play area.

🍺 **Queen's Head Hotel** Park Lane, Congleton
(01260 272546). Canalside at bridge 75. A

traditional and friendly pub offering a good
choice of real ale, often from local breweries,
along with food (V) *L and E daily.* Large garden
with play equipment. Children welcome *until
21.00.* B & B. *Grocers* and *off-licence* close-by.

🍺 **Railway Station Hotel** Biddulph Road
(01260 272567). Near Congleton station, by
bridge 75. A large family pub offering food (V)
L and E daily. Seats overlooking a bowling
green. Quiz *Mon.*

🍺 ✕ **Robin Hood** Buxton Road, Buglawton,
Congleton (01260 273616; www.robinhood-
pub.co.uk). South west of bridge 61. A choice
of real ale is served in this very friendly and
comfortable country pub. Dating from 1787, it
was once the Buglawton Court Room and is
noted for its ghost sightings. The shelves are
liberally sprinkled with local guide books and
leaflets. Meals (V), which include Thai curries
and home-made soup, are served *L and E, and
all day at weekends.* The large, secure garden
has a bouncy castle.

Oakgrove

The Macclesfield Canal completes the climb of Bosley Locks and resumes its lonely journey through open, attractive countryside. Approaching Oakgrove the foothills and mountains of the Pennines, some over 1200ft high, spill right down to the canal. The swing bridge at Oakgrove was once a notorious obstacle on the canal, often requiring two very strong individuals to prise it open. Thankfully those days have long passed. The navigation now follows the contour of the land as it begins to swing around the hills, passing the large flat expanse of Danes Moss and approaching Macclesfield, now clearly visible to the north. If you choose to moor by Gurnett Aqueduct to visit the pubs nearby, take a look at the plaque on a cottage wall 25yds to the east. It commemorates the training here of James Brindley, the canal builder and civil engineer, between 1733–40 – he was apprenticed to Abraham Bennett. Just beyond the aqueduct, bridge 43 is a superb example of a typical 'snake bridge'.

● **Sutton Lane Ends**
Ches. Tel stores. This village was the home of Charles Tunnicliffe, 1901–79, the bird artist.
● **Oakgrove** A delightful spot with a pub and a superb backcloth of tall, green hills which are ideal for energetic walks. The lane west of the bridge leads to Gawsworth. Sutton Reservoir is just north.
● **Gawsworth**
Ches. PO. 2 miles west of Oakgrove. A refreshingly unspoilt village with several small lakes and a lovely 13th-C church, approached by a long avenue of elm trees. Facing the church is the old rectory, a half-timbered house built by Rector Baguley in 1470.
Gawsworth Hall Near Macclesfield (01260 223456; gawsworth@lineone.net). Close to the church, this is a beautiful black and white manor house, parts of which date from Norman times. It was once the home of Mary Fitton, possibly the Dark Lady of Shakespeare's sonnets. The park encloses a medieval jousting ground, and there is a *summer season* of open-air theatre. *Open mid Apr–early Jun and Sep–early Oct, Sun and B Hol weekends 14.00–17.00; early Jun–Aug, daily 14.00–17.00.* Charge. Fine new tea room, selling excellent cake.
Maggoty's Wood In this pleasant wood just outside the village is the grave of the eccentric fiddler and playwright, Maggoty Johnson. After being totally rejected by London critics he returned to Gawsworth where he died in 1773, having ordered that he should be buried far from the vulgar gentry who did not appreciate his genius.
● **Sutton Reservoir**
Close to the canal north of bridge 49, this reservoir holds up to 94 million gallons of water. The public are welcome to ramble and picnic here.
AMF Bowling Brindley Way, Lyme Green Business Park (01625 616438; www.amfbowling.co.uk). By bridge 45. Maybe you, or your children, would enjoy some 10-pin bowling. *Open daily 10.00–24.00 (09.30 Sat and Sun).* Charge for bowling only. Fully licensed bar and *food* with pizzas and burgers *all day*, diner *open 11.00–16.00.* Parties welcome.

Pubs and Restaurants

🍺 **Fools Nook** Leek Road, Sutton (01260 252254). Just east of bridge 49. An inviting old country pub, where wooden beams and comfy settles immediately make you feel at home. Real ale and traditional home-cooked food (V) *L and E*, from an extensive menu. Very pleasant courtyard at the rear. Children welcome.
🍺 **Church House** Church Lane, Sutton Lane Ends (01260 252436). Well worth the 1/2 mile walk from Gurnett Aqueduct to enjoy this friendly and comfortable village local serving real ale, and good food (V) *L and E*. Children welcome away from the bar, and there is a patio with children's playthings.
🍺 **Old Kings Head** Byrons Lane, Gurnett (01625 423890). Below the aqueduct. A coaching house and smithy dating from 1695, which was visited by Bonnie Prince Charlie. This comfortable beamy pub serves real ales and meals (V) in a separate dining area *L and E and all day Sun.* Outside seating.

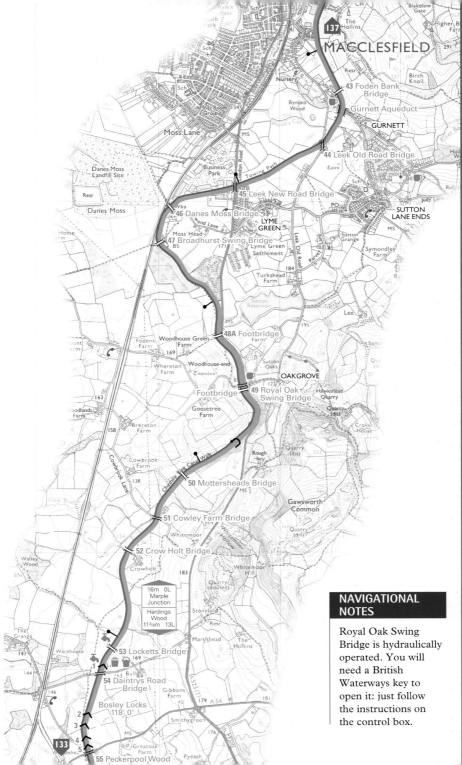

137 The Hollins

MACCLESFIELD

Resr

Birch Knoll

43 Foden Bank Bridge

Gurnett Aqueduct

GURNETT

Moss Lane

44 Leek Old Road Bridge

SUTTON LANE ENDS

Danes Moss Landfill Site

Business Park

45 Leek New Road Bridge

46 Danes Moss Bridge

LYME GREEN

Danes Moss

Moss Head

47 Broadhurst Swing Bridge

Lyme Green Settlement

Sutton Grange

Symondley Farm

Turkshead Farm

Sutton Reservoir

Lee

48A Footbridge

Woodhouse Green Farm

Oaks

OAKGROVE

Footbridge

49 Royal Oak Swing Bridge

Hawkshead Quarry

Goosetree Farm

Brereton Farm

Cowbrook Farm

50 Mottersheads Bridge

Gawsworth Common

Quarry (dis)

Whitemoor

51 Cowley Farm Bridge

52 Crow Holt Bridge

Whitemoor Hill

Crowholt

16m 0L
Marple
Junction

Hardings
Wood
11¾m 13L

53 Locketts Bridge

Marshhead

54 Daintrys Road Bridge

Gibbons Farm

Bosley Locks
118' 0"

133

55 Peckerpool Wood

NAVIGATIONAL NOTES

Royal Oak Swing Bridge is hydraulically operated. You will need a British Waterways key to open it: just follow the instructions on the control box.

Macclesfield

Leaving green and hilly countryside, the navigation enters the outskirts of Macclesfield, where some new housing incorporates a canal crane. A very wide stretch of water is overlooked by a vast and beautifully restored flour mill converted into up-market apartments, marking the site of the original Macclesfield Canal Company. This Hovis Mill was built in the 1820s, and was the birthplace of the famous flour. The word Hovis is derived from the Latin 'hominisunvis' meaning 'power to the man'. Note the archway entrance off the canal, now blocked. The town itself is down the hill; the best place to moor is south of bridge 37, which is also handy for *shops* and *bottled gas*. The tree-lined canal continues northwards to Bollington, passing through glorious open countryside with views of the hills all around, to the Adelphi Mill, once a silk mill and now converted into offices. A 60ft-high embankment and two aqueducts then carry the navigation across the valley towards the huge Clarence Mill, a textile mill now converted into thriving small manufacturing units. High on a hilltop to the south east of the town (directly east of Greens Bridge) is the White Nancy monument, recently renovated. This was erected by the Gaskell family in the 19th C at the northern end of the Kerridge Ridge, probably to commemorate the Battle of Waterloo, and was used by his family as a summerhouse.

Pubs and Restaurants

🍺 **Bee Hive** Macclesfield (01625 424920). South west of bridge 41. Cosy local serving real ale, plus food (V) *L Tue–Sat*. Garden with children's play area. A singer entertains every other *Sat*.

🍺 **Dolphin Inn** 76 Windmill Street, Macclesfield (01625 616179). West of bridge 40. A choice of real ale in a friendly local with an open fire, and a garden. Home-cooked food (V) *L daily*. There are plenty of traditional pub games to play here, and a children's play area in the park opposite. *PO box and telephone* nearby.

🍺 **Navigation** Black Road, Macclesfield (01625 422777). South east of bridge 38. A Victorian local built for the original canal navvies. Real ale, and digital TV. Children welcome. Outside seating.

🍺 **Puss in Boots** 198 Buxton Road, Macclesfield (01625 423261). Canalside at bridge 37. A comfortable pub with an open fire *in winter*, and serving real ale and food (V) *L and E (Sun 12.30–18.00)*. Children welcome, garden. A long-established folk night (bring your guitar!) on the *first Tue in month*, and a quiz *Thur*.

🍺 **Bridgewater Arms Hotel** Buxton Road (01625 422660). West of bridge 38. A sturdy corner house which was being sold as we go to press.

🍺 **Britannia** 260 Hurdsfield Road (01625 423954). West of bridge 34. Unspoilt and attractive terraced pub serving real ale. Children welcome. Pub games. *PO, tel, stores and Chinese takeaway* close-by.

🍺 **Three Crowns** 38 Rainow Road, Higher Hurdsfield. East of bridge 34. A tiny Victorian stone terraced pub with a garden. Real ale.

🍺 **Dog & Partridge** 97 Palmerston Street, Bollington (01625 572177). West of Bollington Aqueduct and bridge 27. A sociable village pub with an open fire. Real ale and hot and cold sandwiches *all day*. There is a bridewell (prison), built in 1831, at the rear. Garden. Folk music on *Fri*. Children welcome.

🍺 **Holly Bush** 75 Palmerston Street, Bollington (01625 573073). A traditional 1930s 'brewer's tudor' pub, with an original interior. Real ale, and food (V) *L and E*. Outdoor drinking area. B & B.

🍺 **Meridian** 48 Palmerston Street Bollington (01625 573883). Originally two cottages, this community-based local still retains many original features – small rooms, brass rails, leather settles, original etched windows, a stove and a piano. Real ale is served.

🍺 **Redway Tavern** 44 Redway Lane Bollington (01625 573591; gaynor@redwaytavern.fsnet. co.uk). A large and popular family-friendly pub, which is extremely handy if you are walking up to see the White Nancy monument (*see* opposite), as the path passes through their land. Real ale is served, and food (V) is available in both the pub *L and E (until 18.00 Sun)* and bistro restaurant, which offers '16 different ways with mussels' amongst other dishes, *L and E*. Children are welcome, and there are extensive children's facilities, and a very pleasant garden, although you can no longer feed the ducks and rabbits, thanks to an unfriendly dog. On *Fri and Sat* you can attend their Dine and Dance evenings, but you must be smartly dressed. B & B.

BOAT TRIPS
White Nancy Cruising Restaurant A restaurant boat operating from Bollington Wharf, Grimshaw Lane. Book well in advance on 0161 368 664, or write to Bollington Packet Boat Company, 25 Everest Road, Hyde SK14 4DX.

WALKING & CYCLING
The White Nancy Monument can be reached by walking south from Kerridge Bridge (27) and following the path. Once at the top you will find it an excellent spot for a picnic, and you can walk along the Saddle of Kerridge, enjoying extensive views. The Redway Tavern nearby is handy for a meal and a pint.

Macclesfield Canal

Macclesfield

Boatyards

(B) **Macclesfield Canal Centre** Swettenham Wharf, Brook Street, Macclesfield (01625 420042). 🛉 D Pump out, gas, narrowboat hire, day-hire craft, overnight mooring, long-term mooring, winter storage, slipway, boat and engine sales and repairs, toilets, books and maps, solid fuel, DIY facilities.

(B) **Peak Forest Cruisers** The Wharf, Buxton Road, Macclesfield (01625 424172). Narrowboat hire (two boats available for week or weekend hire), long-term mooring. *Nearby* 🛉 either side of bridge 37.

(B) **Bollington Wharf** Grimshaw Lane, Bollington (01625 575811). 🛉 🛉 🛉 D Pump out, gas, overnight and long-term mooring, winter storage, boat sales.

(B) **Kerridge Dry Dock** The Barn, Oaklands Farm, Kerridge (01625 574287). Between bridges 28 and 29. Pump out, long-term mooring, winter storage, dry dock, boat repairs.

● **Macclesfield**

Ches. All services. Earliest records of a settlement are to be found in the Domesday Book, when the area was detailed as part of the land of Earl Edwin of Mercia. The town grew rapidly until it became the most important town in east Cheshire, being recognised as a borough in 1220. At that time it was the administrative centre for the Macclesfield Forest, and was granted its charter in 1261. Following set-backs resulting from the Battle of Flodden Field in 1513, the town was granted a new charter in 1595, and this was replaced by yet another, granted by Charles II, in 1684. Now the town is an interesting combination of modern industry and old market town, with cobbled streets and a picturesque medieval Market Place, encircled by busy modern roads. There are several fine classical buildings, making the most of the local stone, and detailed in the fine Town Trail leaflet available at the Tourist Information Centre. In the 18th C the town was one of the leading silk producing centres, but now there are only two small manufacturers left. One interesting feature of the town is the Unitarian Chapel in King Edward Street, approached through a narrow passage and guarded by a lovely wrought-iron gate: it is dated 1689 and is 'for William and Mary's subjects dissenting from the Church of England'.

St Michael's Church Market Place. Very little remains of the original structure founded in 1278 by Queen Eleanor and then known as All Hallows, although the Savage Chapel, the oldest stone building in the town, survives. The church still contains many fine monuments.

Paradise Mill Park Lane (01625 618228; postmaster@silk-macc.u-net.com). Built between 1820–60, this handloom silk-weaving mill finally closed down in 1981. Here you can see Jacquard handlooms in action, authentic room settings and an exhibition of a whole wealth of material connected with one of Macclesfield's major industries. *Open Mon–Sat and B Hols 11.00–17.00, Sun 13.00–17.00.* Charge.

Silk Museum Heritage Centre, Roe Street (01625 613210; postmaster@silk-macc.u-net.com). The first museum in the country devoted entirely to the study of the silk industry: audio visuals, costume, textiles, room settings and even parachutes. Visit also the Heritage Centre in the old 1813 Sunday School building. *Open Mon–Sat and B Hols 11.00–17.00, Sun 13.00–17.00.* Charge. Tearoom and shop.

West Park Museum Prestbury Road (01625 619831; postmaster@silk-macc.u-net.com). Opened in 1898, and situated in a park containing the largest bowling green in Europe, the collections include fine and decorative art, local history and Egyptian antiquities, plus a section devoted to Charles Tunnicliffe (1901–79), the famous bird artist. *Open Tue–Sun and B Hols 13.30–16.30 (closed Mon and G Fri, winter 13.00–16.00).* Free.

Macclesfield Leisure Centre Priory Lane (01625 615602). Three swimming pools, six squash courts and a host of other facilities.

Tourist Information Centre Town Hall, Market Place, Macclesfield (01625 504114; informationcentre@macclesfield.gov.uk). Extremely helpful. *Open Mon–Thur 09.00–17.00 (Fri 16.30), Sat 09.00–16.00. Closed Sun.*

● **Bollington**

Ches. PO, tel, stores, garage, bank. There is a good view of this stone-built town from the huge canal embankment which cuts across it. From here it is only 1 mile to the boundary of the Peak District National Park. The white tower on the ridge south of the town is called White Nancy.

Bollington Leisure Centre Heath Road (01625 574774). Squash courts, a swimming pool and other facilities.

WALKING & CYCLING

'Dave's Hikes' is a series of excellent walks around Macclesfield, and none are too long. You will find details at: www.communityonline.co.uk/daveshikes.asp. The Middlewood Way is a level 10-mile footpath and cycleway along the course of the old Macclesfield, Bollington and Marple Railway, which opened for passenger traffic on 2 August 1869, and goods on 1 March 1870. It closed in January 1970 and was converted for recreational use in 1985. Dr David Bellamy performed the opening ceremony and then, having proclaimed it 'tewiffic', removed his socks and shoes and waded into a nearby pond.

A snake bridge at Congleton (see *page 132*)

Higher Poynton

This isolated stretch is typical of the Macclesfield Canal and in its beautifully quiet, rural isolation it represents much of the charm that most canals possess. Winding northwards along the summit level at over 500ft above the sea, the navigation generally follows the contours of this upland country, but crosses several valleys on embankments with fine aqueducts. There is a pleasant *picnic area* south of Hag Footbridge (16), good *moorings* by the Miners Arms, bridge 18, and between bridges 20 and 19, and a fine shady, wooded section between bridges 22 and 21. There are few centres of population near the canal, just the odd pub here or there, and the countryside is quite unspoilt. Around Higher Poynton the canal becomes wider, the result of ancient subsidence from a coal mine, which necessitated the continual raising of the canal banks and bridges to hold the water in the sinking canal. Be sure to adhere to the main channel here. An old branch near bridge 15 used to lead to the mine; now it is used by a boatyard.

Higher Poynton
Ches. Tel, stores, garage. Considered by some to be the most pleasant moorings on the canal, where the wide water supports large families of ducks, geese and swans. There is a recreation field adjacent, and a handy pub.
Anson Museum Anson Road, Poynton (www.enginemuseum.org). A working display of early internal combustion engines, with emphasis on those made in the Manchester area. *Email geoff@enginemuseum.org for details of open days.*
Lyme Park Disley, Stockport (01663 762023; lymepark@ntrust.org.uk). NT. Two miles east of Higher Poynton. Pedestrian entrance at West Parkgate, 1/4 mile south east of bridge 17 or footpath from bridge 15. In the centre of a 1400-acre park containing deer is this magnificent Italianate palace which was transformed from a Tudor house by the Venetian architect Leoni. Some of the original Elizabethan interiors can still be seen. There are Mortlake tapestries, a large collection of English clocks, Grinling Gibbons wood carvings, countless works of art, and four Chippendale chairs claimed to be covered with material from a cloak worn by King Charles I at his execution. The Victorian garden has a sunken parterre, an Edwardian rose garden, a reflection lake, a ravine garden, a Wyatt conservatory and an 18th-C hunting tower. The house featured in the BBC's recent adaptation of *Pride and Prejudice* as 'Pemberley'. Children's playground. Refreshments available. *Open Apr–Oct, Fri–Tue 13.00–17.00 (closed Wed–Thur); park open Apr–Oct, daily 08.00–20.30 and Nov–Mar, daily 08.00–18.00; garden open Apr–Oct Fri–Tue 11.00–17.00, Wed–Thur 13.00–17.00.* Charge. Restaurant, shops.

Pubs and Restaurants

Windmill Inn Holehouse Lane, Whiteley Green (01625 574222). 250yds west of bridge 25. Dating from the 15th C, when it was recorded as a farm house, it became a pub in 1674. Real ale is served, along with food (V) which is available *L and E*. Children are welcome away from the bar, and there is a garden. There is a useful post box in the wall. Handy for the Middlewood Way path.
Miners Arms Wood Lane North, Four Lane Ends (01625 872731). Near bridge 18. A big, bustling, lively and thriving country pub which is pleasantly family orientated, having extensive gardens and amusements for children. Real ale is served, along with a good choice of food and a children's menu (V) *all day, every day.* Quiz *Sun.*
Lyme View Café Wood Lane East, Adlington (01625 850985). You will receive a warm, friendly and relaxed welcome here for coffee, tea and meals. The food is predominantly home-made, tasty and wholesome. Also cycle hire. *Open Tue–Sun and B Hols 09.30–18.00.*
Boar's Head Shrigley Road North, Higher Poynton (01625 876676). Down the hill from bridge 15. An imposing red-brick pub with a short menu of good pub food (V) *L*. Real ale is served. Children are welcome, and there is a garden with a children's play area. Entertainment on *Sat*, and a theme night *every month*, such as fancy dress or jazz.

WALKING & CYCLING
The Gritstone Trail passes through Lyme Park and continues up onto the moors, passing White Nancy (*see* page 136). The Middlewood Way (*see* page 139) continues to the west of the canal. Details of some interesting walks around Higher Poynton and the canal can be found at www.simonholtmarketing.com/PDFs/Green%20Walks%202.pdf

Boatyards

Ⓑ **Lyme View Marina** Adlington Basin, Poynton (01625 858176). **D** Pump out, gas, day-boat hire, long-term mooring, slipway, solid fuel.

Ⓑ **Constellation Cruises & Braidbar Boats** Lyme Road, Higher Poynton, Stockport (01625 873471; www.constellationcruises.co.uk; www.braidbarboats.co.uk). Near bridge 15. Narrowboat hire, boat building, boat sales and repairs, engine repairs, wet dock.

Ⓑ **The Trading Post** Lyme Road, Higher Poynton, Stockport (01625 872277). Near bridge 15. 🚽 🪣 **D** Pump out, gas, day-boat hire, chandlery, books and maps, gifts, café, solid fuel.

Ⓑ **Classic Maritime Diesels** Lyme Road, Higher Poynton, Stockport (07712 052635). Near bridge 15. Specialists in diesels. Major overhauls and rebuilds, parts made.

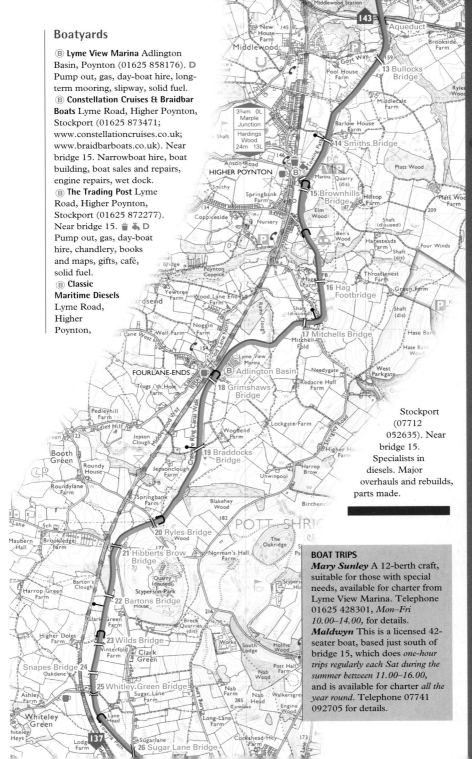

BOAT TRIPS

Mary Sunley A 12-berth craft, suitable for those with special needs, available for charter from Lyme View Marina. Telephone 01625 428301, *Mon–Fri 10.00–14.00*, for details.

Maldwyn This is a licensed 42-seater boat, based just south of bridge 15, which does *one-hour trips regularly each Sat during the summer between 11.00–16.00*, and is available for charter *all the year round*. Telephone 07741 092705 for details.

Marple Junction

Another massive embankment and a tall aqueduct, this time over a railway, are crossed on the way into High Lane. The canal proceeds northwards in a cutting through High Lane, passing the junction with the short High Lane Arm – well protected and now used as a club mooring site – and a children's play park. There are *moorings* between the arm and bridge 11, with *shops* close by. Beyond the town is a restored mill; then open country intervenes, offering views westward of Stockport and the southern outskirts of Manchester. There is a useful *shop*, the Doodfield Stores, down the hill from bridge 6. At bridge 3 there are *two grocers and a fish & chip shop*. Goyt Mill appears, thankfully restored and now housing workshops, heralding the start of Marple, a busy boating centre much enjoyed by the citizens of Manchester. The area of the junction with the Peak Forest Canal is delightful: an old turnover bridge, mellow wharf buildings and the nearby flight of Marple Locks are framed by the distant mountainous country across the Goyt Valley. The canal here is 500ft above sea level.

Boatyards

Ⓑ **British Waterways Marple Yard** Marple Junction, on the Macclesfield Canal (0161 427 1079). 🛏 🚿 ⚓ Overnight mooring.

● **High Lane**
Gt Manchester. PO, tel, stores, garage, station, fish & chips. More of a spread than a village, but there are good moorings and it is useful for supplies. High Lane is effectively at the south east corner of the Manchester conurbation, and is quite indistinguishable from its neighbours. The very long Disley Railway Tunnel passes deep underneath.

● **Marple**
Gt Manchester. All services. A typical residential town, serving as a dormitory base for Stockport and Manchester. Elements of the old village can still be seen, buried amongst the suburbia, but much the most attractive part is by the canal. The rugged Ludworth Moor is not far away, where 'Robin Hood's Picking Rods' still stand, the supposed remains of a Celtic Druid's temple.

● **Marple Locks**
The 16 locks at Marple were not built until 1804, four years after the rest of the Peak Forest canal was opened. The 1-mile gap thus left was bridged by a tramway, while the Canal Company sought the cash to pay for the construction of a flight of locks. This was obviously a most unsatisfactory state of affairs, since limestone from Doveholes had to be shifted from wagon to boat at Buxworth Basin, from boat to wagon at Marple Junction, and back into boat again at the bottom of the tramway. Not surprisingly, a container system was developed – using iron boxes with a 2-ton payload – to ease the triple transhipment. However, this was no long-term solution, and when the necessary £27,000 was forthcoming the company authorised construction of the flight of locks. Today they stand comparison with any flight on the network. Note especially Samuel Oldknow's superb warehouse by lock 9, opposite the lock keeper's house, now tastefully converted to offices.

Pubs and Restaurants

🍺 **Bull's Head** Buxton Road, High Lane (01663 762070) At bridge 11. A lovely comfy, cosy, friendly, locals' pub with an open fire, settles and bookshelves. Real ale and excellent food (V) *L Fri–Sun*. Children welcome, canalside terrace.
🍺 ✕ **Ring O'Bells** 130 Church Lane, Marple (0161 427 2300; www.marple-uk.com/ringobells). By bridge 2. A very comfortable and friendly traditional pub serving real ale and good freshly prepared bar and à la carte meals (V) *L and E (not Mon)*. Chef's specials include lamb Henry, crepes Marango and steak & ale pie. Children welcome *until 19.30*. Garden and canalside patio. Charity quiz night *third Wed in month*.

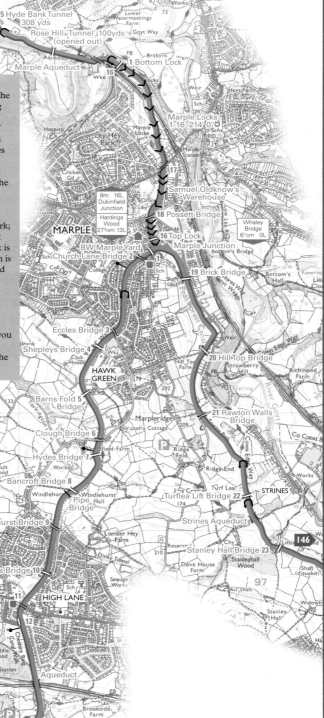

WALKING & CYCLING

There are excellent walks in the Marple area, where stunning scenery combines with the often unexpected remains of early industry. Gordon Mills has written an excellent series of six inexpensive guides for the local community council which take you on some of the finest walks this area has to offer: Marple Dale; The Roman Bridge & Lakes; Marple Locks & Brabyns Park; Chadkirk; From Way to Cut and Donkey Wood. No walk is longer than 4 miles, and each is fully described, with maps and old photographs. You can obtain them from Marple Library or local bookshops, and find details at www. marple-uk.com/Guides.htm. Mr Mills is quite happy for you to download the walks, in exchange for a donation to the British Heart Foundation.

150

Burnvlewick

Chadkirk Aqueduct

E-GV Way

Lower Dale Farm

15 Hyde Bank Tunnel 308 yds

Rose Hill Tunnel 100yds (opened out)

Marple Aqueduct

1 Bottom Lock

16

Marple Locks 1-16 214'0"

Marple Locks 1-16

17

Samuel Oldknow's Warehouse

18 Possett Bridge

8m 16L Dukinfield Junction

Hardings Wood 27¾m 13L

Whaley Bridge 6½m 0L

MARPLE

16 Top Lock

Marple Junction

Bottom's Bridge

BW Marple Yard

Church Lane Bridge 2

19 Brick Bridge

Bottom's Hall

Eccles Bridge 3

Shepleys Bridge 4

20 Hill Top Bridge

HAWK GREEN

Barns Fold 5 Bridge

21 Rawton Walls Bridge

Clough Bridge 6

Marpleridge

Victoria Cottage

Hydes Bridge 7

Bancroft Bridge 8

Windlehurst Pipe Hall Bridge

STRINES

Turflea Lift Bridge 22

Windlehurst Bridge 9

Strines Aqueduct

146

Marriotts Bridge 10

Stanley Hall Bridge 23

High Lane 11 Arm

HIGH LANE

Stanleyhall Wood

97

12

Cheshire Ring Canal Walk

Middle Wood

Middlewood Station

Aqueduct

141

13 Bullocks Bridge

*Hovis Mill at Macclesfield (*see *page 136)*

KEEPING THINGS ON THE LEVEL

The Macclesfield Canal adheres to a mainly level course, with all the locks (aside from the stop lock at Hall Green) in a single group at Bosley. Had the visionary scheme proposed by J. F Pownall, in his work *The Projected Grand Contour Canal to Connect with Estuaries and Canals in England* (1942), come to fruition, the Macclesfield would have formed a part of his grand plan:

'Through the heart of England there runs a *natural canal line*, as I shall term it. This is a line so naturally favourable for canal construction that a canal can follow it easily for miles at a time whilst remaining throughout at the same level. The old canal surveyors saw this line. . . A canal following this contour would therefore proceed right through the country solely on one level. . . it (also) proceeds in direct reaches for long-distances at a time. . . The natural canal line creates the remarkable possibility, never before known, of having a canal go through the length of the country and serve the great industrial areas without any variation from one level.

(There) are very great advantages. The Grand Contour Canal (would be) uniformly level at 310ft above sea level to serve London, Bristol, Southampton, Birmingham, Manchester, Leeds and Newcastle. All the existing canals would be branches from it. The waterway would be large enough to accommodate coastal vessels of a fair size. The Grand Contour Canal would become the primary water distributor of the country. Along the canal there will be formed a special layer in the bed. . . in this layer pipelines for the transport of commercial liquids and gases would be embedded.

Precisely because it expresses a natural feature, the Contour Canal will lie unobtrusively on the land and will have a characteristic scenery of its own.' *Precisely.*

PEAK FOREST AND ASHTON CANALS

MAXIMUM DIMENSIONS Length: 70' Beam: 7' Headroom: 6' **MANAGER** Peak Forest Canal: 01782 785703; roger.teagle@britishwaterways.co.uk Ashton Canal, Hyde to Manchester: 0161 819 5847; enquiries.spring@britishwaterways.co.uk	**MILEAGE** **PEAK FOREST CANAL** *WHALEY BRIDGE to:* Marple Junction: 6¹/2 miles *Dukinfield Junction:* 14¹/2 miles Locks: 16 **ASHTON CANAL** *DUCKINFIELD JUNCTION to:* *Ducie Street Junction:* 6¹/2 miles Locks: 18

THE PEAK FOREST CANAL

This canal runs from the Ashton Canal at Ashton through Marple to Whaley Bridge and Buxworth. Authorised by Act of Parliament in 1794, it was aimed at providing an outlet for the great limestone deposits at Doveholes, south east of Whaley Bridge. However, since Doveholes is over 1000ft above sea level, the canal was terminated at Buxworth, and the line was continued up to the quarries by a 6¹/2-mile tramway.

The canal was completed by 1800 except for the flight of locks at Marple, which were not built until 1804. A second, temporary, tramway bridged this gap in the meantime. Buxworth soon became a busy interchange point where the wagons bringing the stone down from Doveholes tipped their load either into canal boats or into lime-kilns. This traffic, and the boats bringing coal *up* the canal for firing the kilns, accounted for the greatest proportion of the canal company's revenue.

The Peak Forest was also boosted by the opening of the Macclesfield Canal to Marple top lock in 1831, making it part of a new through route from Manchester to the Potteries. The Cromford & High Peak Railway was opened in 1831, joining up Whaley Bridge with the Cromford Canal on the far side of the Peak District.

By the early 1840s the Peak Forest Canal was suffering from competition from the Trent & Mersey Canal Company and two new railways. It was leased in perpetuity to the Sheffield, Ashton-under-Lyne & Manchester Railway, later the Great Central. In 1922 the Buxworth traffic finished, while (through) traffic on the 'lower' Peak Forest Canal had disappeared by World War II. Along with the Ashton, full navigation was restored in 1974, apart from the splendid Buxworth line.

THE ASHTON CANAL

Authorised in 1792 and opened shortly afterwards, the Ashton was a strong rival of the Rochdale Canal – with which it connects in Manchester. The two canals were constructed simultaneously, partly to tap the big coal-producing area around Oldham. The Ashton also opened a new trade route from Manchester to the textile mills of Ashton, while the Rochdale served as a broad canal link over the Pennines between the Mersey and the rivers of Yorkshire. In 1831 completion of the narrow Macclesfield Canal made the Ashton part of a through route from Manchester to the Potteries.

The 1830s saw the peak of the Ashton Canal's prosperity. The canal company sold out to the forerunner of the Great Central Railway Company in 1846, who continued to maintain and operate the canal. Traffic declined in the present century and by 1962 it was unnavigable. A determined effort by the Peak Forest Canal Society, the IWA, local councils and the BWB (as was) resulted in its reopening in 1974.

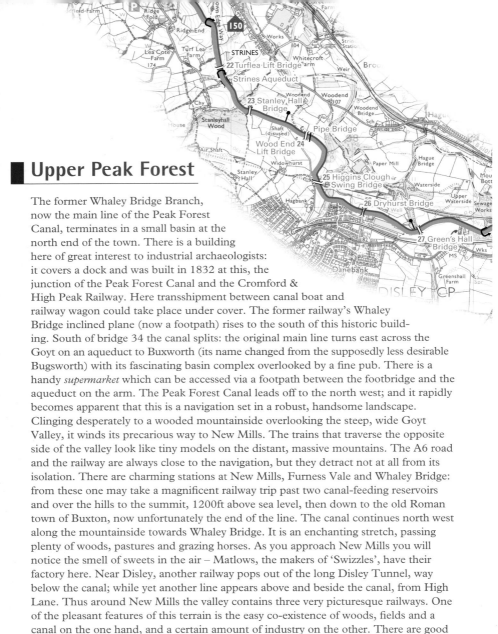

Upper Peak Forest

The former Whaley Bridge Branch, now the main line of the Peak Forest Canal, terminates in a small basin at the north end of the town. There is a building here of great interest to industrial archaeologists: it covers a dock and was built in 1832 at this, the junction of the Peak Forest Canal and the Cromford & High Peak Railway. Here transshipment between canal boat and railway wagon could take place under cover. The former railway's Whaley Bridge inclined plane (now a footpath) rises to the south of this historic building. South of bridge 34 the canal splits: the original main line turns east across the Goyt on an aqueduct to Buxworth (its name changed from the supposedly less desirable Bugsworth) with its fascinating basin complex overlooked by a fine pub. There is a handy *supermarket* which can be accessed via a footpath between the footbridge and the aqueduct on the arm. The Peak Forest Canal leads off to the north west; and it rapidly becomes apparent that this is a navigation set in a robust, handsome landscape. Clinging desperately to a wooded mountainside overlooking the steep, wide Goyt Valley, it winds its precarious way to New Mills. The trains that traverse the opposite side of the valley look like tiny models on the distant, massive mountains. The A6 road and the railway are always close to the navigation, but they detract not at all from its isolation. There are charming stations at New Mills, Furness Vale and Whaley Bridge: from these one may take a magnificent railway trip past two canal-feeding reservoirs and over the hills to the summit, 1200ft above sea level, then down to the old Roman town of Buxton, now unfortunately the end of the line. The canal continues north west along the mountainside towards Whaley Bridge. It is an enchanting stretch, passing plenty of woods, pastures and grazing horses. As you approach New Mills you will notice the smell of sweets in the air – Matlows, the makers of 'Swizzles', have their factory here. Near Disley, another railway pops out of the long Disley Tunnel, way below the canal; while yet another line appears above and beside the canal, from High Lane. Thus around New Mills the valley contains three very picturesque railways. One of the pleasant features of this terrain is the easy co-existence of woods, fields and a canal on the one hand, and a certain amount of industry on the other. There are good moorings at bridge 24, where a public footpath gives easy access to Strines.

BOAT TRIPS
nb Judith Mary II Canal Wharf, Canal Street, Whaley Bridge, High Peak, SK23 7LS (01663 734737, www.peakleisure.co.uk/judithmary). A long-established and fully equipped 70ft, 42-seater narrowboat available for private charter *all year*. Fully licensed. On 14 June 1990 the late Princess Diana had a meal on board whilst visiting the area.

NAVIGATIONAL NOTES

1 You will need a handcuff lock key for the locks on this and the Ashton Canals.
2 Buxworth Basin is closed to navigation as we go to press. Contact BW for the latest information.
3 Bridges 22 and 24 are windlass operated.

WALKING & CYCLING

The towpath is in good condition throughout. Peter Roger's Guide gives details of some walks and bicycle rides from Whaley Bridge – details at users. breathemail.net/peter.rogers/whaley.htm. Details of local walks exploring Bugsworth (as was) Basin and the parish paths can be obtained from: PFCC, 41 Tatton Street, Knutsford, Cheshire, WA16 6AE or at users.iclway.co.uk/don.baines/maps& guides.htm. The Millennium Walkway, which starts by the Heritage Centre in New Mills (*see* page 148) gives access to previously inaccessible parts of the gorge near New Mills. You can also obtain a series of leaflets from the centre giving full details of The Torrs Industrial Trail, The Bridges Trail, The Sett Valley Trail and The Waterside Way. The Goyt Way, which has an interpretation board at the canal terminus, and the Mid-Shires Way (from Buckinghamshire!) both pass through here.

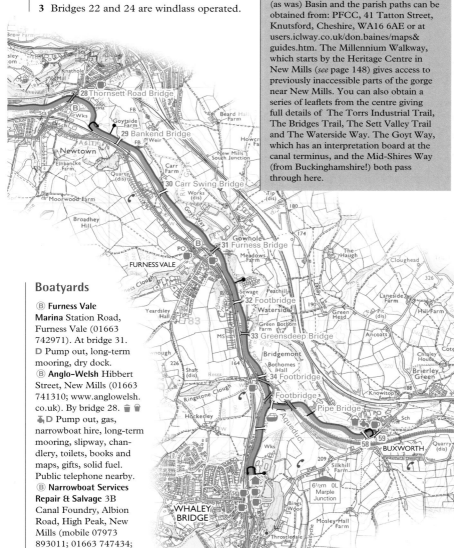

Boatyards

Ⓑ **Furness Vale Marina** Station Road, Furness Vale (01663 742971). At bridge 31. D Pump out, long-term mooring, dry dock.
Ⓑ **Anglo-Welsh** Hibbert Street, New Mills (01663 741310; www.anglowelsh. co.uk). By bridge 28. 🚽 🛁 D Pump out, gas, narrowboat hire, long-term mooring, slipway, chandlery, toilets, books and maps, gifts, solid fuel. Public telephone nearby.
Ⓑ **Narrowboat Services Repair & Salvage** 3B Canal Foundry, Albion Road, High Peak, New Mills (mobile 07973 893011; 01663 747434; www.narrowboat.info). Mobile boat and engine repairs. *Emergency break-down service.*

A SILK PURSE FROM A SOW'S EAR

The Ashton Canal is now a part of the Cheshire Ring, a superb 100-mile cruising circuit which can be comfortably completed in a week. Those with extra energy, or a day or two more, can add in a diversion along the Peak Forest Canal, and their efforts will reap just reward. The ability to cruise these waterways is due to those who campaigned between 1959 and 1974 to clear and restore canals that had become both an eyesore and a danger. Extensive lobbying resulted in the formation of the Peak Forest Canal Society, and with the staging of the 1966 IWA National Rally at Marple, restoration gained momentum. 'Operation Ashton', held over a weekend in September 1968, saw 600 waterway enthusiasts clear more than 2000 tons of rubbish from the canal. Local people were amazed, and began to realise that what had long been regarded as an eyesore and a danger could now become a valuable local amenity. *The corner had been turned*. Following a rally on the Rochdale Canal at Easter 1971, local authorities and the British Waterways Board (as it then was) decided to proceed with full restoration of the Ashton and Peak Forest Canals. We owe a great debt to all those involved.

● **Whaley Bridge**
Derbs. PO, tel, stores, garage, station, laundrette, fish & chips, banks. Built on a steep hill at the end of the canal, with good views across the Goyt valley, this is now a quiet and pleasant place, a new bypass having removed much of the traffic. The beautiful nearby hills are, however, more noteworthy than the town.
Cromford & High Peak Railway In the early 1820s a physical connection was planned between the Peak Forest Canal at Whaley Bridge and the Cromford Canal, way over to the south east on the other side of the Peak District, using a junction canal. However a waterway would have been impracticable through such mountainous terrain, and so a railway was constructed. Known as the Cromford & High Peak Railway, it was opened throughout in 1831, and was 33 miles long. With a summit level over 1200ft above sea level, this extraordinary standard-gauge goods line was interesting chiefly for its numerous slopes and inclined planes, up which the wagons were hauled by either stationary or tenacious locomotive steam engines (the steepest gradient on the line was 1 in 7). The C & HPR closed in 1967; now much of the route has been turned into a public footpath and bridleway. Around Whaley Bridge one may still see the remains of the short inclined plane (now a footpath) which brought the goods down the hill, then through the town to the wharf at the terminus of the Peak Forest Canal.
Toddbrook Reservoir Just south of Whaley Bridge. A very pleasant area for picnicking and walking. Private sailing club; fishing rights on this BW reservoir are exercised by an angling club (day tickets available).
● **Buxworth**
Derbs. Tel, stores. The main feature in Buxworth is the fascinating old terminal basin system. This used to be a tremendously busy complex, and is of great interest to industrial archaeologists. The canal line to Buxworth (once Bugsworth) was built to bring the canal as near as possible to the great limestone quarries at Doveholes, a plate tramway being constructed in 1799 via

Chapel Milton to complete the connection. Known as the Peak Forest Tramway, this little line, 6¹/₂ miles long, brought the stone down the hills to Buxworth, where it was transshipped into waiting canal boats. Throughout the history of the line, the wagons on the tramway were drawn exclusively by horse-power – except for a 500yd inclined plane in Chapel-en-le-Frith, where the trucks were attached to a continuous rope so that the descending trucks pulled empty ones up the 1 in 7¹/₂ slope. The tramway was closed by 1926, and the sidings and basins at Buxworth became disused and overgrown. The Inland Waterways Preservation Society and BW have now almost completed the restoration of this superb complex.
● **Furness Vale**
Derbs. PO, tel, stores, station. A main road (A6) village, useful for supplies.
● **New Mills**
Derbs. PO, tel, stores, garage, banks, laundrette, stations. A mostly stone-built town on the Cheshire/Derbyshire border; its industries include textile printing, engineering and engraving. A boatyard occupies old canal buildings to the east of bridge 28.
New Mills Heritage Centre Rock Mill Lane, New Mills, High Peak (01663 746904, www.newmills.org.uk). North of Thornsett Road Bridge (28). Located by the path leading down into the Torrs Gorge, next to the bus station. A splendid centre where you can see a display illustrating the history of the town, with a superb model. There is also a mock mine tunnel. Local books and walk details can be purchased in the shop, and there is also a café. The Millennium Walkway starts here. *Open Tue–Fri 11.00–16.00, Sat and Sun 10.30–16.30 (16.00 in winter).*
● **Disley**
Ches. PO, tel, stores, garage, station. On the south bank of the canal. The centre of the village is quite pretty, spoilt slightly by the A6 traffic. The village is up the hill, south west of bridge 26. The attractive church stands among trees above the little village square. It was greatly renovated in the last century, but the ancient tower with the griffin leering down at passers-by dates from the 16th C.

Disley

Vehicular and pedestrian access to Lyme Park (*see* page 140) is from the A6 near Disley, 1¹/₂ miles south west of bridge 26.

Pubs and Restaurants

Railway Whaley Bridge (01663 732245). Real ale in a fine straightforward pub. Children welcome.

Goyt Inn 8 Bridge Street, Whaley Bridge (01663 732840). An attractive pub with an open fire and a garden, close to the canal basin and shops. Real ale is served along with food (V) *L (E by request)*. Children are welcome, and there is a garden. Live acts *at the weekend,* quiz *Wed,* karaoke *Thur.*

Navigation 6 Johnson Street, Whaley Bridge (01663 732308). Near the canal terminus, this small traditional pub has a narrowboat theme, with some original canal artwork. Have a look on the notice board for pictures of visitor's boats. Real ale and food (V) *L (E by request)*. Children welcome *until 19.00*. Garden, and *weekend* entertainment and quizzes.

Navigation Buxworth, High Peak (01663 732072; www.navigationinn.co.uk). By the canal terminus, this is a superbly situated pub overlooking the old basins, beautifully decorated with some fine canal memorabilia, and with real fires *in winter*. It was built around 1794, and was once run by Pat Phoenix, *Coronation Street's* Elsie Tanner. A choice of real ale, along with restaurant and bar meals (V)

available *L and E, daily*. Family room, and a garden with a playground and a pet's corner. Occasional live bands. Games room. B & B.

Dog & Partridge Bridgemont, Whaley Bridge (01663 732284). Near the junction to Buxworth Basin. A local pub, with open fires, serving a choice of real ales. Good food (V) is served *L and E and all day Sat and Sun*. Children welcome away from the bar, and there is a garden. Blue grass music *first Sun* in month, fun quiz *last Thur* in month. Annual beer festival, food theme nights.

Crossing Station Road, Furness Vale (01663 743642). By the level crossing, up the hill from bridge 31. A friendly pub serving real ale. Children welcome, garden.

Beehive Albion Road, New Mills (01663 742087). Just along the lane opposite New Mills Wharf, by bridge 28. A welcoming stone-built pub, recently refurbished. Usually there is a choice of real ale available, including some from small local breweries. Meals are served upstairs in the Indian restaurant (V) *E only*. Children are welcome, and there is outside seating.

● **Strines**
Gt Manchester. PO, tel, stores, station. A useful place for supplies.

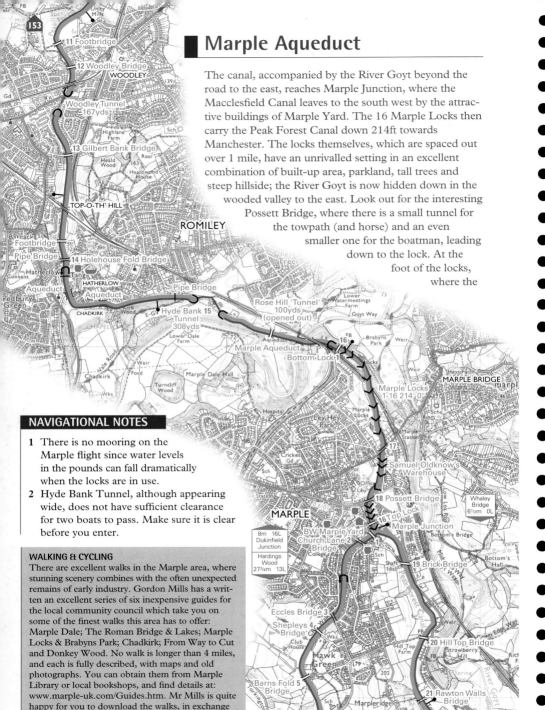

Marple Aqueduct

The canal, accompanied by the River Goyt beyond the road to the east, reaches Marple Junction, where the Macclesfield Canal leaves to the south west by the attractive buildings of Marple Yard. The 16 Marple Locks then carry the Peak Forest Canal down 214ft towards Manchester. The locks themselves, which are spaced out over 1 mile, have an unrivalled setting in an excellent combination of built-up area, parkland, tall trees and steep hillside; the River Goyt is now hidden down in the wooded valley to the east. Look out for the interesting Possett Bridge, where there is a small tunnel for the towpath (and horse) and an even smaller one for the boatman, leading down to the lock. At the foot of the locks, where the

NAVIGATIONAL NOTES

1 There is no mooring on the Marple flight since water levels in the pounds can fall dramatically when the locks are in use.
2 Hyde Bank Tunnel, although appearing wide, does not have sufficient clearance for two boats to pass. Make sure it is clear before you enter.

WALKING & CYCLING

There are excellent walks in the Marple area, where stunning scenery combines with the often unexpected remains of early industry. Gordon Mills has written an excellent series of six inexpensive guides for the local community council which take you on some of the finest walks this area has to offer: Marple Dale; The Roman Bridge & Lakes; Marple Locks & Brabyns Park; Chadkirk; From Way to Cut and Donkey Wood. No walk is longer than 4 miles, and each is fully described, with maps and old photographs. You can obtain them from Marple Library or local bookshops, and find details at: www.marple-uk.com/Guides.htm. Mr Mills is quite happy for you to download the walks, in exchange for a donation to the British Heart Foundation.

River Goyt is crossed, there is the superb spectacle of a major canal aqueduct with an even bigger railway viaduct alongside. West of here a narrow stretch was once Rose Hill Tunnel, long since opened out. The canal then traverses a wooded hillside before diving into Hyde Bank Tunnel, 308yds long. The towpath is diverted over the hill, passing a farm. On the other side, a couple of minor aqueducts lead the canal northwards, away from the Goyt Valley and past Romiley, Bredbury and Woodley, where there is a narrow 176yd-long tunnel, this time with the towpath continuing through it. There is a swimming pool close to the canal at bridge 14.

● **Marple**
Gt Manchester. All services. Once a famous hat-making centre, the town is most interesting by the canal. The town centre can be accessed from bridge 18.
● **Marple Locks**
The 16 locks at Marple were not built until 1804, four years after the rest of the navigation was opened. The 1-mile gap thus left was bridged by a tramway, while the Canal Company sought the cash to pay for the construction of a flight of locks. This was obviously a most unsatisfactory state of affairs, since the limestone from Doveholes had to be shifted from wagon to boat at Buxworth Basin, from boat to wagon at Marple Junction, and back into boat again at the bottom of the tramway. Not surprisingly, a container system was developed – using iron boxes with a 2-ton payload – to ease the triple transshipment. However, this was no long-term solution, and when the necessary £27,000 was forthcoming the company authorised construction of the flight of locks. Today they stand comparison with any flight on the network. Note especially Samuel Oldknow's superb warehouse, by lock 9, now tastefully converted to offices.
● **Marple Aqueduct**
Deservedly scheduled as an ancient monument, this three-arched aqueduct over the River Goyt is a very fine structure, in an exquisite setting almost 100ft above the river. Designed by Benjamin Outram, its construction utilises circular pierced shoulders above each arch to reduce the weight of the rubble filling whilst providing a decorative feature. Contrast and interest are further added by the use of two different colours of gritstone in the parapets and ledges.
● **Romiley**
Gt Manchester. All services. A useful place for supplies.

Boatyards

ⓑ **British Waterways Marple Yard** Marple Junction, on the Macclesfield Canal (0161 427 1079). Overnight mooring.

Pubs and Restaurants

● ✕ **Ring O'Bells** 130 Church Lane, Marple (0161 427 2300; www.marple-uk.com/ringobells). By bridge 2. A very comfortable and friendly traditional pub serving real ale and good freshly prepared bar and à la carte meals (V) *L and E (not Mon)*. Chef's specials include lamb Henry, crepes Marango and steak & ale pie. Children welcome *until 19.30*. Garden and canalside patio. Charity quiz night *third Wed in month*.
● **Pineapple Inn** 45 Market Street, Marple (0161 427 3935). Walk towards the town centre from bridge 2. A friendly locals' pub serving real ale. Children are welcome *until 19.00*, and there is a garden.
● ✕ **Navigation Hotel** By lock 13, Stockport Road, Marple (0161 427 2270). Useful for 'lock wheelers' (remember, there is no mooring on the flight!). A large comfortable pub serving real ale. Food (V) *L and E, daily*.

Children welcome, and there is seating outside in the courtyard. A singer performs on *Thur*.
● **Duke of York Hotel** 250yds east of bridge 14, Stockport Road, Romiley (0161 430 2806, duke.of.york@quista.net). A choice of real ale in an unspoilt 18th-C pub. Food (V) is served *L and E, daily*. Children are welcome, and there is outside seating.
✕ **Bridge Café** Stockport Road, Romiley (0161 430 5937). Moor north of bridge 14. A friendly and welcoming café decorated in canal style and with a pretty garden to the rear, offering reasonably priced, authentic, home-made food (V) (and you can bring your own wine). Fresh vegetables, Scotch salmon, hams and turkeys roasted on the premises. *Open Mon–Fri 9.00–15.00, gourmet evenings for group bookings only (minimum 12)*. Swimming pool adjacent and shops and services close by.

Hyde

The canal continues northward through a landscape which becomes less rural, but increasingly interesting. Bridge 6 is a pretty roving bridge, grown wider over the years. To the north, beyond the M62 motorway, the industrial tentacles of Hyde – Greater Manchester – ensnare the canal traveller. The approach to Dukinfield Junction and Portland Basin is very pleasant. The towpath is tidy, with plenty of grass, trees and seats. A Llangollen-type lift bridge, an aqueduct over the River Tame and a stone roving bridge provide plenty of canal interest. Portland Basin was constructed to allow boats to make the sharp turn here, and was nicknamed the 'weavers rest', since so many weavers had reputedly drowned themselves here during hard times, such as the famine of 1860 and the depression of the 1930s. The warehouse which faces you across the junction, built in 1834, has been restored as a canal heritage centre and museum, and is well worth visiting. Heading off to the south west, the Ashton Canal takes you into Manchester proper: this is a fine, solid industrial section of waterway, with steaming factories, tall chimneys and a good clear towpath. To the east is the Huddersfield Narrow Canal, which now, newly restored, once again crosses the Pennines to Huddersfield (*see* page 53). If you pass Dukinfield Junction during *July*, you may see the colourful Ashton Canals Festival, which has been running successfully for over 10 years now. Portland Basin is a recommended mooring place for those on the Cheshire Ring.

Ashton–under–Lyne
Gt Manchester. All services. Walk north west from Portland Basin and you will find the church of St Michael, which was begun by Sir John de Assheton in the early 15th C and completed by his great grandson before 1516. The church is large, with a tall west tower rebuilt by Crowther in 1886–8. Particularly notable is the stained glass, depicting the Life of St Helena and dating from the 15th–16th C. A market was granted to the town in 1284, but by 1801 the population still numbered only 4800. It then expanded rapidly, due to the growth of cotton weaving in the area, and by 1851 totalled over 30,000.

Portland Basin Social & Industrial History Museum Heritage Wharf, Ashton-under-Lyne (0161 343 2878; www.tameside.gov.uk/museumsandgalleries/portlandbasin.htm). This museum is housed in a superb reconstruction of a canal warehouse dating from 1834, at the junction of the Ashton, Peak Forest and Huddersfield canals. It tells the rich story of Tameside's social, political and industrial history, drawing upon many different facets of local life. The museum features a 1920s street, working models, computer interactives, sound and film. The original waterwheel is restored to working order on the wharfside. Displays include topics such as glassmaking, textiles, hatting, printing, canals, coalmining, Chartism, education and politics. *Open all year, Tue–Sun and B Hols 10.00–17.00.* Free. Shop, café.

Astley Cheetham Art Gallery Trinity Street, Stalybridge (0161 343 2878; www.tameside.gov.uk/museumsandgalleries/astleycheetham.html). Above Stalybridge Library, this gallery was built as a gift to the town in 1901. Exhibition programme of sculpture, textiles, painting and drawings, featuring work by prominent local artists and community groups. *Open Mon–Wed and Fri 10.00–12.30 and 13.00–17.00, Sat 09.00–12.30 and 13.00–17.00 (closed Thur and Sun).* Free.

WALKING & CYCLING
Pasture and fine woodland are a feature of Haughton Dale Nature Reserve, to the west of the canal near Hyde. Paths follow the River Tame here. Details from: Park Bridge Heritage Centre, The Stable, Park Bridge, Ashton-under-Lyne (0161 330 9613; john.jones@nxcorp1.tameside.gov.uk). *Open daily.*

Boatyards

Ⓑ **Portland Basin Marina** Alma Street, Dukinfield (0161 330 3133) 🚿 🚽 ⚓ D Pump out, gas, overnight and long-term mooring, winter storage, crane, 100-year-old dry dock, boat building and fitting, engine repairs, chandlery, toilets, showers, books and maps, gifts, solid fuel, DIY facilities. Laundrette and supermarket close-by. *Emergency call out.*

Map labels:

ASHTON-UNDER-LYNE
Portland Basin / Dukinfield Junction
29 Footbridge
Asda Tunnel 166yds
30
29 Footbridge
Walk Mill Bridge 28
Marple Junction 8m 16L
Jeremy Brook Bridge 27
1 Lift Bridge
Pipe Bridge
155
2 Ashton Street Bridge
3 Dukinfield Hall Bridge
Newton Wood
Dunkirk Farm
4 Newton Hall Bridge
Flowery Field
2
M67 Bridge
Kingston
6
3
HYDE
Hyde Central Station
Footbridge
Pipe Bridge
Captain Clarkes Bridge
8 Footbridge
Apethorne Aqueduct
Footbridge
Haughton Green
Recn Gd
150
10
Haugh Dale

111 Whitelands Bridge
110 Minerva Road Bridge
Ashton Lock 1W
Wellington Mill Bridge
Cockbrook
Clarence Street Bridge
STA
108
107
106
STALYBRIDGE
Texas Street Bridge
Plantation Lock 2W
Tame Lock 3W
Caroline Street 102 Bridge
4W 5W
Pipe Bridge
Cemetery
Tame Aqueduct 105
Hydes
103 Bayley Bridge
104 Peel Street Bridge
53

Pubs and Restaurants

Cheshire Ring Hotel Manchester Road, Hyde (0161 368 1826). A few yards east of bridge 6. A friendly family pub, the oldest pub in Hyde, and handy for snacks and sandwiches *L*. Children are welcome *until 20.30. Shops and station nearby.*

Globe Hotel Globe Square, Dukinfield (0161 330 5561). By bridge 2. A comfortable and friendly family-run hotel with satellite TV and serving real ale. Food in the steak restaurant (V) *L and E, daily.* Children welcome. Patio seating. Quiz *Thur.* B & B.

Feathers 62 High Street, Stalybridge (0161 338 6403). A corner local serving real ale. Children are welcome *until 18.30.* Various artistes perform *each Fri.* There is a useful fish & chip shop next door.

Café on the Wharf Welbeck Street, Ashton-under-Lyne (0161 330 9315; www.tameside.gov.uk/tmbc2/cafeonwharf.htm). By Portland Basin. Soup, snacks and starters, baguettes and daily specials, cakes and pastries. *Open Tue–Fri 10.30–16.30, Sat and Sun 11.00–16.30.*

Station Buffet Platform One, Stalybridge Station, Market Street (0161 303 0007). A very fine refurbishment of the Victorian buffet, incorporating the stationmaster's house and ladies waiting room. Having won many awards, it now serves real ale from a variety of breweries, along with real cider and bottled Belgian beers. Excellent food (V) is served all day, and children are welcome. *Opens 09.30 for coffee.* A short walk north of the canal.

Wharf Tavern Caroline Street, Stalybridge (0161 338 2662). Bar snacks are served in this friendly pub, which has had the same landlord since 1947. Large patio leading down to the canal.

BOAT TRIPS
Huddersfield Canal Society *Stillwaters* is a 46-seater which operates from Portland Basin all year round for party bookings. Public trips (*30 mins*) at the weekend *between 11.00–17.00.* Telephone 0161 339 1332 for details, or visit: www.hcanals.demon.co.uk.

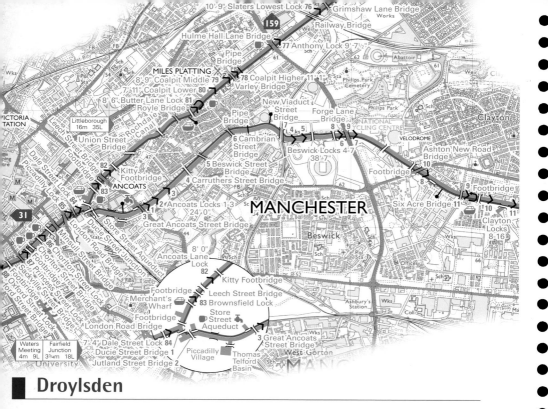

Droylsden

From start to finish, the Ashton Canal passes through a densely built-up area in which the canal is conspicuous as a welcome relief from the townscape which flanks it. Its clear water, excellent towpath, functional but dignified old bridges and the peace that generally surrounds it make it a haven for local school children, anglers, walkers and idlers, indeed for anyone who enjoys an environment that is quite separate from and unrelated to ordinary daily life. The rare pleasure, afforded only by an English canal, of stepping out of a city suburb into the peaceful and unpretentious atmosphere of the 18th C is once again, with continued restoration work, becoming available to all. At Fairfield Junction the top lock of the 18 which climb from Ducie Street Junction is encountered. It is a picturesque canal scene here with traditional buildings, including a shed dated 1833 standing over a canal arm, giving the area a quiet dignity. Descending the locks, you may wish to look out for the remains of several old canal arms: one of the more important was the 5-mile Stockport Branch, leaving from Clayton Junction, just below lock 11. The canal then falls through the remaining locks into Manchester. The surroundings are brightened by the well-cared-for Beswick flight of four locks, standing next to the new Stadium. There are moorings, and a sanitary station by locks 1 and 2 on the Ashton Canal. Large-scale redevelopment has been completed at Paradise Wharf and Piccadilly Village, making this final stretch unusually gentrified, with smart flats, basins and a crane. The Rochdale Canal stretches for 33 miles over the Pennines from Manchester to Sowerby Bridge from Ducie Street Junction to join the Calder & Hebble Navigation, and is once again open to through navigation (*see page 157*) after many years of campaigning. The bottom mile or so of the canal remained navigable, from the junction with the Ashton Canal at Ducie Street down to Castlefield and its meeting with the Bridgewater Canal, and provided a vital link between the Bridgewater and Ashton Canals in the 100-mile Cheshire Ring cruising route.

NAVIGATIONAL NOTES

1 You will need a handcuff lock key for the locks on this and the Peak Forest Canal.
2 Moor only at recognised sites in this area, and do not offer anyone you do not know a ride on your boat.
3 Bridge 21 is very low.
4 Passage through locks 1–18 should be commenced *before 10.00*.

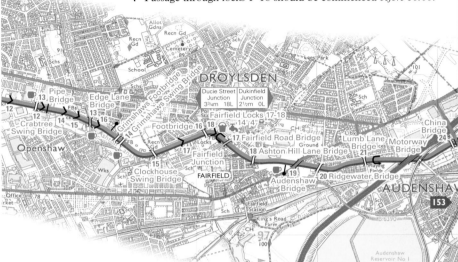

THE CHESHIRE RING – THEN AND NOW

This route has remained one of the most popular cruising circuits for many years now – a one-week trip encompassing parts of the Trent & Mersey, the Bridgewater, the Ashton, the Peak Forest and Macclesfield canals, passing through a wide and exciting variety of canalscape. Part of the journey includes a passage through central Manchester, a pleasant experience these days, but it was not always so . . .

The problem used to be timing your passage through the city so that the 'Rochdale Nine' locks were open, and your subsequent overnight mooring was a safe one! Local children preyed upon you as you tackled the Ancoats, Beswick and Clayton flights, leaping across the locks from one side to the other, begging lifts, and 'picking up' *anything* you might have left lying around . . .

The lock machinery was stiff, water supply uncertain, and the things which fouled your propeller defied description . . .

It is, thankfully, VERY different now, and the city passage is very attractive, interesting and enjoyable. Just take the usual precautions.

Pubs and Restaurants

Strawberry Duck Crabtree Lane, Clayton (0161 223 4415). Canalside at lock 13. A comfortable and traditional two-room pub, over 100 years old, serving home-cooked food (V) *L*, and real ale. Children welcome *until 18.00*. Canalside garden. Entertainment *weekends and Wed*.

Jolly Angler Ducie Street, Manchester (0161 236 5307). Near the junction. A small, plain and very friendly pub visited every few months by Mike Harding, the folk singer, and offering real ale and snacks *at all times* (or you can eat your own sandwiches!). Café nearby. Regular Irish music sessions *Thur and Sat*, folk on *Sun* and ad hoc sessions whenever enough customers are willing. Children welcome. Moorings nearby, but don't leave your boat here overnight.

● **Fairfield**

PO, tel stores. Gt Manchester. Immediately south of Fairfield Junction is a group of neat and tidy buildings around a fine chapel. This is an original Moravian settlement, established in 1785 by Benjamin Latrobe and consisting of tidy rows of cottages built in brick, intended to house the members of a self-contained community.

Velodrome Stuart Street, Manchester (0161 223 2244; www.manchestervelodrome.com). Access from the new bridge, west of bridge 9, and in view from bridge 8, when climbing the locks. This is the National Cycling Centre, where the track is widely regarded as one of the finest and fastest in the world. There is a full programme of exciting cycle races staged in this magnificent stadium, which recently hosted the track events of the Commonwealth Games 2002. *See also* Walking & Cycling.

● **Manchester**

All services. One of Britain's finest Victorian cities, a monument to 19th-C commerce and the textile boom, its size increasing remorselessly with the building of the canals, and later railways. Unfortunately virtually no early buildings survived the city's rapid growth, although there is an incredible wealth of Victorian architecture surviving, in spite of redevelopment. The town hall and surrounding streets are a particularly rich area. St Peter's Square, by the town hall, was the site of the 'Peterloo Massacre' in 1819, when a meeting demanding political reform was brutally dispersed by troops carrying drawn sabres. Eleven people were killed and many more were injured. The Free Trade Hall, once the home of the Hallé Orchestra, is a little further along the road. Built in 1856, it was badly damaged in World War II, but was subsequently re-built to its original Palladian design. There is theatre, ballet and cinema, art galleries, and a wealth of interesting buildings, Victorian shopping arcades, many pubs with a choice of good beer and a variety of restaurants just a short walk from the canal. Sporting facilities are excellent, partly as a consequence of Manchester being the venue for the 2002 Commonwealth Games. The new developments at Salford Quays, on the Manchester Ship Canal, are quite breathtaking.

Tourist Information Centre Town Hall Extension, Lloyd Street, St Peter's Square, Manchester (0161 234 3157; www.manchester.gov.uk). To the north of Oxford Street Bridge. *Open 10.00–17.30 (Sun and B Hols 16.30).*

WALKING & CYCLING

Keen cyclists might like to visit the magnificent Velodrome (*see* above) for a 'Taster Session' where, for a very modest fee, you can hire a track bike and a helmet and ride the steeply banked circuit for an hour. Telephone 0161 223 2244 for details and times.

---

*Todmorden Locks (*see *page 166)*

ROCHDALE CANAL

Rochdale Canal Introduction

MAXIMUM DIMENSIONS
Length: 72'
Beam: 14' 2"
Headroom: 7' 6" (6' 6" under the M62 culvert)
Draught: 2' 6" (recommended by BW as some sections of the western side of the canal are only dredged to 3' 3")

MILEAGE
MANCHESTER to:
Failsworth: 5 miles
Castleton: 11½ miles
Littleborough: 16½ miles
Todmorden: 22 miles
Hebden Bridge: 26½ miles
SOWERBY BRIDGE: 32 miles

MANAGER
0161 819 5847;
enquiries.spring@britishwaterways.co.uk

There is an excellent set of Navigational Notes available from British Watereways which should be studied carefully before navigating this canal.

The Rochdale Canal is one of three Pennine canal crossings. It was authorised by an Act of Parliament in 1794 and completed exactly ten years later. With wide locks it was able to handle barges, Humber keels and even small coasters, the latter sometimes trading between the Continent and Irish ports, using the River Mersey and the Irwell Navigation at the eastern end. However, the Achilles' heel of the waterway lay in its requirement for a copious supply of water at the summit pound, together with the sheer physical effort required to operate the three locks per mile that are averaged over the canal's relatively short length.

The boom years for the canal were in the 1820s and 1830s before the inevitable railway competition began to make an impression. Passenger carrying packet boats (Manchester to Rochdale: 13 miles and 41 locks in 7 hours) and fast, light-goods-carrying fly boats (20 tons transported from Manchester to Todmorden in 12 hours) were both successful enterprises in the early 1800s.

In 1887 the canal's fortunes appeared to take an upturn when the canal company bought its own boats. Traffic included cotton, grain, coal, wool, cement, salt and timber, and whilst end to end carriage steadily declined, shorter journeys continued to thrive. At the outbreak of World War I the canal company was still ordering new craft (powered by 25hp inverted compound steam engines) which were capable, loaded, of pulling a further two laden dumb barges. However, in 1921, as competition from the roads took its toll, the fleet ceased operation and traffic became spasmodic. The last loaded boat to trade over the canal's entire length was nb *Alice*, in April 1937, carrying 20 tons of wire from Manchester to Sowerby Bridge. The navigation was officially closed by an Act in 1952, except for the stretch connecting the Bridgewater and Ashton canals in Manchester. Restoration was commenced nearly 30 years ago and the canal society had not only succeeded in protecting nearly all its original line, but also re-opened 16 miles of the eastern end. It has also, in conjunction with the local authority-based Canal Trust, inspired the construction of Tuel Lane Lock and Tunnel.

Subsequently British Waterways and its partners have completed restoration at a cost of £23 million, rebuilding locks, bridges and tunnels and completing many new structures. This investment has only been possible because of projected benefits to the local community over a number of years, totalling in the region of £200 million.

Ancoats

Departing from Ducie Street Basin, the canal begins its unremitting climb into the Pennines flanked by the not unattractive, although somewhat unusual, stone-filled gabions. Attractively painted cast iron bridges (note how the colour scheme suddenly changes) regularly span the navigation as it heaves its way up past a series of abandoned, but still impressive, cotton mills. Moving steadily onwards and upwards the waterway is accompanied by a mix of urban housing, parkland and industry; the redeveloped Victoria Mill at Miles Platting is a most impressive example. Passing Newton Heath with its canalside *market* and handy *shops*, the canal soon reaches Failsworth where there is a collection of fine mill buildings, many now in their second or third incarnations. The section of the waterway west of the A62 bridge had been built over and part of a supermarket had to be demolished during restoration; the remaining portion together with a *PO, banks and a chemist* still lies to the north beside the new footbridge. Beyond Failsworth, and several more solid mill buildings, development starts to step back from the navigation as it enters a pleasantly tree-lined section. Between here and Littleborough, the line of the canal has been designated an SSSI in recognition of its importance as a site for certain rare aquatic plants, particularly floating water plantain (*Luronium natans*).

Boatyards

See Bridgewater Canal page 31.

Pubs and Restaurants

✕ **Cyberia** 12 Oxford Street, Manchester (0161 950 2233). City-centre internet café.
Try also **Internet Café** at Debenhams Market Street (0161 832 8666) and **Internet Exchange** in Coffee Republic 1–3 Piccadilly (0161 833 3111).

✕ **Kimberley's Café** Victoria Mill, Miles Platting, Manchester (0161 205 4768). *Open Mon–Fri 08.00–16.00.*

🍺 **Spanking Roger** Miles Platting, Manchester (0161 205 7627). Food

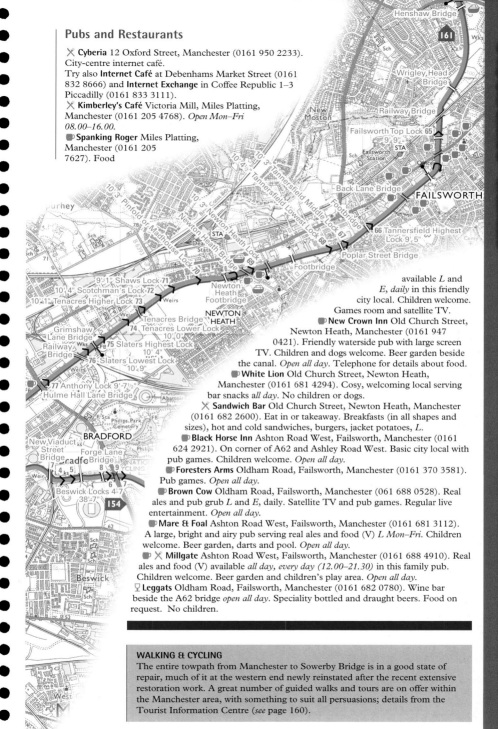

available *L* and *E*, *daily* in this friendly city local. Children welcome. Games room and satellite TV.

🍺 **New Crown Inn** Old Church Street, Newton Heath, Manchester (0161 947 0421). Friendly waterside pub with large screen TV. Children and dogs welcome. Beer garden beside the canal. *Open all day.* Telephone for details about food.

🍺 **White Lion** Old Church Street, Newton Heath, Manchester (0161 681 4294). Cosy, welcoming local serving bar snacks *all day*. No children or dogs.

✕ **Sandwich Bar** Old Church Street, Newton Heath, Manchester (0161 682 2600). Eat in or takeaway. Breakfasts (in all shapes and sizes), hot and cold sandwiches, burgers, jacket potatoes, *L*.

🍺 **Black Horse Inn** Ashton Road West, Failsworth, Manchester (0161 624 2921). On corner of A62 and Ashley Road West. Basic city local with pub games. Children welcome. *Open all day.*

🍺 **Foresters Arms** Oldham Road, Failsworth, Manchester (0161 370 3581). Pub games. *Open all day.*

🍺 **Brown Cow** Oldham Road, Failsworth, Manchester (061 688 0528). Real ales and pub grub *L* and *E*, daily. Satellite TV and pub games. Regular live entertainment. *Open all day.*

🍺 **Mare & Foal** Ashton Road West, Failsworth, Manchester (0161 681 3112). A large, bright and airy pub serving real ales and food (V) *L Mon–Fri*. Children welcome. Beer garden, darts and pool. *Open all day.*

🍺 ✕ **Millgate** Ashton Road West, Failsworth, Manchester (0161 688 4910). Real ales and food (V) available *all day, every day (12.00–21.30)* in this family pub. Children welcome. Beer garden and children's play area. *Open all day.*

🍷 **Leggats** Oldham Road, Failsworth, Manchester (0161 682 0780). Wine bar beside the A62 bridge *open all day*. Speciality bottled and draught beers. Food on request. No children.

WALKING & CYCLING

The entire towpath from Manchester to Sowerby Bridge is in a good state of repair, much of it at the western end newly reinstated after the recent extensive restoration work. A great number of guided walks and tours are on offer within the Manchester area, with something to suit all persuasions; details from the Tourist Information Centre (*see* page 160).

Manchester

All services. One of Britain's finest Victorian cities, a monument to 19th-C commerce and the textile boom, Manchester can trace its origins to the Roman fort of Manucium, built at Castlefield during the first century. *See* Bridgewater Canal page 31 for Central Manchester.

Bridgewater Hall Lower Mosley Street, Manchester (0161 950 0000; www.bridgewater-hall.co.uk). A visually striking hall – built beside the Rochdale Canal coal wharves and its junction with the Manchester & Salford Junction Canal (its name was almost as long as the waterway itself) – and home to the Hallé Orchestra and an impressive pipe organ. Telephone for programme details.

Gallery of Costume Platt Hall, Wilmslow Road, Rusholme, Manchester (0161 224 5217; www.manchestergalleries.org.uk). Housed in the Georgian mansion of a Manchester textile merchant, this is one of the largest collections of costume and accessories in Britain. The collection includes clothes worn from the 17th C to the present day, ranging from rare items, through the everyday dress of local working people to contemporary designer wear. Over 23,000 items are displayed on rotation. Shop. *Open Mar–Oct 10.00–17.00 and Nov–Feb 10.00–16.00. Open B Hol Mon.* Free.

Library Theatre Central Library, St Peter's Square, Manchester (0161 236 7110; www.libtheatreco.org.uk). Intimate theatre space in the basement of the Central Library. Telephone for programme details or visit their website.

Manchester Art Gallery Mosley Street, Manchester (0161 235 8888; www.manchester-galleries.org.uk). Outstanding collection of 19th-C Pre-Raphaelite paintings; works from 18th-C masters (Gainsborough, Reynolds and Stubbs); contemporary art and sculpture; fine examples of Dutch and Italian painting and an internationally renowned collection of decorative art (ceramics, metalwork, furniture and textiles). Also the Clore Interactive Gallery for 5–12 year olds and their families. Shop and Gallery Restaurant. *Open Tue–Sat 10.00–17.00 and B Hol Mon.* Free.

Manchester Museum University of Manchester, Oxford Road, Manchester (0161 275 2634; www.museum.man.ac.uk). Enjoying the fruits of a £19.5 million refurbishment, this university museum helps to uncover the mysteries of Ancient Egypt, discover the world of neotropical frogs, tease out the intricacies of the human body and encourage you to marvel at the dinosaurs and other prehistoric beasts. Stunning displays and interactive exhibits. Shop and café. *Open Mon–Sat 10.00–17.00, Sun and B Hols 11.00–16.00.* Free.

Bridge Street, Manchester (0161 839 6061; www.peopleshistorymuseum.org.uk). The extraordinary story of ordinary people: clock in at the factory; peer into the secret meeting room of the Tinplate Worker's Society; tremble at the scene from the Peterloo Massacre of 1819; remember the sounds of the 1960s and 1970s and a great deal more. Café and shop. *Open Tue–Sun 11.00–16.30.* Children free; adults charge (except Fri).

Royal Exchange Theatre St Ann's Square, Manchester (0161 833 9833). Theatre in-the-round set in the recently restored Royal Exchange Centre. Telephone for programme details.

Manchester Cathedral Cathedral Gardens, Manchester (0161 833 2220). Founded as a Chantry College in 1421, it became the cathedral for the newly formed diocese in 1847. 16th-C misericords render a humorous depiction of medieval life; carving in the choir stalls and canopies is exquisite as is the choir screen and the six bays that make up the nave, which are the widest of any church in England.

Urbis Cathedral Gardens, Manchester (0161 907 9099; www.urbis.org.uk). New interactive museum devoted to urban living, beginning with a sky glide in The Glass Elevator with the city as a backdrop, thence through four cascading themed 'involvements' entitled Arrive, Change, Order and Explore. *Open daily 10.00–18.00 (20.00 Sat).* Café (*open 11.00–17.00*) and shop. Charge. Last admission 1½ hours before closing.

Whitworth Art Gallery University of Manchester, Oxford Road, Manchester (0161 275 7450; www.whitworth.man.ac.uk). Home to internationally renowned collections of British watercolours, textiles and wallpapers. Also an impressive range of paintings, drawings, sculptures and prints. Exhibitions and events throughout the year. Gallery Bistro (0161 275 7497) serving drinks, home-made cakes and light lunches *Mon–Sat 10.00–16.30 and Sun 14.00–16.30*. Specialist art bookshop (0161 275 7498). Gallery *open Mon–Sat 10.00–17.00 and Sun 14.00–17.00.* Free.

Ancoats Mills Not far out of Ducie Street Basin the canal passes, on the off side, a collection of fine old cotton spinning mills. These are of national importance and include some of the earliest mills built in Manchester. Murray's Mills were constructed between 1798 and 1804 and Old Mill – built 1798 – is the city's oldest surviving mill and is of a non-fireproof design. Of slightly later construction is Sedgewick Mill (1818–20), while Paragon and Royal Mills were the last of a whole series of buildings on this site, being completed in 1912. They ceased production around 1960.

Tourist Information Centre Town Hall Extension, Lloyd Street, Manchester (0161 234 3157; www.manchester.gov.uk). *Open daily Mon–Sat 10.00–17.30, Sun & B Hol Mon 11.00–16.00.*

Newton Heath

Gt Manchester. PO, tel, stores, butcher, baker, bank, takeaway, station. A satellite to Failsworth, once engaged in cotton spinning and weaving and now a useful place to stop outside the city.

Failsworth

Gt Manchester. PO, tel, stores, banks, stores, garage, takeaways, station. Virtually the most southerly outpost of the cotton industry in Rochdale and close to the crescent-shaped Lancashire coalfield, exploited around Ashton-under-Lyne.

Slattocks

This stretch is a mix of industry and housing, with the navigation sometimes part buried in a leafy cutting. There is only one lock in this 3-mile stretch. Beyond Mills Hill there is an abrupt and welcome change as, on crossing the infant River Irk, the water-way bends around to confront a stone bridge and lock in a delightfully rural setting. As it gains height the navigation has partially looped back on itself and at Higher Boarshaw the locks are interspersed with two striking examples of the Manchester & Leeds Railway's bridges. Above the second bridge, as the waterway rounds a slight bend, the Pennines first come into full view and although still distant, herald the challenge yet to come – for which the compact flight of the six Slattocks Locks provides a telling overture!

- **Slattocks**
  Gt Manchester. PO, tel, stores, takeaway, garage. A long, narrow village. It is reputed to derive its name from a Northern-style amalgamation of the two words 'South Locks'.

Pubs and Restaurants

- **Boat and Horses** Broadway, Chadderton, Oldham (0161 681 2363). Busy pub serving real ale and food (V) *all day, every day 12.00–21.30.* Beer garden and outdoor play area.
- **Railway & Linnet** Grimshaw Lane, Chadderton, Oldham (0161 643 2047). Immediately west of Grimshaw Vertical Lift Bridge. Friendly local 'twixt canal and railway serving real ale.
- **Rose of Lancaster** 7 Haigh Lane, Chadderton, Oldham (0161 624 3031). Real ales. Food (V) *available all day, every day 12.00–21.30.* Children welcome. Beer garden and terraced seating overlooking the canal. Moorings.
- **Hopwood Arms** Rochdale Road, Middleton (01706 359807). Village pub at Slattocks Top Lock serving real ale and food *L and E.* Children welcome. Outside seating.
- ✕ **Village Pantry** Rochdale Road, Middleton (0161 643 2359). Close to the Hopwood Arms. Home bakery selling cakes, buns, muffins, bread, confectionery and sandwiches.

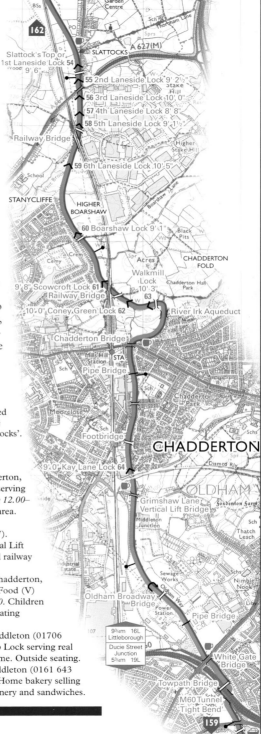

Rochdale

Above the locks there are fine open views as the waterway bends first towards the railway then swings back to duck under the motorway, in what was a road crossing over a farm lane. No provision was made for the canal, then derelict, when the M62 was constructed and to build one retrospectively, when the navigation was restored, would have been prohibitively expensive. The ingenious solution devised was to commandeer an existing culvert, divert the line of the waterway through it, relocate lock 53 south of the motorway to correct the levels, and provide an alternative approach to the farm. Above Castleton, the canal heads into Rochdale but skirts the town itself which used to be served by an arm below Moss Locks, now derelict. The main line maintains a discrete distance and retains its Pennine vistas, stretching out ahead in a wide arc. Passing through a shallow cutting in open moorland, the navigation arrives at the charming cluster of buildings at Clegg Hall: early 19th-C weavers' cottages, an old mill from the same era and the gaunt, blackened remains of the original hall peeping out from behind the trees. Beyond, the waterway negotiates a series of new bridges – replacing previous infilling – and passing Little Clegg, a chemical works and Smithy Bridge station, arrives in Littleborough accompanied by the railway

NAVIGATIONAL NOTES

1 The M62 culvert is only 14' 7" wide with a maximum draught of 3' 3" and an air draught of 7' 1". All craft should proceed with extreme caution.
2 The new section under the A627M is made up of new narrow channel, a passing place and a 121yd tunnel. As there are short sightlines throughout, boaters should proceed with caution. The channel and tunnel are only 16' 6" wide so wide boats must give way in the passing place between the two.
3 The new channel west of Well i'th Lane Bridge (approximately 1/2 mile east of the A627M Tunnel) is 20' wide but there is a tight curve at the eastern end. Care should be taken, especially by wide boats.

Pubs and Restaurants

There are plenty of pubs at Castleton, and an excellent selection of pubs and restaurants in Rochdale, so it is worth walking up into the town.

▪ **Blue Pits Inn** 842 Manchester Inn, Castleton (01706632151). Echoing the name of the nearby lock flight, this friendly pub serves real ale and once shared its cellar with the morgue. Pub games and open fires *in winter*.

▪ **Crown & Shuttle** 170 Rochdale Road, Milnrow (01706 648259). South east of Wallhead Bridge. A small upstairs military museum, three comfortable rooms downstairs and excellent real ale from the local JW Lees Brewery makes this friendly and traditional local well worth the walk. Outside seating, open fires *in winter* and pub games *all the year round. Open all day.*

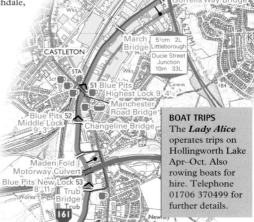

BOAT TRIPS
The *Lady Alice* operates trips on Hollingworth Lake Apr–Oct. Also rowing boats for hire. Telephone 01706 370499 for further details.

161

- **Castleton**
  Gt Manchester. PO, tel, stores, off-licence, takeaway, laundrette, station. A cotton-spinning town and once home to Tweedales & Smalley, a textile machinery manufacturer that specialised in the production of ring spinning machines. The works is now used by Woolworths as a distribution centre. The Arrow Mill, standing beside the canal with its somewhat truncated chimney, is a fine example of a cotton mill built in 1908.

- **Rochdale**
  Gt Manchester. All services. Home of the Co-operative Movement and birthplace of Gracie Fields, this is also another cotton-spinning town par excellance, although by the 18th C Rochdale was the flannel capital of Britain – a centre for the production of coarse and plain weave flannel. Lord Byron became Lord of the Manor of Rochdale in 1808 and, while residing at Hopwood Hall, Middleton, wrote a large part of *Childe Harolde*.

Esplanade Arts and Heritage Centre The Esplanade, Rochdale (01706 342154; www.rochdale.gov.uk). Borough art gallery and museum, extensive local collections and archives. *Open Tue–Sat 10.00–16.30, closed for lunch 13.00–14.00.*

Gracie Fields Theatre Hudson's Walk, Rochdale (01706 645522; www.rochdale.gov.uk).

Rochdale Pioneers Museum 31 Toad Lane, Rochdale (01706 524920; www.rochdale.gov.uk). The Rochdale Society of Equitable Pioneers held their first meeting here on 15 August 1844 and 31 Toad Lane went on to become the world's first viable Co-operative shop. *Open Tue–Sat 10.00–16.00 and Sun 14.00–16.00.*

St Chad's Parish Church Sparrow Hill, Rochdale (01706 645014). There has been a church overlooking the town, perched on this site, for over 1,000 years and parts of the present tower date back to Saxon times, although there have been several different buildings over the centuries. There is a striking Burne-Jones stained-glass window in the tower and further glass by William Morris. The town stocks, dating from 1688, are within the church curtilage.

Corgi Heritage Centre 53 York Street, Heywood, Rochdale (01706 365812; www.corgi-heritage. co.uk). The chance to discover the fascinating history of Corgi die-cast model vehicles from a manufacturer established before the World War II. Archive collections offer the visitor a long walk down memory lane. *Open Mon and Wed–Fri 09.00–17.30, Sat 09.00–17.00.* Free. On main bus route from Rochdale to Bury.

Tourist Information Centre The Clock Tower, Town Hall, Rochdale (01706 356592; www.rochdale.gov.uk). *Open Mon–Sat 10.00–16.00.* There is a 'Rochdale and Co-operation Town Trail' available from here.

- **Milnrow**
  Gt Manchester. PO, tel, stores, takeaway, station. Very much a centre for stone quarrying, open-cast and shaft mining, lying on the south east end of the crescent-shaped Lancashire coalfield. At Tunshill Farm there is a bank of old coking kilns and the remains of a fulling mill, with evidence of a paved pack-horse track and numerous local paths. Also six beehive coking ovens nearby.

Ellenroad Engine House Elizabethan Way, Milrow, Rochdale (01706 881952; www.ellenroad. org.uk). Home of the world's largest working steam mill engine and the Whitelees beam engine. The engine house is *open and in steam on 1st Sun in each month (except Jan) 12.00–16.00.* Charge. Regular bus service from Rochdale terminus and Newhey railway station is nearby.

Summit

Leaving Littleborough, the canal climbs steadily upwards past the strung-out Courtaulds factory, leaving the industrial chimneys of Rochdale far behind. The transition between sheltered valley bottom, with its compact, functional towns, and the open moorland that the waterway now heads towards, is fairly abrupt. Above West Summit Lock two contrasting, though striking features planted on the landscape are the Steanor Bottom Toll House (at the intersection of two roads to the west) and the 763yd span of the high-voltage line totally straddling the valley here. The typical moorland of the area is an acid peat overlying gritstone, poor draining and therefore agriculturally unproductive. At Longlees Lock the remote summit pound finishes. This was once the site of both a chemical and a brick works. Now reverted to coarse grasses, rushes and mosses, this section of the waterway is a haven to birdlife that can include meadow pipit, snipe, sandpiper, wheatear, dunlin, curlew and redshank. The descent into Todmorden is as scenically exhilarating as it is physically exhausting and the extended views, both in front and behind, steadily give way to the valley's intimacy.

● **Littleborough**
Lancs. All services. Laundrette. A bustling little town, busy with visitors in summer though, strangely, without a market. Opposite the solid stone parish church is the excellent Coach House Heritage Centre – a local initiative to provide tourist information established in a grade II listed building. Just round the corner, in Victoria Street, are a good butcher and baker.
Coach House Heritage Centre Lodge Street, Littleborough (01706 378481).

Winterbutlee Lock 30
36 Lightbank Bridge
9' 6" Lightbank Lock 31
37 Deanroyd Bridge
Sands Lock 32
9' 3"
38 Lane Bottom Bridge
Bottomley Lock 33
11' 0"
39 Stonehouse Bridge
40 Warland Bridge
Pipe Bridge
10' 1" Warland Lower Lock 34
41 Warland Gate Bridge
10' 1" Warland Upper Lock 35
Longlees Lock 36
12' 0"
Steanor Bottom Toll House
West Summit Lock
11' 8" 37
R1 Chelburn Bridge
1st Below West Summit Lock 9' 1" 38
2nd Below West Summit Lock 9' 3" 39
Punchbowl Lock 10' 5" 40
R2 Punchbowl Bridge
1st Below Punchbowl Lock 10' 7" 41
2nd Below Punchbowl Lock 10' 0" 42
Thickone Lock 10' 2" 43
Sladen Lock 10' 3" 44
R3 Sladen Bridge
Pike House Lock 10' 3" 45
R4 Pike House Bridge
R5 Bent House Bridge
Bent House Lock 9' 7" 46
R6 Windy Bank Bridge

15½m 47L
Sowerby Bridge

Ducie Street Junction
15½m 35L

Footbridge
Littleborough Higher Lock 9' 9" 47
R7 Durn Bridge
Ealees Footbridge R9
Littleborough Lower Lock 10' 1" 48
Ben Healey Bridge

LITTLEBOROUGH

Pipe Bridge
Pipe Bridge

SUMMIT

Open summer, Tue–Fri and Sun 14.00–17.00, Sat 11.00–17.00; winter closes at 16.30. Exhibits and gifts.

● **Summit**
Lancs. PO, tel, stores. Once a bustling woollen weaving community, the village has played an important part in three very different forms of transport. It sits beside the summit level of the canal, a place of sustenance to the thirsty boater and source of the much-needed water supply for locks descending east and west. The railway burrows underneath in a tunnel 2869yds long – the longest rail tunnel in the world when built in 1839. Some 23 million bricks were used in its construction. In 1984 a petroleum-carrying goods train caught fire and burnt uncontrollably in the tunnel for several weeks, smoke and flames belching from the ventilation shafts. It took £4 million and six months to re-open the tunnel to traffic.

Steanor Bottom Toll House Just to the north of the village and built in 1824 at the junction of the old and new routes to Littleborough, this is considered to be the finest example of a turn-pike toll house in England.

● **Walsden**
W. Yorks. PO, tel, stores, garage, takeaways, station. Meaning 'Valley of the Welsh' this textile village, just outside Todmorden, offers the boater all the important forms of sustenance.

Pubs and Restaurants

🍺 **Wheatsheaf** Church Street, Littleborough (01706 377695). A comfortable, family pub serving bar food (V) *L daily*, and real ale. Children and dogs welcome. Garden. Disco *Fri.*

🍺 **Royal Oak** Littleborough (01706 371346). Small town pub serving real ales. Children welcome. Outside seating. Karaoke *Fri.* Darts and pool.

✗ **Coach House Coffee Shop** Lodge Street, Littleborough (01706 378481). Inexpensive home-made snacks and cakes, teas and coffees served in this friendly annexe to the Heritage Centre. *Open Tue–Sat 10.30–16.30.*

🍺 **Falcon Inn** Littleborough (01706 378640). Bar meals (V) are available *Fri and Sat L* and traditional *Sunday* lunch *is served 12.00–18.00* in this mid-17th-C coaching inn which is now a large, comfortably furnished, family pub with disco on *Fri* and folk group on *Tue*; karaoke *Sat and Sun.* Pool and big screen TV.

🍺 **Red Lion Hotel** 6 Halifax Road, Littleborough (01706 378195). Once a farmhouse, this very traditional old pub has been licensed since the 18th C to dispense a wide selection of regular and guest real ales. Also an excellent range of Belgian bottled beers and foreign ales – both bottled and on draught, and real cider. Pub games, open fires *in winter* and no machines. Non-smoking area. Live music *Sun.* Camping. *Open all day (from 15.00 Mon–Thur).*

🍺 **Waterside Inn** 1 Inghams Lane, Littleborough (01706 376250). Small, friendly public house sitting above the newly opened waterway. Canalside seating. B & B.

🍺 ✗ **Summit Inn** Summit (01706 378011). Canalside at West Summit Lock 37. Real ale and a wide range of interesting à la carte and bar food (generous portions) (V) *available L and E (no food Mon or Tue). Sunday* carvery. Children welcome, garden. Quiz *Thur*; live music *Fri.* Pub games. Telephone for details of special, pre-booked, ethnic menus.

🍺 ✗ **Bird i'th Hand** (01706 378145). Between Walsden and Summit, near Warland Upper Lock 35. Food-orientated establishment offering anything from snacks to a gourmet meal (V) *L and E, daily* in a warm, cosy three-roomed pub. Dating from 1823, this coaching house (once owned by a pigeon fancier) now serves real ale. Children welcome, and quiz *Wed.*

🍺 ✗ **Waggon and Horses** Rochdale Road, Walsden (01706 813318). A pub that welcomes boaters and families with an extremely inexpensive menu (V) served *L and E (no food Mon)*. The landlord operates an excellent *lending and exchanging library:* ideal for the boater stranded in a low pound!

🍺 **Border Rose** Rochdale Road, Walsden (01706 812142). Busy, upmarket pub and restaurant serving a wide range of home-made food (V) *L and E Mon–Thur and all day Fri–Sun.* Also real ale. Children welcome. Beer garden and aviary with cockatiels.

🍺 **Cross Keys Inn** Walsden (01706 815185). A homely, welcoming establishment serving a wide range of real ale together with traditional, home-cooked food (V) *L and E and all day Sun.* Children welcome: dogs welcome when food is not being served. Canalside patio and moorings. B & B. *Open all day.*

✗ **Grandma Pollard's Fish & Chips and Home-made Pies** Rochdale Road, Walsden (01706 815769). Something of an institution in the area, this is a chippy and pie provider of great character. *Open Mon and Tue 09.00–15.30 and Wed–Fri 09.00–20.00.* Grandma pleads exhaustion as her excuse for remaining *closed over the weekend*!

🍺 ✗ **Hollins Inn** Walsden (01706 815843). 70yds from Hollins Lock. Comfortable, family pub resurrected from the ashes of the original which burnt down in 1978. Recently refurbished, it now extends a warm welcome to all canal users and offers a variety of real ales. The ghost of a previous licensee is reputed to cause disarray by moving glasses and bottles around on the shelves. However, an excellent selection of reasonably priced à la carte and bar food (V) is still *available L and E (until 20.00 but not Mon E).* Home-made steak and ale pie a speciality. Children welcome *until 21.30,* as are dogs. Outside seating and bowling green.

Todmorden

Now the descent begins in earnest with 17 locks in less than 3 miles and a spectacular railway crossing for good measure. A sweeping bend leads the waterway into the town with an immense brick retaining wall of massive proportions running all the way around the outside. The 'Great Wall of Todmorden' supports the railway embankment at this point and estimates of the total number of bricks used put the figure at more than 4 million. Beyond the compact town of Todmorden the countryside initially opens out revealing the disused Cross Stone Church, perched high on hills to the north of the navigation. Its badly blackened stonework is a reminder of the concentration of local industry, both past and present. Lobb Mill has finally been re-built (and turned into luxury apartments) while opposite Callis Lock there is a useful, boater-friendly *coal merchant* selling just about everything that is combustible. The waterway is now tucked tightly under a steep hillside covered by ancient deciduous woodland as the canal hugs the narrow valley bottom, interspersed, on the towpath side, with textile mills and dyeworks. The navigation approaches Hebden Bridge descending Stubbing (meaning a cleared

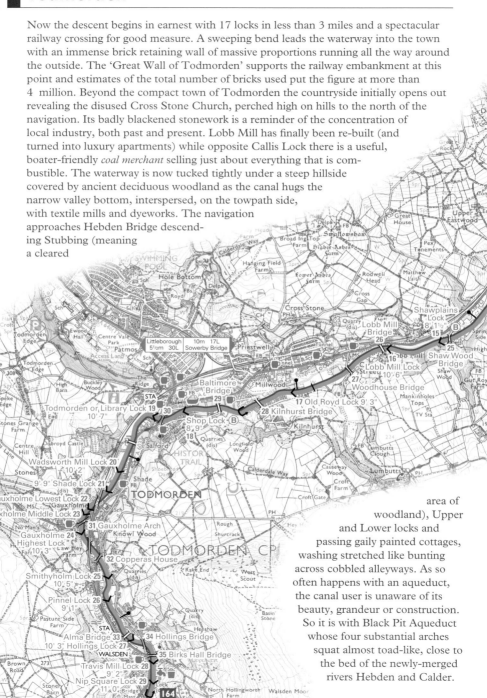

area of woodland), Upper and Lower locks and passing gaily painted cottages, washing stretched like bunting across cobbled alleyways. As so often happens with an aqueduct, the canal user is unaware of its beauty, grandeur or construction. So it is with Black Pit Aqueduct whose four substantial arches squat almost toad-like, close to the bed of the newly-merged rivers Hebden and Calder.

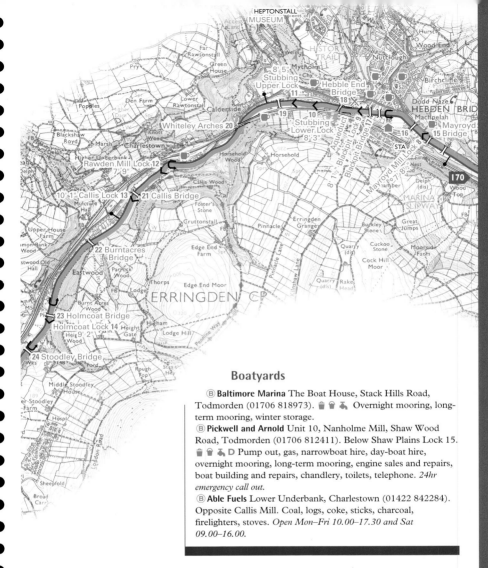

Boatyards

ⓑ **Baltimore Marina** The Boat House, Stack Hills Road, Todmorden (01706 818973). 🚽 💧 ⛽ Overnight mooring, long-term mooring, winter storage.

ⓑ **Pickwell and Arnold** Unit 10, Nanholme Mill, Shaw Wood Road, Todmorden (01706 812411). Below Shaw Plains Lock 15. 🚽 💧 ⛽ D Pump out, gas, narrowboat hire, day-boat hire, overnight mooring, long-term mooring, engine sales and repairs, boat building and repairs, chandlery, toilets, telephone. *24hr emergency call out.*

ⓑ **Able Fuels** Lower Underbank, Charlestown (01422 842284). Opposite Callis Mill. Coal, logs, coke, sticks, charcoal, firelighters, stoves. *Open Mon–Fri 10.00–17.30 and Sat 09.00–16.00.*

CHARLESTOWN RAILWAY DISASTER

In 1912 there was a serious derailment on the Charlestown curve when the 14.25 Manchester to Leeds express left the track, having effectively shattered the alignment of the rails at this point. The accident, involving a 2-4-2 radial tank engine, occurred on the stretch of line just before the railway crosses the canal on Whiteley Arches. The inspector, Colonel Druit, found at the subsequent enquiry that while the 45mph line speed at this point was suitable for normal express running, it was too high for tank engines of this type. Indeed, he went on to question the suitability of tank engines per se – with their high centre of gravity and inherent instability – for sustained high-speed traction. The derailed locomotive, together with all its carriages, toppled down the embankment, coming to rest strewn across the grounds of the old Woodman Inn.

● **Todmorden**

W. Yorks. All services. Laundrette. 19th-C manufacturing success led to the concentration of wealth in the pockets of a few individuals whose ostentation was often manifested locally in civic and domestic architecture. Todmorden is fortunate, indeed, to have benefited greatly from the philanthropy of the Fielden family, whose legacy of good taste in buildings represents a feast in stone. Their choice of architect, in John Gibson of London, proved most successful. His work both echoes the solid vernacular building from a previous era, while introducing a further wealth of styles, which in turn complement the fine stone railway viaduct that dominates the town's centre. Simple classical building sits side by side with the richly ornate, a striking example of the latter being the elaborately pedimented town hall. Originally built astride the county boundary (moved in a later reorganisation) between Lancashire and Yorkshire, this Italian Renaissance style building is fronted by six sturdy pillars, surmounted by statuary depicting, on the one half, the agriculture and engineering of Yorkshire, while on the other various facets of cotton spinning in Lancashire. In contrast the Unitarian Church, erected by Joshua and Samuel Fielden, again to a design by Gibson, is pure Victorian Gothic revival and a fitting memorial to their father, John Fielden MP. His concern for his fellow man extended to Westminster and industrial reform, being largely responsible for the Ten Hours Act of 1847 which limited the maximum working day to ten hours for any person under 18 and any woman over 18.

Craft Centre Lever Street, Todmorden (01706 818170). Small family-run centre: stalls, workshops and a tearoom.

Free Library Rochdale Road, Todmorden. Typifies the many individual buildings in the town displaying the skills of the stone mason in conjunction with the philanthropy of local benefactors. The library was a gift from the local Co-operative Society in 1897 and its asymmetry is pleasing in a simple way. It gives a second name to Todmorden Lock beside it, namely Library Lock.

Hippodrome Theatre Halifax Road, Todmorden (01706 814875). A striking building of its period, recently refurbished, though seemingly under-used.

St Mary's Church Rochdale Road, Todmorden. Built on land given to the town c. 1476 it still retains its 15th-C tower. Subsequently much altered, the present Gothic Revival chancel bears little relationship to the original, although it contains a pleasing carved oak screen and attractive stained-glass windows.

Stoodley Pike The original monument was erected in 1815 to commemorate the end of the Napoleonic Wars. However, weakened by lightning, it collapsed 40 years later and was replaced by the present 120ft high structure. Visible from the canal, as you approach the town, it makes the object of a bracing walk, rewarded by stunning views across Calderdale.

Tourist Information Centre 15 Burnley Road, Todmorden (01706 818181; todmorden@ytbtic.co.uk). *Open Easter–mid Sep daily 10.00–16.30 (16.00 Sat and Sun). Winter Mon–Fri 10.00–16.00; Sat and Sun 11.00–15.00.*

ON YOUR TOD

It is said that the only man-made feature distinguishable on the Earth, when viewed from the moon, is the Great Wall of China. Clearly this must be due to its length rather than its – relatively speaking – minuscule width. For a guard detachment, patrolling some of its more remote lengths, it must have been a singularly lonely and, in some cases, solitary occupation. The 'Great Wall of Tod' – the name given to the canalside railway retaining wall before Library Lock – is unlikely to hold quite such long-standing historical significance. Nor will it become a talking point amongst future lunar cosmonauts. Owing its existence to the less than prosaic function of keeping 'railway out of t'cut' it still remains, nonetheless, one of the wonders of a more local world. Building with brick in the Calder Valley, rather than the local gritstone, was largely down to the advent of the railway: a phenomenon repeated throughout many other areas of the country.

Pubs and Restaurants

🍺 **Mason's Arms** 1 Bacup Road, Gauxholme (01706 812180). Close to bridge 31. Almost lost under the railway arches, this quaint drinkers' pub dispenses four real ales – two regulars and two rotating guests: local breweries are always well represented. They describe themselves as a 'nice locals' drinking hole serving good quality beer and make reference to the three distinctive tables that have always inhabited the tap room, and were reputed to have been mortuary slabs – *whilst in their present location.* Children welcome *until 20.00;* dogs without restriction. Beer garden with lovely views. Pool, darts, open fires and no machines. *Open all day (from 15.00 Sun–Thur in winter).* Useful *PO and stores* through railway viaduct and turn left.

🍺 **Fox and Goose** 9 Heptonstall Road, Hebden Bridge (01422 842649). A serious beer drinker's pub dispensing an excellent (and ever-changing) selection of real ales. A 'conversational establishment' eschewing theme nights. They also serve German and Czech bottled beers and at least 30 malt whiskies. Outside seating. Traditional pub games.

✗ 🍷**Canal Cafe** 9 Pebble End, Hebden Bridge (01484 845065). Teas, coffees and large portions of appetising home-made fare (cakes, snacks and meals) at very reasonable prices. Beers, wines and ciders. Children welcome (accompanied by an adult if under 14); dogs outside only. Canalside seating. Gifts. *Open daily Easter–Oct; winter weekends and B Hols all year. Late opening in summer.*

🍺 ✗ **Stubbing Wharf** King Street, Hebden Bridge (01422 844107). A range of regular and guest real ales together with real cider dispensed in a comfortable, family pub beside the canal. A wide selection of inexpensive food (V) served in the bar and no smoking dining room and story-telling *last Fri in the month.* Outside courtyard seating. Open fires; no machines and pub games (including pool). Moorings.

🍺 ✗ **Rose and Crown** Todmorden (01706 812428). Opposite Woodhouse Bridge. A

squat stone building, originally three cottages built in the late 18th C, entered through a pair of delightful stained-glass doors. This is an original pub with all the traditional trappings serving a selection of real ale together with excellent meals available (V) *L and E, daily.* Children welcome. Outside seating. Quiz *Wed;* darts *Thur.*

🍺 **Shannon and Chesapeake** 257 Halifax Road, Todmorden (01706 813386). North of canal, between bridges 27 and 28. A small pub with a friendly atmosphere – always with something going on *at the weekends* – serving real ale. Breakfast *Sun 11.00–14.00.* Children and dogs welcome without restriction. Small garden at the rear. Pool.

🍺 **Rope and Anchor** Halifax Road, Todmorden (01706 816054). North of canal, near bridge 29. Real ale and food (V) available *L and E Mon–Sat and all day Sun.* Children welcome. Pub games. *PO, butcher, grocer and two takeaways opposite.*

🍺 **Bramsche Continental Bar** Rochdale Road, Todmorden (01706 815117). Close to bridge 30. Bearing the name of Todmorden's twin town, this bar not only serves a wide range of continental lagers and fruit beers but also dispenses a selection of real ales. Children welcome. Interesting selection of spirits but no ghosts!

🍺 **Golden Lion** Rochdale Road, Todmorden (01706 813532). Close to bridge 30. Variously post office, armoury and drawing office for Stoodley Pike, this 300-year-old coaching house now concentrates on serving real ales and bar food (*always available*). Children welcome. Outside seating. Quiz *Wed.*

🍺 **White Hart** Station Road, Todmorden (01706 812198). Imposing mock-Tudor building replacing the 1728 original that once housed the local court. Market place and focal point of the town's development, it now dispenses real ale and food (V) *L Wed–Mon.* Children welcome; outside seating. Quiz *Wed;* disco *Thur and Fri.* Pool and pub games.

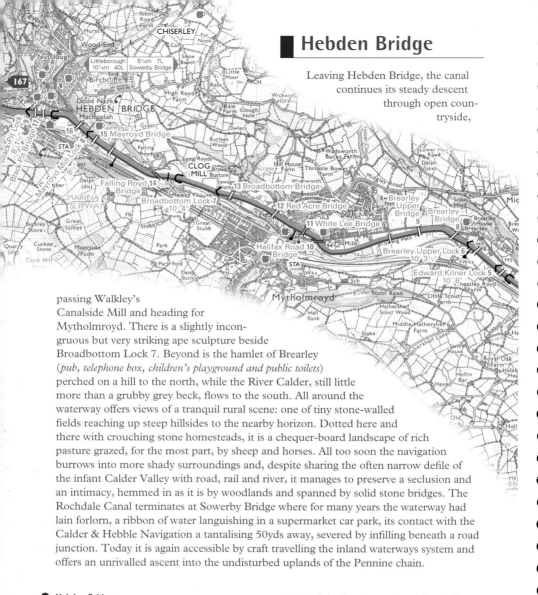

Hebden Bridge

Leaving Hebden Bridge, the canal continues its steady descent through open countryside,

passing Walkley's Canalside Mill and heading for Mytholmroyd. There is a slightly incongruous but very striking ape sculpture beside Broadbottom Lock 7. Beyond is the hamlet of Brearley (*pub, telephone box, children's playground and public toilets*) perched on a hill to the north, while the River Calder, still little more than a grubby grey beck, flows to the south. All around the waterway offers views of a tranquil rural scene: one of tiny stone-walled fields reaching up steep hillsides to the nearby horizon. Dotted here and there with crouching stone homesteads, it is a chequer-board landscape of rich pasture grazed, for the most part, by sheep and horses. All too soon the navigation burrows into more shady surroundings and, despite sharing the often narrow defile of the infant Calder Valley with road, rail and river, it manages to preserve a seclusion and an intimacy, hemmed in as it is by woodlands and spanned by solid stone bridges. The Rochdale Canal terminates at Sowerby Bridge where for many years the waterway had lain forlorn, a ribbon of water languishing in a supermarket car car park, its contact with the Calder & Hebble Navigation a tantalising 50yds away, severed by infilling beneath a road junction. Today it is again accessible by craft travelling the inland waterways system and offers an unrivalled ascent into the undisturbed uplands of the Pennine chain.

● Hebden Bridge

W. Yorks. All services. Developed as a settlement in late medieval times, providing both a meeting point of packhorse routes and a river crossing. However, it was not until the late 19th C, with the advent of steam power, the building of canal and railway, together with the mechanisation and centralisation of the textile industry, that the town attained its present size and character. Displaying a variety and delicacy of stonework – towers, turrets and pediments at every turn – houses and mills peel off from the market square to straggle haphazardly up steep hillsides. The first bridge to cross the River Hebden was wooden, dating from 1477 and replaced by the present stone packhorse bridge some 30 years later. This solid structure contrasts with the delicate ironwork of the cast iron Victorian road bridge, sited upstream beside the ornate council offices, which incorporate the original fire station. Double-decker housing and a diversity of religious non-conformism are also characteristic of this strikingly compact mill-town.

Hebden Bridge Alternative Technology Centre
Hebble End Mill, Hebden Bridge (01422
842121; www.alternativetechnology.org.uk).
Information line 08453 304930. Working
from a strong base within the local community,
this charitable organisation – in making
sustainability sustainable and simply
irresistible – aims to provide inspiration,
practical innovation, information and advice.
By setting a stimulating and exciting example,
it seeks to enable people to improve all
aspects of their lives and environment.
Permoculture garden, plastic pipe
recycling, 'renewables' and shop.
*Open daily Mon–Fri 10.00–
17.00; Sat 12.00–17.00 and
Sun 12.00–16.00. Extended
opening on B Hol week-
ends.*
**Walkley Canalside
Mill** Burnley
Road,

Hebden Bridge (01422 842061). Specialist
shopping and attractions. Restaurant. *Open
daily (except 25–26 Dec), Mon–Fri 10.00–
17.00, Sat, Sun and B Hols 10.00–17.30. Free.*
Hour Glass Art Studio Hebden Bridge (01422
846060; www.hourglass-studio-gallery.co.uk).
Contemporary art exhibitions; local original
art work; shop selling local jewellery, small
paintings and sculpture; educational art.
Open Wed–Sun 11.30–17.30.
Hardcastle Crags NT, Hollin Hall Office,
Hebden Bridge (01422 844518; yorkhc@
smtp.ntrust.org.uk). Large tract of Trust-
managed countryside, 1^1/2 miles north of
Hebden Bridge, easily accessible by bus.
Rich in natural history and famous as the
seat of the hairy wood ant. Regular events
and guided walks – telephone for details.
Open all year. Free.
Tourist Information Centre 1 Bridge Gate,
Hebden Bridge (01422 843831; www.calder.
gov.uk). *Open mid Mar–mid Oct Mon–Fri
09.30–17.30, Sat 10.15–17.00 and Sun 10.30–
17.00. Winter Mon–Fri 10.00–17.00, Sat and
Sun 10.30–16.15.*
Metro (0113 245 7676; www.wymetro.com).
Contact for all local travel information or a
selection of free timetables.

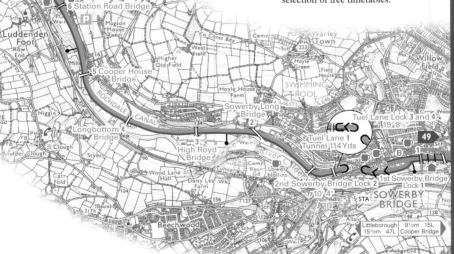

NAVIGATIONAL NOTES

Tuel Lane Lock is operated by a
resident lock keeper and passage will
only be permitted when the lock is
manned. Contact 0161 819 5847;
enquiries.spring@britishwaterways.
co.uk *for operating times.*

BOAT TRIPS
Calder Valley Cruising *Gracie Fields* and
Sarah Siddons provide a variety of
imaginative trips, some horse-drawn, all
the year round from Hebden Bridge.
Information centre and shop aboard
barge *Branwell.* Telephone 01422 845557
for full details.

Heptonstall

W. Yorks. PO, tel, stores. An extraordinary 'textile village', little changed over the centuries, set high on hills overlooking Hebden Bridge. Walk up the Buttress (beyond the packhorse bridge) or take a bus and visit this settlement barely touched by time. In one small area there is a ruined 15th-C church, its early Victorian replacement and the Octagonal Chapel, one of the oldest continually used Methodist churches in the world, dating from 1764. Also a 16th-C cloth market hall, school museum, a dungeon and David Hartley's (the infamous coiner) grave. There is also the grave of Sylvia Plath, American poet and wife of Ted Hughes. The village provides one of the most spectacular viewpoints in Calderdale.

Old Grammar School Museum Heptonstall, Hebden Bridge (011484 719222; www.calder. gov.uk). Depicts an old school classroom together with varying local history displays. *Open Easter– Oct, weekends and B Hols 13.00–17.00.* Charge.

Cloth Hall Heptonstall. Built between 1545 and 1558 as a market for local handloom weavers to sell their cloth to dealers. It is now a *private* house.

Weavers' Square Heptonstall. A unique museum of stone depicting many types of Yorkshire paving.

Mytholmroyd

W. Yorks, PO, tel, stores, takeaways, hairdressers, station. Since the 11th C the ingredients of a farming and weaving community have existed in the area, confined largely to individual settlements above the marshy valley bottom. The site of the present village was initially a fordable crossing of the River Calder and, with the coming of the canal and the railway, developed as a focus for steam-powered textile production. Initially producers of cotton goods (with the canal as both supplier of raw materials and shipper of finished goods) the mills went on to manufacture worsted in the late 19th C, which in turn stimulated the growth of local dyeworks. Infamous as the base for the activities of David Hartley and the 'Coiners', Mytholmroyd was also the birthplace of Ted Hughes, the late Poet Laureate, and home to the annual Dock Pudding championships – *held in May.*

The Coiners of Cragg Vale Coining was the illicit manufacture of coins, often using metal filed or clipped away from the perimeter of genuine coins. This was melted down and cast into new coins with an appropriate design hammered onto the face and reverse sides. A new rim was then hammered onto the adulterated coin. On 10 November 1769 an excise man, William Dighton, who had been sent to curtail the activities of the Cragg Vale coiners, was murdered in Halifax by members of the gang. Loyalty was not a notable feature within coiner circles and the miscreants were quickly betrayed to the authorities in return for an enticing reward.

Dock Pudding Championships Dock Pudding is made from the weed *Polygonum bistorta* (sweet dock) and is not to be confused with the large coarse cow docks. Mixed with other ingredients and cooked to a variety of secret recipes, the finished product, looking not unlike a slimy, spinach concoction, is entered into a competition and judged on its culinary merits. Believed by many locals to be an essential spring medicine, efficacious in the cure of acne and as a cleanser of the blood.

Luddenden Foot

W. Yorks. Tel, stores, off-licence, takeaway, library. Centred around more recent lines of communication in the valley bottom, the village once featured the railway station where Branwell Brontë was booking clerk. Passengers arriving on one of the earliest passenger lines to be opened in Britain, were greeted with the cry of 'Foo-it! Foo-it!' as porters sought to differentiate this upstart settlement from the ancient, textile-producing village, perched on the hillside 1/2 above.

Boatyards

See Calder & Hebble Navigation, page 48.

THE BEER NECESSITIES

Take an old ice cream cooler, a scrapyard copper, a home-made cask washer and two locally constructed mash tuns; place them in a canalside mill (once a sweet factory) and what have you got? A family-run brewery – whose proprietor (for many years a joiner) is not short of ingenuity. Always fermenting new ideas for the future, his imagination stretches into the often mind-bending task of naming new brews, tapping into local history with names like 'Luddite' and 'Coiners'. When the ailing sweet factory finally called time on its production it was sold, complete with its old manufacturing equipment. Ideas were already brewing as to how it might be pressed into use for ale production. The family are all adept at meeting new challenges, right down to Sooty the brewery cat. Keeping the mouse population in check is a doddle for a four-legged feline; not so easy if you've had the misfortune to lose a leg in a brush with a car.

Pubs and Restaurants

See also Calder & Hebble Navigation, page 49.

There is a wide choice of pubs to choose from in Hebden Bridge, together with an even wider choice of real ales.

The selection of tearooms, bistros, pizzerias and restaurants is equally copious.

White Lion Bridge Gate, Hebden Bridge (01422 842197; www.whitelionhotelhb.co.uk). A friendly and relaxed family pub with many interesting features set in a 17th-C listed building. An excellent selection of real ales and good food served *L and E, daily*. Children's room and riverside garden. Open fires *in winter* and non-smoking area. B & B. *Open all day Mon–Sat.*

These two pubs both represent worthwhile walks or bus rides:

Hare & Hounds Billy Lane, Chiserley Old Town, Hebden Bridge (01422 842671; www.hare.and.hounds.connectfree.co.uk). Cosy pub serving real ale and tasty bar meals (V) *L Sat and Sun and E Tue–Sun*. Children welcome. Beer garden with stunning views over the Calder Valley – close to the Pennine Way. Pub games. B & B. *Hourly* Halifax service bus no 593 *during day* or minibus H3 and H7 *evenings and weekends.*

Old Hall New North Road, Heckmondwike, Hebden Bridge (01924 404774). An exciting grade I listed building with several rare features which in themselves make the walk well worth while. Real ale is dispensed amidst portraits of Tudor royalty, and food (V) is available *L and E Mon–Sat and 12.00–16.00 Sun.* Children welcome. Pub games and non-smoking area. Quiz *Tue and Thur.* Outside seating. *Open all day.*

Dusty Miller Mytholmroyd (01422 882247). Once the regular haunt of the Crag Vale Coiners, it now offers real ale and occasional karaoke. Children welcome. Pool.

Shoulder of Mutton Mytholmroyd (01422 883165). Opposite railway station. Award-winning hostelry that takes its beer and food seriously. This pub has been under the same management for nearly 30 years and displays an interesting collection of memorabilia featuring the local Coiners. An excellent selection of both regular and guest real ales are served; there are three cosy eating areas, portions are generous and the prices low.

Tasty, home-cooked food (V) available *L and E (19.00–20.30 except Tue)*. Children and dogs welcome. Streamside garden.

White Lion Mytholmroyd (01422 883131). An interesting range of very reasonably priced bar meals and snacks (V) served *L, daily*, in comfortable surroundings, by a friendly, welcoming landlady. Real ale, moorings outside, pub games, Quiz *Mon* and live music alternate *Fri.* Children welcome *until 20.00.* Beer garden.

Grove Inn Brearley House (01422 883235). Cosy, single room pub, beside the main road, serving real ale. Snacks and traditional bar food (V) served *L and E Tue–Sun.* Children welcome; garden. Games room with pool and darts. Quiz night *Thur.* Busy in *summer.*

Weavers Arms Luddenden Foot (01422 882241). Open *all day* serving real ale and sandwiches at the bar. Comfortable pub, once the haunt of Branwell Brontë during his sojourn at the local station. Pub games and outside seating. Children welcome *until 19.00. Takeaway* next door.

Coach and Horses Luddenden Foot (01422 884102). Large, open-plan (originally six rooms) family pub serving an appetising array of inexpensive home-cooked food (V) *L and E Mon–Sat and Sun 12.00–18.00* together with a selection of real ales. Regular foreign cuisine evenings. Children under supervision welcome. Outside seating. Singer *every three weeks.*

Shandaar Indian Restaurant Station Road, Luddenden Foot (01422 886640). Above Old Brandy Wine. Restaurant and takeaway.

Old Brandy Wine Station Road, Luddenden Foot (01422 886173). Real ales are served in this ex-factory and working-man's club, now refurbished. Discos *Fri and Sat*; karaoke *Sun.* Children welcome *until 21.00.* Outside seating.

Puzzle Hall Inn 21 Hollins Mill Lane, Sowerby Bridge (01422 835547). South of canal before Sowerby Long Bridge. A wide cross section of customers gather at this 300-year-old hostelry of great character set between river and canal. Real ale and food (V) *L (E Wed only)* are served in this tiny, two-roomed pub where *Wed E* is curry night. Well-behaved children and dogs welcome (but no dogs *Wed E*). Garden. Live jazz *Tue* and various entertainment *Thur and Sat.*

Hebden Bridge (see page 170)

TRENT & MERSEY CANAL

MAXIMUM DIMENSIONS

North end of Harecastle Tunnel to Croxton Aqueduct
Length: 72'
Beam: 7'
Headroom: 7'

Croxton Aqueduct to Preston Brook Tunnel
Length: 72'
Beam: 9'
Headroom: 6' 3"

MANAGER:
01782 785703;
enquiries.p&p@britishwaterways.co.uk

MILEAGE
HARDING'S WOOD, junction with Macclesfield Canal to:
King's Lock, Middlewich, junction with Middlewich Branch: 10½ miles
Anderton Lift (for River Weaver): 22¾ miles
PRESTON BROOK north end of tunnel and Bridgewater Canal: 29¾ miles

Locks: 36

This early canal was originally conceived partly as a roundabout link between the ports of Liverpool and Hull, while passing through the busy area of the Potteries and mid-Cheshire, and terminating either in the River Weaver or in the Mersey. Its construction was promoted by Josiah Wedgwood (1730–95), the famous potter, aided by his friends Thomas Bentley and Erasmus Darwin. In 1766 the Trent & Mersey Canal Act was passed by Parliament, authorising the building of a navigation from the River Trent at Shardlow to Runcorn Gap, where it would join the proposed extension of the Bridgewater Canal from Manchester.

The ageing James Brindley was appointed engineer for the canal. Construction began at once and in 1777 the Trent & Mersey Canal was opened. In the total 93 miles between Derwent Mouth and Preston Brook, the Trent & Mersey gained connection with no fewer than nine other canals or significant branches.

By the 1820s the slowly-sinking tunnel at Harecastle had become a serious bottle-neck, so Thomas Telford recommended building a second tunnel beside the old one. His recommendation was eventually accepted by the company and the new tunnel was completed in under three years, in 1827. Although the Trent & Mersey was taken over in 1845 by the new North Staffordshire Railway Company, the canal flourished until World War I.

Look out for the handsome cast iron mileposts, which actually measure the mileage from Shardlow, not Derwent Mouth. There are 59 originals, from the Rougeley and Dixon foundry in Stone, and 34 replacements, bearing the mark of the Trent & Mersey Canal Society – T & MCS 1977.

Harding's Wood Junction

At the north end of Harecastle Tunnel (2926yds long) the Trent & Mersey passes Kidsgrove station and a coal yard; there is also a *shower* in the facilities block beside the north tunnel portal. Beyond is Harding's Wood and the junction with the Macclesfield Canal, which crosses the T & M on Poole Aqueduct. There are *showers*, *laundry facilities* and a self-operated *pump-out* at the BW offices at Red Bull. The canal continues to fall through a heavily locked stretch sometimes called

Pubs and Restaurants

🍺 ✕ **The Harecastle Hotel** Liverpool Road, Kidsgrove (01782 773925). Family pub close to bridge 132. Reasonably priced food (V) *all day until 20.00*, accompanied by their own traditional Mowcop gravy. Real ales. Children welcome. Karaoke and quizzes *Fri and Sat*. B & B.

🍺 **The Blue Bell** Canalside, at Hardings Wood Junction (01782 774052). Friendly, quiet, one-bar local, winnner of many CAMRA awards. Real ale, plus a range of specialist bottled beers, including many from Belgium, plus real cider and perry. No juke box, pool table or gaming machines. Four separate drinking areas, including a no-smoking section. Note the trapdoor in the lounge ceiling. Well-behaved children welcome *until 21.00*. Snacks are available *at weekends*. *Open Tue–Fri 19.30–23.00; Sat 13.00–16.00, 19.00–23.00; Sun 12.00–16.00, 19.00–22.30. Closed Mon.*

🍺 **The Canal Tavern** Hardingwood Road (01782 775382). Canalside by bridge 133. Food (V) served *L and E*. Children welcome *until 19.30*. Large garden. Karaoke at *weekends*.

🍺 ✕ **The Red Bull Hotel** Congleton Road South, Church Lawton (01782 782600). By lock 43 on the Trent & Mersey. Popular pub close to Hardings Wood Junction, serving real ale and bar meals (V), including fish dishes *L and E*, along with good wine. Children welcome. Canalside seating area. Quiz night *each Tue*.

✕ ♀ **Mrs B's Victorian Supper Rooms** 8 Congleton Road, Butt Lane, Kidsgrove (01782 775654). Enchanting period establishment, *open L and E* (book in advance), and offering an exciting 7-course dinner in a friendly atmosphere. Good choice of wine.

🍺 **The Broughton Arms** (01270 878661). Canalside at Rode Heath. Friendly family pub, with comfortable bars and canalside seating. Range of real ale. Food (V) available in bar and dining area *L and E*. Children welcome away from the bar. Waterside garden with patio heaters.

✕ ♀ **Brindley's Lockside Restaurant** The Canal Centre, Hassall Green (01270 762266; www. brindleysrestaurant.co.uk). A well-restored 18th-C building beside the canal. Appetising range of reasonably priced dishes (V, and vegan by arrangement) served *L and E (seasonal)*. *Sunday* roast. Children's menu. Lockside seating. 🦽 D Gas, coal, provisions, books and maps.

🍺 **The Romping Donkey** Hassall Green (01270 765202). Haunted 17th-C pub serving real ale, and home-made bar meals (V) and snacks *L and E*. Children welcome, and there is a garden. Karaoke *Thur and Sun*.

'heartbreak hill' but known to the old boatmen as the 'Cheshire Locks'. Two minor aqueducts are encountered, and most of the locks are narrow pairs – the chambers side by side. At Hassall Green there is a *PO, tel and stores* incorporating a canal shop, restaurant and boatyard services.

● **Kidsgrove**
Staffs. All services. Originally an iron and coal producing town, Kidsgrove was much helped by the completion of the Trent & Mersey Canal. James Brindley is buried here.
● **Rode Heath**
Cheshire. PO, tel, stores. A useful shopping area right by bridge 140. A butcher's shop at bridge 139. **Rode Heath Rise** Once the site of a salt works, it has now been landscaped and restored as a wildflower meadow. Telephone (01477) 534115 for further information.

NAVIGATIONAL NOTES

HARECASTLE TUNNEL Do not enter in an unpowered craft. With the complete removal of the towpath, headroom is no longer the problem it once was. A one-way system operates, so follow the instructions of the tunnel keepers. *For updated tunnel opening times, telephone (01782) 785703.*

Boatyards

Ⓑ **Smithsons Solid Fuel and Caravan Centre** Kidsgrove (01782 787887). Near bridge 132. **D** Calor gas, solid fuel, lubricants and caravan fittings which can be used as chandlery. Also bicycles and bicycle spares for sale.

Ⓑ **Canal Centre** Hassall Green, Sandbach (01270 762266). **D** Gas, groceries, books and maps, coal. Also PO, general store, off-licence, gifts, licensed restaurant and tearoom, coal.

WALKING & CYCLING
The towpath is in good condition through to Preston Brook and offers the opportunity to sample a varied landscape, ranging from the beauties of the Dane Valley through to the industry inherent in this long-established salt-producing area.

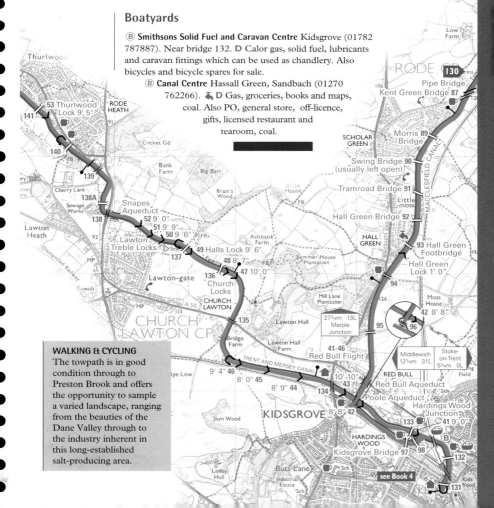

Wheelock

The canal now descends the Wheelock flight of eight locks, which are the last paired locks one sees when travelling northwards. The countryside continues to be quiet and unspoilt but unspectacular. The pair of locks half-way down the flight is situated in the little settlement of Malkin's Bank, overlooked by terraced houses. The boatman's co-op used to be here, in the small terrace of cottages. The adjoining boatyard now specialises in the restoration of traditional working boats. At the bottom of the flight is the village of Wheelock; west of here the navigation curls round the side of a hill before entering the very long-established salt-producing area that is based on Middlewich. The 'wild' brine pumping and rock-salt mining that has gone on hereabouts has resulted in severe local subsidence; the effect on the canal has been to necessitate the constant raising of the banks as lengths of the canal bed sink. This of course means that the affected lengths tend to be much deeper than ordinary canals. Non-swimmers beware of falling overboard. The navigation now begins to lose the rural character it has enjoyed since Kidsgrove. Falling through yet more locks, the canal is joined by a busy main road (useful for *fish & chips*, west of Kings Lock; and *Chinese takeaway*, west of bridge 166) which accompanies it into an increasingly flat and industrialised landscape, past several salt works and into Middlewich, where a branch of the Shropshire Union leads off westwards towards that canal at Barbridge. The first 100yds or so of this branch is the Wardle Canal, claimed to be the shortest canal in the country.

● **Wheelock**
Ches. PO, tel, stores, garage, fish & chips. Busy little main road village on the canal.
● **Sandbach**
Ches. PO, tel, stores, garage, bank, station. 1½ miles north of Wheelock. An old market town that has maintained its charm despite the steady growth of its salt and chemical industries. After walking from the canal you can refresh yourself with a pint of real ale from any of the seven pubs visible from the seat in the market place.
Ancient Crosses In the cobbled market place on a massive base stand two superb Saxon crosses, believed to commemorate the conversion of the area to Christianity in the 7th C. They suffered severely in the 17th C when the Puritans broke them up and scattered the fragments for miles. After years of searching for the parts, George Ormerod succeeded in re-erecting the crosses in 1816, with new stone replacing the missing fragments.
St Mary's Church High Street. A large, 16th-C church with a handsome battlemented tower. The most interesting features of the interior are the 17th-C carved roof and the fine chancel screen.
The Old Hall Hotel An outstanding example of Elizabethan half-timbered architecture, which was formerly the home of the lord of the manor, but is now used as an hotel.

Boatyards

Ⓑ **Malkins Bank Canal Services** (01270 764595). 🛠 Long-term mooring, slipway, boat building and historic boat restoration, boat repairs. Breakdown service.

Pubs and Restaurants

✗ **Di Venezia** 464 Crewe Road, Wheelock (01270 762030). *Open L and E* serving pizzas and traditional Italian dishes (V). Children welcome. Mooring.

Nags Head Wheelock (01270 762457). ¼ mile west of bridge 154. Small black and white pub serving real ale and traditional bar meals (V) *L and E (not Sat and Sun E or E Nov–Mar)*. Children and dogs welcome. Garden and aviary. Barbecue *summer Sats*. Pool and traditional pub games. Chinese takeaway opposite.

Commercial Wheelock (01270 760122). Near bridge 154. Set in a Georgian house with an old-fashioned and spacious feel this pub serves real ale, and also real cider. *Open all day*. Children and dogs welcome. Beer garden, snooker room, darts and dominoes.

Cheshire Cheese Wheelock (01270 760319). Heavily beamed, canalside pub serving real ale and a range of meals and snacks (V) *L and E, daily*. Children and dogs welcome (dogs in the garden). Large beer garden.

Market Tavern The Square, Sandbach (01270 762099). Opposite the crosses. Lively, old, traditional town pub serving real ale and home-cooked bar food (V) *L Mon–Sat*. Children's menu and beer garden. One of the seven real ale pubs in, or close to, the square.

Kinderton Arms (01606 832158). Close to canal 1 mile south of Middlewich, by lock 70. Ignore its dour appearance and enter to enjoy real ale and a friendly welcome. Excellent pub grub (V) served *09.00–17.00 daily* at remarkably low prices. Traditional *Sunday* lunches, tea and coffee. Children welcome.

Middlewich

The Trent & Mersey skirts the centre of the town, passing lots of moored narrowboats and through three consecutive narrow locks, arriving at a wide (14ft) lock (which has suffered from subsidence) with a pub beside it. This used to represent the beginning of a wide, almost lock-free navigation right through to Preston Brook, Manchester and Wigan (very convenient for the salt industry when it shipped most of its goods by boat), but Croxton Aqueduct had to be replaced many years ago, and is now a steel structure only 8ft 2in wide. The aqueduct crosses the River Dane, which flows alongside the navigation as both water courses leave industrial Middlewich and move out into fine open country. Initially, this is a stretch of canal as beautiful as any in the country. Often over-hung by trees, the navigation winds along the side of a hill as it follows the delightful valley of the River Dane. There are pleasant *moorings* with *picnic tables* and *barbecue facilities*, created by the Broken Cross Boating Club in old clay pits, just north of bridge 176, on the off-side. The parkland on the other side of the valley encompasses Bostock Hall, a school for children with learning difficulties. At Whatcroft Hall (privately owned), the canal circles around to the east, passing under a derelict railway before heading for the industrial outskirts of Northwich and shedding its beauty and solitude once again.

NAVIGATIONAL NOTES

There are several privately owned wide 'lagoons' caused by subsidence along this section of the Trent & Mersey, in some of which repose the hulks of abandoned barges and narrowboats, lately being salvaged. Navigators should be wary of straying off the main line, since the off-side canal bank is often submerged and invisible just below the water level.

Boatyards

ⓑ **Kings Lock Boatyard** Booth Lane, Middlewich (01606 737564; www.kingslock.fsnet.co.uk). 🛒 D Gas, overnight mooring, long-term mooring, winter storage, slipway, engine sales and repairs, boat repairs, chandlery (including mail order), books, maps, gifts, solid fuel. *Emergency call out.*
ⓑ **Andersen Boats** Wych House, St Anne's Road, Middlewich (01606 833668; www.andersonboats.com). Pump out, gas, narrowboat hire, books and maps. Useful DIY shop nearby.

ⓑ **Middlewich Narrowboats** Canal Terrace, Middlewich (01606 832460; www.middlewichboats.co.uk). 🛒 🛒 🔧 D Pump out, gas, narrowboat hire, overnight mooring (*not Fri*), long-term mooring, dry dock, groceries, chandlery, books and maps, engine repairs, toilets, laundry service, breakdown service, grit blasting, hull and cabinside painting. *Closed Sun.* Useful tool hire shop next door.

Pubs and Restaurants

🍺 **The Kings Lock** Middlewich (01606 833537). Overlooking the lock. Real ales and bar food (V) available *L and E.* Children welcome *until 21.00.* Dogs in bar areas only. Canalside seating.

🍺 **The Cheshire Cheese** Lewin Street, Middlewich (01606 832097). Newly refurbished and friendly, traditional establishment serving real ales and good pub grub (V) *L daily and E Thur–Sat.* Children welcome. Landscaped garden with large patio and marquee. *Weekly* karaoke and occasional live bands.

🍺 **The Newton Brewery Inn** Middlewich (01606 833502). ¼ mile south of Big Lock. Small friendly pub with an attractive garden running down to the towpath. Real ale. Telephone for details of food. Children welcome.

🍺 ✕ **The Boars Head** Kinderton Street, Middlewich (01606 833191). Large rambling pub offering real ale and bar snacks (V if pre-booked). Pool room. Patio. B & B.

🍺 ✕ **The Big Lock** Middlewich (01606 833489). Canalside. Variously a bottle-making factory and canal-horse stables, this pub now serves real ale. Bar snacks and an à la carte menu (V) available *L and E (not Sun).* Children and dogs welcome. Garden area. Quiz *Mon.*

● **Middlewich**
Ches. PO, tel, stores, bank, garage. A town that since Roman times has been dedicated to salt extraction. Most of the salt produced here goes to various chemical industries. Subsidence from salt extraction has prevented redevelopment for many years, but a big renewal scheme is now in progress. The canalside area is a haven of peace below the busy streets.

St Michael's Church A handsome medieval church which was a place of refuge for the Royalists during the Civil War. It has a fine interior with richly carved woodwork.

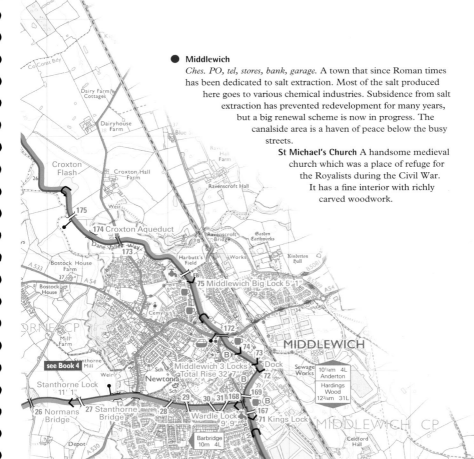

Anderton Lift

The outlying canal settlement of Broken Cross acts as a buffer between the beauty and solitude of the Dane Valley and the industrial ravages around Northwich. Beyond is another length in which salt mining has determined the nature of the scenery. Part of it is heavily industrial, with enormous

ICI works dominating the scene; much of it is devastated but rural (just), some of it is nondescript, and some of it is superb countryside. Donkey engines can still be seen in surrounding fields pumping brine. Leaving the vicinity of Lostock Gralam (*licensed grocer 100yds east of bridge 189 open daily until 22.00*) and the outskirts of Northwich, one passes Marston (*late opening stores and tel*) and Wincham (*PO, tel, stores*). Just west of the village, one travels along a 1/2-mile stretch of canal that was only cut in 1958, as the old route was about to collapse into – needless to say – underground salt workings. Beyond the woods of Marbury Country Park (attractive short-stay *moorings*) is Anderton (*PO, tel, stores*) – the short entrance canal to the famous boat lift down into the Weaver Navigation is on the left. The main line continues westwards, winding along what is now a steep hill and into Barnton Tunnel. There is a useful range of shops, up the hill from the east end of the tunnel, including a *laundrette, chemist* and *butcher*. You then emerge onto a hillside overlooking the River Weaver, with a marvellous view straight down the huge Saltersford Locks. Now Saltersford Tunnel is entered: beyond it you are in completely open country again. There are good moorings in the basins to the east of both tunnels.

NAVIGATIONAL NOTES

1 Saltersford Tunnel is crooked, affording only a brief glimpse of the other end. Two boats cannot pass in this or Barnton Tunnel, so make sure they are clear before proceeding.

2 *See* notes on page 184 covering use of the Anderton Boat Lift.

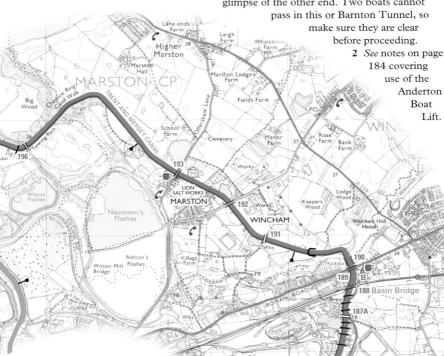

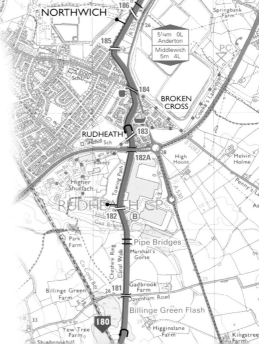

● **Marston**

Ches. Tel. A salt-producing village, suffering badly from its own industry. The numerous gaps in this village are caused by the demolition or collapse of houses affected by subsidence. Waste ground abounds.

The Lion Salt Works Offershaw Lane, Marston (01606 41823; www. lionsaltworkstrust.co.uk). Beside the canal at bridge 193. The Thompson family established an open pan salt works in Marston in 1842, producing fishery salt, bay salt, crystal salt and lump salt. The salt was pumped as wild brine from 45yds beneath the works and evaporated in a large iron pan. The crystals thus formed were raked into tubs to form blocks, and subsequently dried in brick stove houses, before being exported (with the first part of the journey by canal) to India, Canada and West Africa. The works closed in 1986 but is currently being restored and is well worth visiting. Audio visual display.

and many exhibits. *Open Mon–Thur 13.30–16.30.* Charge. Also information on the attractive countryside of Vale Royal and its rich industrial heritage.

Marbury Country Park A 200-acre park occupying the landscaped gardens of the former Marbury Hall and estate, once the home of the Barry and Smith-Barry families. Overlooking Budworth Mere, the house was demolished in 1968 and the much-neglected gardens restored to their former glory by Cheshire County Heritage and Recreation service. The Information Centre (1/2 mile north of bridge 196) houses a display of Marbury's wildlife and history, including its use as a POW camp during World War II. Visitor's moorings and picnic area.

● **Anderton Lift**
An amazing and enormous piece of machinery built in 1875 by Leader Williams (later engineer of the Manchester Ship Canal) to connect the Trent & Mersey to the flourishing Weaver Navigation, 50ft below. As built, the lift consisted of two water-filled tanks counterbalancing each other in a vertical slide, resting on massive hydraulic rams. It worked on the very straightforward principle that making the ascending tank slightly lighter – by pumping a little water out – would assist the hydraulic rams (which were operated by a steam engine and pump) in moving both tanks, with boats in them, up or down their respective slide. In 1908 the lift had to have major repairs, so it was modernised at the same time. The troublesome hydraulic rams were done away with; from then on each tank – which contained 250 tons of water – had its own counterweights and was independent of the other tank. Electricity replaced steam as the motive power. One of the most fascinating individual features of the canal system, it draws thousands of sightseers every year. Restoration to full working order is now complete, following the original 1875 hydraulic design.

● **Northwich**
Ches. All services. Regular buses from Barnton. A rather attractive town at the junction of the Rivers Weaver and Dane. (The latter brings large quantities of sand down into the Weaver Navigation, necessitating a heavy expenditure on dredging.) As in every other town in this area, salt has for centuries been responsible for the continued prosperity of Northwich. The Weaver Navigation has of course been another very prominent factor in the town's history, and the building and repairing of barges, narrowboats, and small seagoing ships has been carried on here for over 200 years. Nowadays this industry has been almost forced out of business by foreign competition, and the last private shipyard on the river closed down in 1971. (This yard – Isaac Pimblott's – used to be between Hunt's Locks and Hartford Bridge. Their last contract was a tug for Aden.) However, the big BW yard in the town continues to thrive; some very large maintenance craft are built and repaired here. The wharves by Town Bridge are empty, and are an excellent temporary mooring site for anyone wishing to visit the place. The town centre is very close; much of it has been completely rebuilt very recently. There is now an extensive shopping precinct. Although the large number of pubs has been whittled down in the rebuilding process, there are still some pleasant old streets. The Weaver and the big swing bridges across it remain a dominant part of the background.

Tourist Information Centre 1 The Arcade, Northwich (01606 353534; www.valeroyal.gov.uk). *Open Mon–Fri 09.00–17.00; Sat Apr–Oct 10.00–14.00 and Nov–Mar 09.30–12.30.*

Dock Road Edwardian Pumping Station Weir Street, Northwich (0161 794 9314). Intriguing listed building housing unique pumps and

---

BOAT TRIPS

Weaver Sovereign offering trips to various destinations along the River Weaver. *All trips leave from Northwich Marine and include a commentary, food and bar.* Weston Docks, Runcorn is also visited. *Sunday lunch and dinner* trips. Boat also available for private charter (maximum 60 people). For details telephone (01606) 40295.

Canal Explorer (01565 750461). Operates boat trips from the Anderton area. Telephone for details.

NAVIGATIONAL NOTES

1 The Anderton Boat Lift is available for use 7 days a week and pre-booked passage is essential by telephoning 01606 786777. *Open Apr–Sep 09.00–18.00 with reduced operating hours Oct–Mar.*

2 Boaters should differentiate between the holding moorings at the top and bottom of the lift, which are solely for lift use, and the visitor moorings beside Anderton Nature Park on the Weaver. Similar short stay visitor moorings are available on the Trent & Mersey.

gas-powered engines fully restored to working order. Building open and engines working *Easter–Sep on Sat, Sun and B Hols 14.00–17.00.* Charge.
Salt Museum Weaver Hall, London Road, Northwich (01606 41331; www.saltmuseum.org.uk). The history of the salt industry from Roman times to the present day, housed in the town's former workhouse. Look out for the remarkable model ship, made from salt of course. *Open all year Tue–Fri 10.00–17.00; Sat and Sun 14.00–17.00 (12.00–17.00 during Aug); B Hol Mon 10.00–17.00.* Audio visual introduction. Charge.

Boatyards

ⓑ **Orchard Marina** (01606 42082; orchardmarina@aol.com). Beside bridge 182. ⚓ 🛏 ⚒ D Pump out, gas, overnight/long-term mooring, slipway, dry dock, boat and engine repairs, boat fitting out, boat and engine sales, dry dock, DIY facilities, books, maps, solid fuel, toilets, showers, laundrette. *Emergency call out.*
ⓑ **Colliery Narrowboat Co** Wincham Wharf, Lostock Gralam, Northwich (01606 44672; winchamwharf@talk21.com). Beside bridge 189. ⚓ 🛏 ⚒ D Pump out, gas, overnight/long-term mooring, slipway, crane, storage, dry dock, boat building, boat sales, boat and engine repairs, wet dock, DIY facilities, toilets.
ⓑ **Alvechurch Boat Centres** Anderton Marina, Uplands Road, Anderton (01606 79642; www.alvechurch.com). Services are on the canal. ⚓ 🛏 ⚒ D E Pump out, gas, narrowboat hire, overnight mooring, long-term mooring, slipway, sales, engine repairs, boat painting, covered wetdocks for hire, chandlery, gifts, restaurant, telephone, toilets.
ⓑ **Barnton Wharf** Barnton Road, Northwich (01606 783320; barntonwharf@talk21.com). ⚒ D Pump out, gas, day-craft hire, long-term mooring, boat and engine sales, boat and engine repairs, boat fitting out, solid fuel. *24hr emergency call out.*
ⓑ **Travelreign** Uplands Road, Anderton (07931 323747). ⚒ Overnight and long-term mooring, winter storage, slipway, wet dock.

Pubs and Restaurants

🍺 **Old Broken Cross** (01606 40431). Canalside, at bridge 184. Attractive old pub, serving well-kept real ale and food (V) *L and E, daily.* Children and dogs welcome. Monthly entertainment. Small canalside garden. *Chemist, grocer, laundrette and other shops are 1/2 mile past pub, towards Northwich.*
🍺 ✕ **Wharf** Wincham Wharf (01606 46099). Canalside by bridge 189. Converted warehouse, reputed to be the oldest on the Trent & Mersey. Real ale is served, together with inexpensive bar meals (V) *L and E (until 19.00 unless by prior arrangement).* Children welcome. Music, karaoke and quiz nights. Pool and large-screen TV upstairs.
🍺 **Salt Barge** Marston (01606 43064). Opposite the Lion Salt Works, beside bridge 193. Deceptively large pub with a friendly atmosphere, neatly divided into cosy areas, and with an inviting family room. Real ales and good food (V) available *L and E, daily.* Children's menu and *Sunday* lunch. Garden. ✕ ♀ **The Moorings** Anderton Marina (01606 79789). Canalside seating. Boaters please moor outside the basin. Small, independent restaurant and bar overlooking Anderton Marina and the Trent & Mersey Canal. *Open all day.* Wide variety of food (V) with emphasis on fresh fish and fresh produce, served *L and E (not Mon E or Tue all day).* Children and dogs welcome. Patio and terrace.
🍺 **Stanley Arms** (01606 75059). Canalside, right opposite the Anderton Lift *(also PO, stores).* Friendly real ale pub with a family room, where children are welcome. Bar food (V) served *all day, every day.* Outside seating and children's play area. The landlord keeps a collection of local tourist information leaflets. Excellent 'bottom of garden' moorings.

Dutton

This, the northernmost stretch of the
Trent & Mersey, is a very pleasant one
and delightfully rural. Most of the way the
navigation follows the south side of the hills
that overlook the River Weaver. From about
60ft up, one is often rewarded with excellent
views of this splendid valley and the occasional
large vessels that ply up and down it. At one
point one can see the elegant Dutton railway
viaduct in the distance; then the two waterways diverge as the Trent & Mersey enters
the woods preceding Preston Brook
Tunnel. There is a stop lock south
of the tunnel just beyond a pretty
covered dry dock; there are often
fine examples of restored working
boats moored here. At the north
end of the tunnel a notice
announces that from here onwards
one is on the Bridgewater Canal
(*see* page 21). There are good
moorings north of bridge 213,
and to the south of
Dutton stop
lock.

NAVIGATIONAL NOTES

1 Access to Preston Brook Tunnel is restricted to *northbound on the hour to
   10 minutes past the hour; southbound on the 1/2 hour to 20 mins to the hour.*
2 North of Preston Brook Tunnel you are on the Bridgewater Canal, which is
   owned by the Manchester Ship Canal Company. See page 21.

Pubs and Restaurants

🍺 ✕ **Leigh Arms** (01606 853327). ¼ mile south of bridge 209, overlooking the Weaver and Acton Swing Bridge. Attractive old coaching inn with large restaurant area serving real ales and an extensive menu of home-made food (V) *all day, every day*. Children and dogs welcome. Patio and garden seating, large children's play area. Music (country & western) *Thur. Weekend summer* barbecues.

🍺 ✕ **Horns Inn** (01606 852192). 200yds south of bridge 209 on the A49, by Acton Swing Bridge. Friendly, roadside pub serving home-made bar food (V) *L and E, daily*. Cosy bars, large garden and children's play area.

✕ **Hollybush** Acton Bridge (01606 853196). ¼ mile north of bridge 209. Listed, timber-framed building, one of the oldest farmhouse pubs in the country, with unique charm and character. Four cosy rooms, including traditional tap-room, make up the bar area together with the tasteful addition of a new restaurant. Wide range of interesting, home-cooked food (V) served in bar and restaurant *L and E, daily*. Children welcome. Garden with children's play area. Traditional pub games. Accommodation.

🍺 **Talbot Arms** Dutton (01928 718181). Comfortable pub atop Preston Brook tunnel, serving real ale. Traditional bar food available *L daily and E Thur–Sat*. Outside seating and discos *Fri and Sat*. Quiz night *Wed*.

🍺 **Tunnel Top** Northwich Road, Dutton (01928 718181). Family pub with warm friendly atmosphere, serving real ale and excellent food (V) *L and E Mon–Thur* and all day *Fri–Sun*. Children and dogs welcome. Large garden.

Boatyards

ⓑ **Black Prince Holidays** Bartington Wharf, Acton Bridge, Northwich (01606 852945; grandadpip@tinyworld.com). 🚿 🚽 ♿ DE Pump out, gas, electric boat recharging, narrowboat hire, day-hire craft, long-term mooring, engine repairs, groceries, books and maps, toilets, gifts, laundry, coal.

ⓑ **Dutton Dry Dock** Tunnel End, Dutton (01928 716701; timleech@dutondok.u-net.com). Dry dock, historic boat repairs, boat blacking, boat repairs, engineering and machine shop, vintage engine repairs.

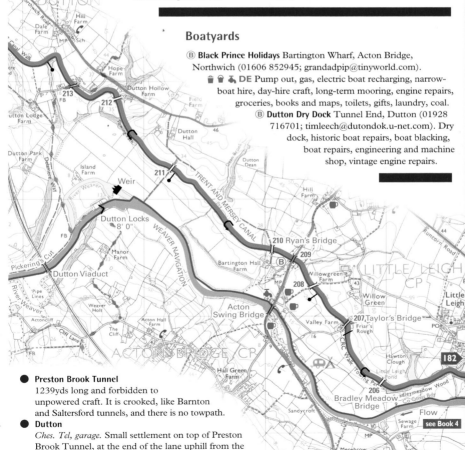

● **Preston Brook Tunnel**
1239yds long and forbidden to unpowered craft. It is crooked, like Barnton and Saltersford tunnels, and there is no towpath.

● **Dutton**
Ches. Tel, garage. Small settlement on top of Preston Brook Tunnel, at the end of the lane uphill from the south end of the tunnel.

Anderton Lift restored (see pages 183–5)

INDEX